The Letters of Rosa Luxemburg

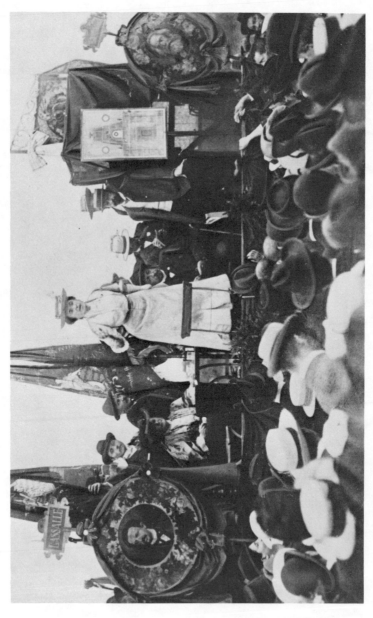

Rosa Luxemburg addressing a rally. The pictures on either side of her are of Lassalle and Marx. (Courtesy Dietz Verlag)

The Letters of Rosa Luxemburg

*edited and with an Introduction
by Stephen Eric Bronner*

with a Foreword by Henry Pachter

Westview Press / *Boulder, Colorado*

Copyright © 1978 by Westview Press, Inc.

Published in 1978 in the United States of America by
  Westview Press, Inc.
  5500 Central Avenue
  Boulder, Colorado 80301
  Frederick A. Praeger, Publisher

Library of Congress Cataloging in Publication Data
Luxemburg, Rosa, 1870-1919.
  The letters of Rosa Luxemburg.
  1. Communists—Correspondence. I. Bronner, Stephen.
HX273.L83A4 1978   335.43'092'2   78-17921
  ISBN 0-89158-186-3
  ISBN 0-89158-188-X pbk.

Printed and bound in the United States of America

Contents

v

Foreword

On January 15, 1919, mercenaries of the counterrevolution murdered Karl Liebknecht and Rosa Luxemburg, the two leaders of the Spartacus uprising. One year later, a small volume of Rosa Luxemburg's "Letters from Prison" appeared in print. These were addressed to Liebknecht's wife Sonja, while Karl was at the front and then in jail, and they showed the dreaded "Red Rosa" as a warm and sensitive woman who was concerned with the birds she watched from her cell, romantic poetry, and the worries of her friends. In short, they showed Rosa Luxemburg to be human.

Three years later, her friend Luise Kautsky published the letters that Rosa Luxemburg had sent to her and her husband over the years. Karl Kautsky had been the theoretical panjandrum of the Social Democratic Party (SPD) and the editor of its prestigious journal, *Die Neue Zeit*. He and Rosa Luxemburg had at first been comrades-in-arms on the party's left but then quarrelled over many issues including the timid course taken by the journal, the mass strike and, finally, the party's support of the Kaiser's war. Nevertheless, Luise erected this monument to her mourned friend. Rosa Luxemburg's criticisms of Kautsky emerge from those letters, and yet one hears once again the voice of a tender individual whose heart beat as much with her private circle of intimates as with the great causes of mankind.

After Luise's death, her son Benedikt—with whom Rosa had played when he was a child—discovered another bundle of letters. Some of them revealed her budding love for a younger man, Hans Diefenbach, while the collection as a whole permitted an even greater appreciation of her multifaceted nature. Benedikt Kautsky was able to publish these letters after World War II, and soon thereafter the Polish Communist party released two volumes of Rosa Luxemburg's letters to her first love and permanent political mentor, Leo Jogiches.

Then too, Charlotte Beradt published Rosa's intimate letters to her secretary Mathilde Jacob, which illuminate the everyday cares and needs so much a part of one's life. Finally, I understand that about a thousand letters still lie in the archives of the Institute for Marxism-Leninism in East Berlin.

I have always wanted the human face of this great revolutionary to be made more visible to the general public. It is this that the present volume seeks to accomplish. In it we see the woman, the lover, the companion, the friend of nature and poetry, the prisoner who charms her jailer, the employer, the cook, and, of course, the political activist.

A number of things were necessary for the completion of this collection. First, the letters had to be selected—but the temptation to display all the riches that might overburden a book of this sort had to be resisted. Secondly, there was a need for new translations on account of the unsatisfactory original rendering of the texts. In this respect, Stephen Eric Bronner and Hedwig Pachter have labored hard to do justice to the spirit of the letters while making the translations readable. Finally, the letters themselves had to be placed within a context. To this effect Professor Bronner has contributed a brilliant introduction, in which he explains Rosa's life and thought and why it is time for this continent to receive her message.

I very much hope that Rosa Luxemburg will find a better reception in this country than she did in her own. In Poland and East Germany, she is thought of as a martyr and a saint, duly celebrated on appropriate state occasions. In West Germany, her picture graces a postage stamp, but not even the Young Socialists march under her name. The irony has been grippingly expressed by the young poet Peter Steinbach, who fled East Germany in 1958.

> Somewhere behind the Red City Hall
> Stands
> the entire Central Committee
> before your remains
> MEMORIAL ROSA
> Those who here bend their heads
> Shoot at
> Whoever thinks differently
> Or would like to live elsewhere

And they conclude contracts
with those who
Oh Rosa-on-the-post-stamp
lick your behind
after nosily justifying themselves
Has mankind
Ever sunk so low?

Henry Pachter

Preface

If Rosa Luxemburg's entire correspondence were compiled, it would surely amount to at least six huge volumes. To a certain extent, of course, any selection procedure contains an arbitrary element, but the difficulty is increased when one considers that certain collections of Rosa Luxemburg's letters—all of which were compiled after her death—sought to emphasize a particular aspect of her personality to the detriment of other facets.

The purpose of this collection, however, is to show the personality of Rosa Luxemburg in its political as well as in its personal dimensions. Consequently, the selection of these letters involves an attempt to present the spirit of her time as it is reflected in her political thinking, activism, and personal concerns. This intent dictated the criteria used in the selection process; thus, letters that relate to truly minor political incidents have been eliminated along with those that are repetitive or deal with everyday occurrences of secondary interest.

The benefit that has been derived from the two major biographies will be obvious, both in the introduction and in the evaluation of the letters. The earlier book by Paul Fröhlich, a founder of the German Communist Party (KPD) who later became the leader of the German Socialist Workers' Party (SAP), is oriented towards Rosa Luxemburg the public figure. The second biography, Peter Nettl's two-volume work, is the standard work dealing with all aspects of Rosa Luxemburg's life and career.

The main sources of the letters compiled in this collection are the following: *Briefe aus dem Gefängnis* (Berlin 1920); *Briefe an Karl and Luise Kautsky* (Berlin 1923), which was translated by Louis P. Lochner as *Letters to Karl and Luise Kautsky* (New York 1923); "Aus den Briefen Rosa Luxemburgs an Franz Mehring," edited by F. Schwabel, *Internationale* 2, no. 3 (1923):67-72; "Unbekannter Brief

Rosa Luxemburgs. Als Rosa aus dem Gefängnis kam . . ." *Rote Fahne*, 18 July 1926, no. 165, Supplement p. 1; *Briefe an Freunde*, ed. Benedikt Kautsky (Hamburg 1950); "Einige Briefe Rosa Luxemburgs und andere Dokumente," *Bulletin of the International Institute of Social History* 8, no. 1 (1952):9-39; W. Blumenberg, "Einige Briefe Rosa Luxemburgs," *International Review of Social History* 8, pt. 1 (1963):92-108; Gotz Langkau, "Briefe Rosa Luxemburgs im IISG—Ein Nachtrag," *International Review of Social History* 21, pt. 3 (1976):413-494; *Briefe an Leon Jogiches*, ed. Feliks Tych (Frankfurt/Main 1971); *Rosa Luxemberg im Gefängnis, ed. Charlotte Beradt (Frankfurt/Main 1973); Vive la Lutte: Correspondance 1891-1914*, ed. Georges Haupt et al. (Paris 1976); and *J'étais, je suis, je serai!: Correspondance 1914-1919*, ed. Georges Haupt et al. (Paris 1977).

I would also like to thank these friends and colleagues for reading and commenting on the manuscript: Raya Dunayevskaya, A. Thomas Ferguson, Loren Goldner, Douglas Kellner, John McClure and George McKenna. My thanks are also extended to Dorothea Frankl for her help with the translation and Larry Hartenian for reading the manuscript and for his assistance with various phases of the book's progress. Then, too, I extend my appreciation to Jean Baldauf, Deierdre O'Shea, and Lynne DeCicco for their time in helping to prepare the manuscripts.

Stephen Eric Bronner
New Brunswick, N.J.

Reflections on Rosa

Rosa Luxemburg and the Other Tradition

There is always a tradition of liberation that stands in opposition to the heritage that a given society preserves and propagates. This other tradition is one that is hidden, that has not been dominant and has never been associated with power. Indeed, the very reason it continues to exist is that it opposes the given system by aspiring toward a freedom that has not yet been attained.

In view of the oppression that has been justified in the name of socialism, a recovery of this emancipatory tradition has become crucial for Marxists. For there can be little doubt that, despite the new interest in such an emancipatory Marxism among certain segments of the intelligentsia, most continue to view socialism in terms of a Marx-Lenin-Stalin lineage. The image that this lineage conjures up is a "socialism of gray," a socialism of dictatorship and concrete, of repression, censorship, and party orthodoxy.

Were this abomination really equivalent to the potential within Marxism, there would truly be no reason to work for the transformation of capitalism. But the deformation that exists in the East is not equivalent to socialism, nor does it exhaust the forms that socialism can take. There remains a Marxian heritage that strains against the shackles of both capitalist and "socialist" oppression.

Rosa Luxemburg, following Marx, stands at the beginning of this emancipatory heritage. In her letters, which reflect the development of both her politics and her personality, a perspective emerges that is neither bureaucratic nor party oriented. This perspective does not dote on some "objectivistic" historical determinism: it demands instead that the masses of the oppressed take control of their destiny and that the individual not be sacrificed to party decree. These letters of Rosa Luxemburg become the testament of a dedicated socialist whose influence extended beyond the revolts that shook Europe from 1918 to 1923 to the student revolts of the late sixties. Indeed, Rosa Luxemburg has helped give birth to an intellectual tradition that has been carried over by thinkers and movements outside the mainstream of Marxism, such as the "council communists" in Germany, the CNT (Confederacion Nacional del Trabajo) in Spain, and the Workers' Opposition in Russia.

The tradition that Rosa Luxemburg fostered has usually been defeated wherever it has emerged in concrete revolt, while her thought has, on the whole, been ignored in the West and castigated in the East.

It is no wonder, for the demands that this heritage presents would call into question those political constellations of oppression existing in both worlds. Furthermore, in contrast to the social democratic parties that simply seek to improve the distribution of wealth, and the liberal parties that mouth the phrases of formal representative democracy, the Marxian tradition in which Rosa Luxemburg stands at the forefront seeks to intensify and extend democracy by socializing production and knowledge. What becomes so very clear in the letters in this collection is the demand that the working class not remain content with a better share of the wealth it produces. It must also seek control over the production process itself and extend democracy beyond the realm of the formally political, making it a component of everyday life. There is, of course, a romantic element to these demands—an element that receives expression in the letters and contradicts the "socialism of gray." It is manifested in many ways. But whether it be in a description of a street corner, a view of the night from her prison cell, or her delight in the revolts of the working class, one thing is always evident: for Rosa Luxemburg the world, like the self, is open, capable of change, and in constant need of being changed. When Rosa Luxemburg writes, "I, too, am a land of boundless possibilities," the thought of a new socialism—a socialism of color and life—begins to emerge. It is precisely this thought that the tradition in which she plays such a fundamental role seeks to actualize.

Childhood and Youth

Rosa Luxemburg was born in the small Polish city of Zamosc in 1871, the year of the Paris Commune. Her father was a middle-class Jew who was cosmopolitan in his views. Thus, he found Zamosc somewhat stifling and moved his family to Warsaw in 1873, the year in which Rosa would develop the hip affliction that would remain with her for the rest of her life. A Jew in Poland who spoke German at home, Rosa learned of Schiller, the Enlightenment, and cosmo-politanism in her family circle. Although it is true she lived with her brother in Warsaw during the revolution of 1905-1906, it would be too much to say that she remained on intimate terms with her family. She barely mentions them in her letters, and yet there was a tie. When, for instance, the father of her friend Hans Diefenbach fell ill, she advised Hans to return home. Indeed, Rosa Luxemburg could write to Diefenbach—the man closest to her toward the end of her life—that:

Later one always blames oneself bitterly for every hour which one took away from the old people. I wasn't lucky enough even to have done as little as that. After all, I constantly had to look after the urgent business of humanity and make the world a happier place. And so I received the news of my father's death in Berlin, where I had been wrangling with Jaurès, Millerand, Daszýnski, Bebel, and God knows who else until the feathers flew. In the meantime, the old gentleman wasn't able to wait any longer. Probably he said to himself that there would be no sense anyway in waiting, however long he waited; after all, I never did "have time" for him or myself—and he died. When I came back from Paris, he had already been buried a week. Now, of course, I would be much wiser, but one is usually wiser after it's too late.

This tension between personal life and political commitment would remain with Rosa Luxemburg. And yet, she was able to stay on reasonably good terms with her family. For his part, her father was able to show a certain broadmindedness when Rosa, still in high school, became involved in radical politics.

Indeed, it was in high school that Rosa Luxemburg first became politically active. During this time she made the acquaintance of Martin Kasprzak, a founder of socialism in Poland, who was to die on the scaffold in 1905. She also joined the Proletariat party, which, like most of the East European socialist parties before the turn of the century, was highly centralized and patterned somewhat after the famous and terroristic Russian Narodnaya Volya (People's Will). Soon enough, Proletariat came under police surveillance and harassment. Thus, after leaving high school in 1887, Rosa Luxemburg escaped to Zurich. There she began her socialist apprenticeship in earnest; she read Marx and Engels for the first time and entered into the world of radical emigré life with its endless cafe colloquies, personal quarrels, and intense intellectual friendships. It was also in Zurich that she met her future lover and political mentor Leo Jogiches. The meeting would result in a stormy and intense relationship that would come to an abrupt end around 1906-1907, though their political collaboration was to last until Rosa's death in the midst of the Spartacus rebellion of 1919.

And then too, Zurich offered her its university. There Rosa would study mathematics, natural science, and political economy. Particularly in prison, she returned again and again to studying the natural sciences, although her central concern was always political economy. Rosa Luxemburg was immediately recognized as a brilliant student and her dissertation on the industrial development of Poland, written under the tutelage of Julius Wolf, received the rare honor (at that time) of being published as a book.

Its argument served as a complement to and theoretical justification of the political position she had taken as early as her high school years. Rosa Luxemburg had always been opposed to a socialism that advocated Polish nationalism, and her dissertation sought to show that Polish industrial development was dependent upon the growth of the Russian market and Russian capitalism. This insight led her to stress the need for solidarity between Polish and Russian workers and to reject the need for Polish separatism.

The unity between the theoretical in Rosa Luxemburg's writing and the concrete needs of political practice formed early, and it was never broken. In concrete terms, the political implications that she drew from her economic research served as the theoretical basis for the journal *Sprawa Robotnicza (The Workers' Voice)*, which Luxemburg and Jogiches founded in 1893. That same year, a strike wave encompassing 60,000 workers hit the city of Lodz. In the wake of these events, the Proletariat party joined with the Polish Workers' League to form the Socialist Party of Poland (PPS). This was the party that would fall more and more under the direction of the two men who were to become Rosa Luxemburg's arch-enemies within the movement for Polish socialism, Ignaz Daszyński and Josef Pilsudski. Like Mussolini, Pilsudski would later defect from socialism altogether and become the dictator of Poland in the twenties. It was this attempt to steer the PPS into the nationalist camp that led Luxemburg to support a new party that would oppose the PPS: the Social Democratic Party of the Kingdom of Poland and Lithuania (SDKPL), the party to which she would devote herself for the rest of her life.

Apprenticeship

The basic political thrust of the SDKPL involved a radical opposition to capitalism and nationalist reformism, coupled with a demand for solidarity between the Russian and Polish proletariat as the basis of a thoroughgoing internationalism. This opposition to nationalism has become one of the hallmarks of Rosa Luxemburg's brand of socialism. In contrast to the PPS and to what would become Stalinism with its slogan of "socialism in one country"—as well as to the contemporary Left's sometimes uncritical support of "national liberation"—Luxemburg realized that an equal partnership between nationalism and socialism was impossible. To be sure, Rosa, following Marx, believed in agitation within national boundaries. At the same time, however, national boundaries and national identity could simply not be accepted as the political and cultural divisions of the proletariat, if the latter was to negate the bourgeoisie and its ideology.

Internationalism has often been accused of remaining abstract. Although it is true that all revolutions have used national symbols, it is also true that the Russian Revolution, which began as a national bourgeois revolution, deepened into an international and proletarian one. Although there would be many conflicts between Luxemburg and Lenin, both perceived the need for and demanded an international revolution, while consistently expressing their hatred of chauvinism. This was particularly the case in the period following the collapse of the Second International.

Rosa Luxemburg's critique of nationalism still retains a fundamental validity. Indeed, her analysis assumes importance both in terms of those revolutionary values that the contemporary Left seeks to foster and in regard to the type of society that it wishes to actualize. For Rosa Luxemburg saw that nationalism would chain the socialist movement to the ideology of that bourgeois class it seeks to oppose. She also realized that a purely "national" revolution would undermine socialism by tying the nation to a bourgeois economy that was becoming ever more interdependent and transnational. Finally, and perhaps most important, the simple acceptance of a nationalistic consciousness would necessarily prevent the proletariat from recognizing the fact that the nation state and nationalism are strictly historical phenomena that might, at any given time, become obsolete. The emphasis upon nationalism would thus effectively deny the possibility of creating an alternative to the bourgeois form of socioeconomic organization and cripple the ability of the workers' movement to conceptualize the common humanity that socialism is to serve. This notion of a common humanity remained central to Luxemburg. Toward the end of her life, she could write to Mathilde Wurm:

> What do you want with this particular suffering of the Jews? The poor victims on the rubber plantations in Putamayo, the Negroes in Africa with whose bodies the Europeans play a game of catch, are just as near to me. Do you remember the words written on the work of the Great General Staff about Trotha's campaign in the Kalahari desert? "and the death-rattles, the mad cries of those dying of thirst, faded away into the sublime silence of eternity."
>
> Oh, this "sublime silence of eternity" in which so many screams have faded away unheard. It rings within me so strongly that I have no

special corner of my heart reserved for the ghetto: I am at home wherever in the world there are clouds, birds and human tears.

Emphasis upon internationalism need not lead to the abolition of
specific cultures or languages. In fact, during her own school years,
Rosa Luxemburg rebelled against the imposition of Russian and the
ban on Polish. From such a position various cultural products
become the possessions of the proletariat as a whole, and one's
identity is no longer based upon the accident of birth within a specific
race or area but instead upon membership in a class. Thus, from the
very first, Rosa Luxemburg would embody her slogan, "the
International is the fatherland of the proletariat." Consequently,
when she sought entry into the world of international socialism, she
was led to that country whose socialist party was the most advanced in
theory and, by the lights of the age, closest to revolution. It was clearly
the German Social Democratic Party (SPD) that served as the fortress
of "orthodox" Marxism and the model for the entire Second
International.

Robert and Mathilde Seidel—he the editor of the influential
Arbeiterstimme (*Voice of the Workers*)—had introduced Rosa
Luxemburg into German socialist circles in Zurich. Although still
very young, she had achieved a minor level of renown as an expert on
Poland and Russia after the publication of her dissertation. This was
seen as making her somewhat valuable to the movement. Still,
restrictions on German immigration were very tight, and Rosa was
forced to make a marriage of convenience to Gustav Lübeck, the son
of a Polish expatriate, shortly after finishing her thesis. This enabled
her to make the move to Berlin, the city in which she would make her
career as a social democrat, and also the city in which she would be
brutally murdered in a revolt that was suppressed by the very same
party she had initially held in such high esteem.

The East European Dimension

Few individuals—Trotsky would be one of them—ever rose to fame
in the socialist world as quickly as did Rosa Luxemburg. Still, she
had to earn her spurs as a party worker, and thus it was that in 1898 the
SPD sent her to Poznan—an area that she called "the boundary
between civilization and barbarism" in one of her letters—to organize
the Polish workers living on German soil. Traveling in the area
proved exhausting, the incessant meetings tiring, and the organiza-

tional work mundane. Yet it all seemed to serve a function, even though the SPD was actually only using the SDKPL in its rivalry with Pilsudski's PPS.

Ultimately, the organizational efforts of both parties would prove a failure. But, with this initial trial that she bore so cheerfully, Rosa Luxemburg gained the practical credentials she needed as the party's expert on East European questions, as well as a mandate to attend the meetings of the International. Then, too, her experience was a factor when the movement chose her to sit on the commission that was to arbitrate the bitter quarrel that broke out between the Bolsheviks and Mensheviks in 1902.

Tension had existed within the Russian Social Democratic Party since its inception in 1898. This tension stemmed from the conflict between those who advocated trade-union activity and political reform within the framework of Russian economic development and those who sought to create a revolutionary proletarian class consciousness by stressing the need for autonomous political action on the part of the working class. Where most of the "orthodox" Marxists supported the "economist" view that Russia's coming revolution must be "bourgeois," Lenin became the leader of the younger and more political faction that held a more Jacobin conception of revolution.

For her part, Rosa Luxemburg tried to emphasize the need for unity between the two factions after the split. Yet, as this hope diminished, it becomes clear from her letters that, despite the ambivalent feelings that she had about Lenin and her dislike of the arrogance and intrigues of the Bolsheviks, she drew ever further away from the Mensheviks who ultimately became the champions of the PPS. Luxemburg's support of the Bolsheviks would never be uncritical; and yet, whatever the disagreements that would later arise between Lenin and Luxemburg, there was one point—a very decisive point—on which they could agree theoretically at this initial stage in the development of Russian socialism: the significance of the trade unions.

Already, in his now famous *What Is To Be Done?*, Lenin had recognized that trade-union consciousness could never be anything but reformist, that the emphasis upon economic benefits—to the detriment of political action—could not create a revolutionary consciousness among the working class, insofar as revolutionary consciousness is predicated upon the translation of economic demands into political ones. From this, Lenin concluded that there was a need for a revolutionary "vanguard" party, composed of a small number of dedicated revolutionary intellectuals, to introject the required revolutionary consciousness into the working class "from without." This was only logical in Russia, given the absence of a working class tradition and a "mass party" organization. From her own experience within the International, Luxemburg also realized that the party must dominate the trade unions if the proletariat was ever to act in an offensive and revolutionary manner. However, her political and theoretical conclusions differed from those of Lenin.

When Lenin's *What Is To Be Done?* first appeared, it caused very little fuss in the West; in fact, it was only translated into German in the twenties. But, from the very first, Rosa Luxemburg saw the importance of Lenin's statement. Her response to it and to Lenin's *One Step Forward, Two Steps Back* occurs in one of her most important essays, *The Organizational Question of Social Democracy.* In this work, the emphasis falls upon the need for a mass party—in accordance with the tradition of Western social democracy—and upon the necessity for democracy within the party as the method for building revolutionary consciousness. The party can seek to influence the masses, but it should not have the hubris to rule them. Although the differences between Luxemburg and Lenin's views on the relation between party and mass can be overdrawn, still for Luxemburg consciousness cannot be manufactured and then introjected into the masses from the outside. Instead, it must emerge in action from the development of the proletariat in its self-conscious opposition to the bourgeoisie.

This emphasis is precisely what led Rosa Luxemburg to the stance that she took in 1905 on the "mass strike." Initially two points become important in considering the mass strike debate. The first is that Rosa Luxemburg did not invent the theory of the mass strike, for it had long been the central concern of the anarcho-syndicalists. Indeed, it was not she, but Parvus, who had originally formulated the mass strike theory in Marxian terms. Secondly, the year 1905, which is usually seen as marking the beginning of the mass strike revolt in Russia, was itself a culmination rather than a beginning. In 1902 a wave of strikes had hit Batum. In December of that year the strikes spread to Rostov-on-Don, and 1903-04 saw widespread striking first in Baku and then in Tiflis, Odessa, Kiev, and other cities. It was in 1905, however, that the strike of 140,000 workers in St. Petersburg resulted in the creation of the St. Petersburg Soviet, which elected the youthful Trotsky as its president.

News spread slowly to the West, but discussion began and reached a crescendo in the party convention of 1905 when August Bebel brought the matter up for discussion. Luxemburg took the most radical stance in support of this experiment in proletarian self-rule. She was backed by the more hesitant Kautsky and Bebel, who viewed the mass strike as a defensive tactic. The response in the bourgeois press was nothing less than outrageous. Luxemburg was castigated as a Jew, a woman—and what was perhaps the worst—as a hypocrite. A man of no less stature than the Reverend Friedrich Naumann, a leader of the "liberal" Progressive Party, attacked her personally for supporting the bloodshed in the East while sitting safely in Germany.

But, after the convention, Rosa Luxemburg—under the pseudonym Anna Matschke—left immediately for Warsaw, then still a part of the Russian empire, where revolution was also in progress. There she worked to put out *Czerwony Sztandar*, which was often, as she wrote to the Kautskys, "carried out by force, with revolver in hand, in the bourgeois printshops." The *Sztandar* had originally been established by Leo Jogiches in 1902 as the popular organ of the SDKPL, while 1905 marked the first publication of *Przeglad Socjaldemokratzyczny*, which would serve the party's theoretical needs.

By 1906, the tsarist police had arrested Rosa. She faced a long prison term, but connections made it possible for her to be released on the 3,000 rubles that her father and the SPD had raised for bail. It was no secret to the authorities that she would jump bail, yet she wrote: "My friends absolutely insist that I telegraph [Premier Sergei] Witte, and that I write the German Consul here. I wouldn't think of it! These gentlemen can wait a long time before a Social Democrat asks them for protection and justice. Long live the revolution!" What emerges here is not simply inflated pride, but a perception of a social democracy that stands implacably opposed to the bourgeoisie. No quarter is to be asked from the enemy, for that friction necessary for proletarian class consciousness must continually be emphasized if the proletariat is to view itself as "sovereign."

Rosa Luxemburg's concern for democracy should not obscure this hatred of the bourgeoisie. Democracy can never be actualized under the material exploitation of the capitalist system; the exploitative system and the bourgeoisie have to be suppressed, but they can only be suppressed by the dictatorship of a class—not the dictatorship over a class by a small group of party leaders—that demands the actualization of democracy in the socioeconomic, as well as in the political, realm. Only in this manner can the sovereignty of the proletariat be assured.

It is this type of self-contained proletarian sovereignty that underlies Rosa Luxemburg's theory of the mass strike, and even of the

relation between the party and the masses. The mass strike for
Luxemburg was neither the apex of revolution, as it was for the
anarchists, nor a "myth" in Sorel's sense. Rather, the mass
strike was a stage within the revolutionary conflict itself. During that
stage, the artificial division between political and economic
organization could be overcome and the proletariat could begin the
manifold social experiment of organizing itself in new ways.

The Revolutions in Russia

Rosa Luxemburg feared "putschism," as did all Second International social democrats. Unlike most of these same social
democrats, however, she also feared the power and hubris of the party
apparatus. The mass strike was the means whereby the proletariat
would avoid falling into either of these organizational dilemmas,
while directly attacking the bourgeoisie. Although Rosa Luxemburg
was delighted and amazed at the manner in which workers'
organizations sprang up by themselves in 1905, it is too much to say—
as is often said—that she prized spontaneity pure and simple, or that
she believed that organization does not precede action but rather is
itself the result of such action.

For Rosa Luxemburg, organized preparatory work was always
essential. But, in her view, this preparatory work—which in itself
demanded party organization—was to be designed to foster the
proletarian class consciousness necessary for revolutionary action.
This action, in turn, would itself create new forms of organization
through the self-administration (*Selbsttätigkeit*) of the proletariat
that would render the old organizational forms obsolete. In this way,
the mass strike emerged in Rosa Luxemburg's thought as the method
by which the self-administration of the masses could be assured.
Where, on the one hand, "putschism" would be avoided through the
process of developing the revolutionary consciousness necessary to
grasp objective revolutionary possibilities, on the other hand,
bureaucratic degeneration would be avoided through the emphasis
upon the subjective revolutionary action of the proletariat itself.

Practically speaking, Rosa Luxemburg's hopes for the 1905
revolution could be condensed into one word: republic. The creation
of a republic would make the Russian bourgeoisie accept the power
that its counterpart did not accept in Germany in 1848. In other
words, it would force the Russian bourgeoisie to remain loyal to the
European revolutionary demands of 1789, and this itself would create

the preconditions for a deepening of proletarian class consciousness. Rosa Luxemburg viewed this as occurring via the exacerbation of the fundamental class contradictions within capitalism aided by the greater possibilities for propaganda and organization that a republic would provide.

The failure of the revolution, however, did not dampen Luxemburg's belief in the mass strike, and for a good reason: not only did the action force the creation of a Duma and so manifest the power of the proletariat, it also exposed the weakness of the bourgeoisie in the type of Duma that it proceeded to organize. In short, it became clear that "the manifold Russian liberal bourgeoisie is not able either to protect the given order from ruin or create a new, up-to-date legal or political order." Rather than retreating to a reformist course in the wake of the ensuing counterrevolution, if anything Rosa Luxemburg radicalized her views. Indeed, in a letter to the Latvian social democrats in 1908, she could write:

And so, after three years of the most difficult attempts, we find ourselves faced once again with the Gordian knot: neither the liberal bourgeoisie nor its artificial unification with the revolutionary proletariat can actualize the task of the Russian revolution. Only the independent activity of the proletariat as a class, supported by the revolutionary movement of the peasants, will be able to destroy absolutism and introduce political freedom into Russia. This is the most irrefutable and most important lesson from the history of revolutionary development.

Unfortunately, however, Rosa Luxemburg's European comrades did not agree. Instead, the increasing bureaucratic petrification, the new nationalism, and the Kautskyian "strategy of attrition" led to her defeat on the mass strike issue in 1910 and, perhaps more importantly, to a state of isolation on the Polish question that became complete in 1912.

The position that she put forward in 1908, however, was precisely the one that would inform her analysis up to and through the Russian Revolution of 1917. Sometimes critics of the revolution have sought to use Rosa Luxemburg's pamphlet *The Russian Revolution*—which was not published in her lifetime for fear of giving support to the counterrevolution—as a blanket condemnation of the Bolsheviks. Needless to say, Rosa Luxemburg herself did not see it that way. Indeed, she viewed the Russian Revolution as the potential "salvation" of Europe, and, like Lenin and Trotsky, saw the revolution in an international context. The Russian Revolution would raise the curtain for the European Revolution. This was the crucial assumption for all of them, and Luxemburg's criticisms of Bolshevik tactics aimed above all to preserve this international perspective.

The destruction of the Second International was a horror, but it was precisely because of the constancy of Rosa's internationalism that she sought to revamp the Second International and resisted appeals to form a successor. Lenin perceived the lack of discipline and leadership as instrumental in the failure of the Second International with regard to the matter of World War I. He sought to remedy these deficiencies in a new communist international. Rosa Luxemburg, however, feared that this would lead to Russian hegemony and create a new nationalism in the name of internationalism—which it certainly did, even before Lenin's death in 1924. Then too, there were the residual effects of the Lenin-Luxemburg controversy over nationalism. In this debate, Lenin took the position supporting "national self-determination" while assuming that the proletarians of the Eastern countries would naturally wish to be allied with the Soviet Union. Essentially, the issue was a practical rather than theoretical one for Lenin insofar as he offered independence to nations over which the Bolsheviks held no control. This contrasted sharply with Luxemburg's stance on internationalism. As the war dragged on in Europe, however, Rosa Luxemburg continued to look with hope to the events in Russia. And yet she could criticize them at the same time. For her, Lenin was still a man and a comrade and not yet a god.

Her other criticisms of revolutionary policy are well known. There was the attack on the agrarian policy of the Bolsheviks—the policy that would unintentionally, and unknowingly, lead to the agrarian problem of the late twenties and thirties (for which Stalin would have his own solution). Then there was her criticism of Lenin's decision to dissolve the Constituent Assembly—an assembly which might have been able to coexist with the soviets but where the Bolsheviks were in the minority—even though the events in Germany would finally be decided in terms of *either* soviets or a parliament. Lastly, there was the critique of the abandonment—or at least constriction—of democracy and the Red Terror.

What Rosa Luxemburg did not do, in contrast to so many liberal critics of the Revolution, was to simply center her analysis of the events taking place in Russia on the Bolsheviks themselves. Rosa Luxemburg could write to Luise Kautsky that if the revolution failed in Russia, it would be because the European proletariat did not carry through its own revolution to support the industrially backward Russians. Moreover, in a telling letter to Adolf Warski in 1918, she could even say of the terror:

> To be sure, terrorism indicates fundamental weakness, but the terror is directed against internal enemies whose hopes rest upon the continuation of capitalism outside Russia, and who receive support and encouragement for their views from abroad. If the European revolution takes place, the Russian counterrevolutionaries will not only lose this support, but—more importantly—their courage as well. In short, the terror in Russia is above all an expression of the weakness of the European proletariat.

Whatever the other differences between them, Lenin and Luxemburg meet in their analysis of the importance of revolutionary action by the international proletariat for the success of the Russian Revolution. Even the most fundamental disagreements between them were disagreements between comrades, and respect was given on both sides. From Rosa Luxemburg's letters, it becomes clear that the degeneration of the Russian Revolution is not simply to be blamed on developments within Russia, but on the European workers' movement as well. In short, a particular proletariat has responsibilities that transcend its national boundaries and national concerns. For Rosa Luxemburg, this applied both to the Russians and to the Europeans. In dealing with either proletarian movement, however, Rosa Luxemburg emerged as an individual who was not afraid to criticize those whom she supported. With this criticism the truth becomes evident that the real revolutionary is never the blind fanatic. Instead, the revolutionary is the one who—while working for solidarity and consistently recognizing the fundamental difference between friend and foe—continually refuses to surrender that critical faculty which Rosa Luxemburg valued so highly.

A Revolutionary in the West

When Rosa Luxemburg entered upon the social democratic scene in Germany in 1898, Karl Marx had already been dead for fifteen years, and the working class movement had entered a new phase of political development. The revolutions of 1848 had failed, the Paris Commune had been crushed, and the First International lay in ruins. The Second International arose from the ashes, and the SPD stood at the forefront of it. Formed in 1875, the SPD was the first of the modern social democratic parties and also the strongest. Thus, it is no wonder that other countries looked to the German socialists for leadership, and that the Austrians, the Belgians, and the Swiss, among others, followed the German organizational model.

The Party itself was created at Gotha by the merger of the two leading German working-class organizations. The first, the *Allgemeiner Deutscher Arbeiterverein,* followed the thinking of its founder Ferdinand Lassalle in its emphasis upon state cooperatives and reformist political activity within the existing state structure. This organization had opposed the more Marxist group, commonly known as the *Eisenachers,* who were in principle far more concerned with the seizure of state power and the proletarian expropriation of the means of production. This double heritage was to influence the entire development of the movement, for the divergence of outlook would be reproduced in the factions that would form within the SPD.

Nevertheless, from the moment of its emergence, the SPD was a force to be reckoned with. As a consequence of the enormous increase in capital accumulation, industrialization, and urbanization in the latter part of the nineteenth century, the proletariat grew rapidly. This was precisely what made the SPD a "mass party" from its very inception. As a "mass party" it had to accommodate conflicting tendencies, and it was this that made questions of theory, ideology, and access to the press so essential to Rosa Luxemburg.

Although papers like the *Sächsische Arbeiter-Zeitung* (on the SPD left) and the *Sozialistische Monatshefte* (on the SPD right) would arise, the prestige of the first theoretical organ of social democracy, *Die Neue Zeit,* would never be rivaled. Its editor, Karl Kautsky, passed for Marx and Engels' philosophical heir and gave SPD theory a consistency that was fundamental for its development. Kautsky's prominence was only increased when, having been charged with synthesizing the views of the SPD, he wrote his now classic *Erfurt Program.*

But perhaps synthesis is not quite the right word for what Kautsky achieved: the *Erfurt Program* was divided into a radical theoretical section that emphasized revolutionary change and a section of immediate demands that were essentially reformist in nature. This dichotomy between the subjective sense of a radical socialist purpose and the reformism that was objectively taking place in the party's political practice would later come to haunt the movement during the "Bernstein debate." Yet the division in the *Erfurt Program* in a sense also gave the seal of approval to the conflict between reformists and "orthodox" Marxists, while opening a place within the party for what would emerge as the socialist "center."

Holding together such an uneasy alliance of factions was no easy task. Charged with this mission were the two men who, with Kautsky, would to a certain extent serve as Rosa Luxemburg's sponsors: August Bebel and Wilhelm Liebknecht. Both had known Marx and Engels, and both had paid a price for their convictions. As members of the Reichstag, they had been imprisoned for treason when they opposed the Franco-Prussian War and the German annexation of Alsace-Lorraine. Where Bebel had gained great fame for his oratory and his journalism, Liebknecht—whose son Karl was to become Rosa Luxemburg's comrade in martyrdom—was far less flamboyant and was known primarily for his organizational skills. But, in fact, both mirrored the contradiction that stemmed from the situation in which social democracy found itself at its birth; that is to say, they were at once revolutionaries and bureaucratic reformists.

Precisely because of the power it could potentially exert, the political position of the SPD was precarious from the very first. It was not only Bismarck's Anti-Socialist Laws that relegated the entire party to an underground and oppositionalist existence, which in turn led the SPD—as a "mass party"—to seek legality, emphasize universal suffrage, and concentrate on trade union legislation. It was also the simple fact that the political organization of the proletariat was forced to struggle for the very bourgeois demands and reforms abandoned by the bourgeoisie itself after the revolution of 1848. The basic issues of the major intraparty debates in which Rosa Luxemburg would involve herself stemmed precisely from the fact that the SPD was not opposing a bourgeois government but, rather, a semiabsolutist police state. The fact that the German state took on the guise of democracy, but was still dominated by the aristocratic Junkers, forced the SPD to emphasize union organizing in the face of political persecution and to seek simultaneously the legislative legitimacy that would allow it to emerge from underground.

In this regard, the socialist historian George Lichtheim has remarked that it was democracy and the demands for popular rule, rather than the purely socioeconomic reforms, which constituted the truly radical aspect of the SPD. Indeed, by the 1890s, Bismarck had already nationalized the railroads in Germany, set up a pioneering social security system, and formulated a welfare policy which included workmen's compensation. But all this occurred in the face of the growing underground SPD, which, following Marx, sought to turn economic demands into political ones. The prevention of such a transformation was what Bismarck sought, and this created a concern for democracy among all segments of the party. Moreover, the very fact that the SPD was the *only* party that suffered under a ban allowed its membership to believe that it was revolutionary, precisely because its enemies judged it as such. With this presupposition, a type of complacency took root that paved the way for the party's integration into the very society it had originally sought to supplant.

Nevertheless, it is no accident that all of Rosa Luxemburg's opponents, and Luxemburg herself, agreed on the basic proposition that democracy could not be separated from socialism. The real differences within social democracy all involved the concrete nature of this linkage. Thus, where Eduard Bernstein would follow the road of parliamentary constitutionalism, and Kautsky would support republican democracy, Luxemburg would seek to deepen democracy and integrate it into the everyday life of the proletariat. For Rosa Luxemburg, democracy became the fundamental form of proletarian education, and, in this sense, she takes the old bourgeois concept of democracy and infuses it with a historically progressive content.

The differences between these views and the unanswered questions that they raise are still debated by the Left, but at that time, these differences still existed under the unique historical circumstance of socialist solidarity. In short, they were debated within the context of an "orthodox" Marxism that prescribed a unity that transcended differences. Particularly when a party is underground, the perception of an enemy, the assurance that justice is on the side of the oppressed and that victory will be achieved, is central to the cohesion and élan of the movement. Marxism fostered this unity and élan for a proletarian organization that, even after the lifting of the Anti-Socialist Laws, was in dire straits. Thus, historical circumstances dictated that Marxism become a positive and objective doctrine. Through this transformation, however, Marxism lost the critical and reflexive element that would allow it to call into question the very uses to which it was being put. In this way, Marxism became a revolutionary ideology that veiled a reformist practice.

Still, for many in the social democratic movement, this ideology was a fundamental constituent of party life when Rosa Luxemburg made her appearance on the international social democratic stage. For her part, Rosa Luxemburg had not gone through the period of the Anti-Socialist Laws during which the thinking of the older German Marxists—like Kautsky, Bebel, and Liebknecht—had been formed. Luxemburg recognized this herself and showed the old men a respect that was mingled with the feeling that their time had passed. Thus, in August 1900, Rosa Luxemburg could write to the

Kautskys that "the *moral* loss resulting from [Wilhelm] Liebknecht's death is greater than you would perhaps initially care to think. The old generation passes and there remains—God have mercy . . ." And yet, in the same letter she can go on to say that Liebknecht "died just in time to retain his fame." This letter manifests the ambivalence that Rosa Luxemburg would experience in dealing with those older radicals who would sponsor her in the face of what would become the reformist challenge. Still, they did sponsor her insofar as these "radicals" were anxious to preserve Marxism from a mounting attack directed by the socialist right.

In the Cauldron of Intraparty Conflicts

The right wing of the party that laid down this challenge was composed of trade union leaders like Karl Legien, old Lassalleans, party bureaucrats, and those "Marxists" who were sincerely convinced that Marxian theory had to be revised to fit a changed reality. The theoretical leader of this coalition was Eduard Bernstein, a former editor of *Die Neue Zeit*. A friend of Engels who had fled to Switzerland and then England in the face of antisocialist persecution, Bernstein held impeccable socialist credentials. Although many of his compatriots actually clung to a non-Marxist world view, Bernstein was himself convinced of the authenticity of his Marxism and the viability of socialism. The basic problem was that Bernstein, who was to introduce the notion of "revisionism," viewed socialism as manifesting itself in an "evolutionary" rather than a "revolutionary" manner. The socioeconomic critique that he made, translated under the title *Evolutionary Socialism*, was both compact and incisive.

In contrast to Marx—as interpreted by Kautsky in the *Erfurt Program*—Bernstein found trends that appeared to contradict the notion that capitalism was "objectively" and "inevitably" doomed to destruction through the increasing immiserization of the proletariat and the concentration of capital in fewer and fewer hands. Basing his observations roughly on the period of the Anti-Socialist Laws, Bernstein noted that a middle class was on the rise; this allowed him to conclude that the expected concentration of capital was not taking place and that the proletariat was not expanding. Moreover, from his empirical analysis, Bernstein also argued that the wages of workers were rising and that the extension of credit was overcoming the nagging set of crises in the business cycle. Because these objective socioeconomic facts seemed to contradict the predictions of Marx's theory, Bernstein believed that the party must come to terms with them in its theorizing. This, he claimed, it had already done in practice anyway, since the SPD was following the course of a reformist trade union party. Thus, Bernstein asked the SPD to appear what it actually was by linking its theory to its practice.

Under the circumstances, Bernstein thought it both useless and dishonest to maintain the revolutionary pretense. Moreover, precisely insofar as the objectivist theory of Marx was not able to stand up to historical reality, it was dangerous to keep talking of a revolutionary goal that was anything but "inevitable." Still, Bernstein did believe that socialism was desirable as a means of redistributing income and insuring parliamentary government in terms of the bourgeois structure of representative democracy. From the standpoint of the "orthodox" Marxists, this meant that the creation of socialism came to be grounded on nothing other than an ethical demand—it was no accident that Bernstein would later look to Kant for his philosophical orientation. Because social conditions were improving, because it was useless to argue about the goal, and because the SPD was bringing socialism about in practice, Bernstein could make his famous statement that "the movement is everything and the goal is nothing."

The extent to which Bernstein's theory shook the socialist world is difficult to imagine today. The Marxian theory that had sustained the workers' movement during twenty years of underground work was being attacked at its very core. As will become clear in the letters in this collection, Rosa Luxemburg fully understood the gravity of the situation and, with the support of Bebel and Kautsky, came to the defense of Marxism, particularly in her brilliant theoretical pamphlet *Social Reform or Revolution*. In opposition to Bernstein, Luxemburg argued that credit does not reduce the potential for crisis, but rather exacerbates it. Moreover, Rosa Luxemburg put forward the position that the manner in which Bernstein had discussed the middle class was mistaken. In fact, capital *was* being concentrated in fewer and fewer hands, and the middle class was indeed falling into the proletariat. In regard to this economic issue, there can be little question that the attenuation of crises did not occur; the depressions of 1918-24 and 1929-32 alone support this view. Nevertheless, the economic argument is truly relevant only when the political consequences are drawn from the analysis. Thus, Luxemburg could attack the optimistic and unwarranted presuppositions that Bernstein had made regarding the possibilities for the "evolution" of socialism within a stabilized capitalism. She reminded her audience that there was no intrinsic relation between capitalism and even parliamentary democracy and that the economic system of capitalism could exist with any number of political forms. She argued, too, that without the "goal" of socialism, the SPD would not only come to implicitly accept the values of a repressive bourgeois society; it would eventually turn into just another bourgeois parliamentary party, inasmuch as it could be ideologically integrated into the existing structure.

Thus, it would be a serious mistake to believe that Rosa Luxemburg carried on her debate simply to justify Marxism theoretically, or to assume, as some critics have, that she unhesitatingly accepted the revolutionary character of the SPD. From her letters, it becomes evident that Luxemburg viewed the debate in practical political terms and that she was speaking for a segment of the party that was revolutionary. Clearly, this debate involved the nature of the political direction social democracy would take. But the very fact that this debate occurred within a political context of assumed unity tactically prevented an attack upon both the theory and the practice of the party. Thus, when Luxemburg suggested that it was only the goal that separated the SPD from all other parties, and that the practice must be related to this theoretically defined goal, she was actually arguing that the SPD must look to its roots in revolutionary theory— as elaborated in the *Erfurt Program*—and correct its practice. It was for this reason that she could appear as an ally of both Bebel and Kautsky in the debate.

Theorizing for its own sake always meant very little to Rosa Luxemburg. What concerned her was the increasing predominance of reformist practice within the Second International. In addition to her assault upon Bernstein, she attacked the decision of the French socialist party to let Alexander Millerand become the first socialist to take part in a bourgeois cabinet—a cabinet that was led by René Waldeck-Rousseau and also included the infamous General Gallifet, who had led the slaughter of the Parisian Communards. Recognizing the German party's increasing reliance on the trade unions, Luxemburg also argued that trade unions can only act in a defensive manner by regulating the given apportionment of labor and the due amount of wages. She denied that the trade unions could govern the actual level of wages or the production process in a bourgeois state. These were the inherent constraints that led Rosa Luxemburg to term the work of the trade unions a "labor of Sisyphus." This earned her their undying hatred—a development of great significance, since the trade unions would ultimately lead the

SPD to oppose the council movement that the socialist Left supported in the 1918 revolution.

But if she did seek to launch a criticism of party practice through an attack upon the theory of revisionism, why did the revolutionary Rosa Luxemburg feel called upon to join the social democratic movement in the first place? After all, there were other groups she could have joined: there were anarchist organizations, and even an ultraleft group called *Die Jungen* (The Young Ones) that had been purged from the SPD.

The simplicity of the answer to this question should not obscure its importance. Rosa Luxemburg knew that there was no such thing as a "correct line" if the party that propagated that line was cut off from the masses. "Staying in contact with the masses" was the political motto she followed to the end of her life. Small sectarian movements meant nothing to her, and "splitting" the workers' movement was always suspect. For Rosa Luxemburg always recognized that, given the existence of a mass workers' party, it was easier to be right in theory while sitting in a cafe than to attempt to come to terms with the exigencies of existing political practice. This was what led her to say that a mistake the workers make in their own actions is worth more than ten victories won under the guidance of a wise central committee. In fact, it is this statement that leads to the "spontaneity theory" for which she has so often been criticized by supporters of Lenin.

The Socialist Left—On the Defensive

"Spontaneity" does not mean the denial of an organized party. On the contrary, only a party can turn economic demands into political ones and give the workers' movement consistency in periods of revolutionary ebb. As Luxemburg explains in *Mass Strike, Party, and Trade Unions*, there must be a continuous inter-action between the party and the proletarian masses. Rosa Luxemburg understood implicitly that organizations are subject to Robert Michels' law of ossification. In her quest for radical action, she constantly appealed to the masses over the heads of the leaders—a tactic that became ever more pronounced with the increasing conservatism of the leadership.

The historical situation only validated this position. If it was the political demand for democracy that was revolutionary—in the sense that it constituted the real threat to the status quo—then the necessity for working with a mass party was primary. Besides, the extent of repression that socialists experienced in the early years is difficult to appreciate in countries that have bourgeois democratic regimes. In fact, when Rosa Luxemburg was imprisoned for the first time in Germany, it was for stating that Kaiser Wilhelm "who talks about the security and good life of German workers has no idea of the real facts."

Under these circumstances, the demands for suffrage and civil liberties were absolutely essential for creating the context in which a more radical political development of the proletariat could arise. In a certain sense, these purely formal liberties were seen by Luxemburg as the sine qua non for revolutionary action. This is why she could support political reform under some circumstances and the mass strike when the potential for more radical action manifested itself.

The Second International was itself a democratic organization like the SPD. The party hierarchy was horizontally intersected by the press, where radicals had access and often control, and in the SPD even the Reichstag delegation could exert a countervailing influence on the bureaucracy until at least a decade into the twentieth century. The basic point is that, although a bureaucratic petrification was under way, a broad variety of viewpoints could be represented and heard within the socialist camp during most of Bebel's leadership. Thus, the existence of radicals within the party was not just for window dressing. In fact, they exerted an influence that went far beyond the size of their group. Consequently, Parvus and Julek Marchlewski, radicals, foreigners, and friends of Rosa Luxemburg expelled from Saxony by the royal government, could push through her appointment as editor of the *Sächsische Arbeiter-Zeitung*. The same was true in regard to the *Leipziger Volkszeitung*, where Franz Mehring arranged for Luxemburg's appointment as coeditor after Bruno Schönlank's death.

As the letters show, Rosa Luxemburg was enormously concerned about her relations with the socialist press. Indeed, the years following the Bernstein debate were marked by an extraordinary output and ceaseless political activity. Her writing and her oratory brought her fame, and it is fair to say that by 1905 Rosa Luxemburg had reached the peak of her influence within the party as the recognized expert on Russian and Polish affairs and as the principal representative for the left wing of the International.

Yet, the very year that highlighted the influence of the Left—due to the revolutionary events in Russia—also marked the start of a decline that resulted in an ever-increasing isolation of Luxemburg's political position within the International. Following the wave of strikes in Russia, the question of the mass strike emerged in Europe. The Russian events had an enormous impact upon Rosa Luxemburg; her impressions, which were articulated initially in the letters, were theoretically formulated in what is perhaps her most important pamphlet, *Mass Strike, Party, and Trade Unions.*

Where Rosa Luxemburg viewed the Russian mass strike and the self-organization of the proletariat as examples to be followed by the Germans, the entrenched bureaucracy and the reformist trade union leaders made their position clear: "The general strike is general nonsense." These revisionists were still rejoicing over the 1903 election that had given the SPD its largest electoral victory (81 seats in the Reichstag and three million votes). Yet, by 1907, the party was to suffer its most severe defeat. Through an appeal to nationalism, militarism, and imperialism, the von Bülow government scored a resounding victory at the polls by drawing upon that very middle class which Bernstein and the reformists sought to woo to the socialist cause. In the wake of this defeat, discussion over the mass strike was ended and the party self-consciously began to shift toward the right. Support emerged for strengthening Germany's navy as praise for imperialistic ventures began to increase. At the same time, the party executive consolidated itself as a separate bureaucracy. The unity of the left wing began to dissolve as Luxemburg became ever more disenchanted with Kautsky. On the right, two names that would later gain a sinister significance for Rosa Luxemburg were starting to become prominent: Friedrich Ebert and Gustav Noske.

In the midst of a set of political crises that were occurring with ever-increasing frequency, in 1907 the Second International took up the matter of world war. Resolutions were passed, and among them was the famous Bebel resolution that was amended by Rosa Luxemburg to strengthen international socialism. But the resolution stood in the abstract, since no one really understood the implications of a concept such as world war—a lack of imagination for which the International would later pay a heavy price.

The year 1907, however, also marked Rosa Luxemburg's association with the Socialist Party School in Berlin, whose other teachers included Franz Mehring. Among her students were members of the party right wing and future Spartacists like the later president of the GDR, Wilhelm Pieck. The lectures she gave at the school were much discussed and later served as the basis for her *Introduction to Political Economy.*

Meanwhile, her power was dwindling within the SPD. The

essential reason was the growing split in what was once the radical faction of the SPD, a split that culminated in 1909-10 with the open conflict between Rosa Luxemburg and Karl Kautsky. Personal dislike had been building on both sides since the aftermath of the mass strike debate, and it intensified when Kautsky elaborated a "strategy of attrition" involving the "defense" of existing privileges against the growing right wing reaction, both within the party and society at large. This basically "passivist" position was countered by Rosa Luxemburg in her article *What Next?* It was this that provided the actual issue for a break. Things were further aggravated by Kautsky's alleged interference with Luxemburg's attempt to publish a rather personal rejoinder to criticisms of her position.

Once the break occurred, Luxemburg attacked with a vengeance. In contrast to Kautsky's "strategy of attrition," she claimed that existing privileges could only be defended by demanding new ones. She urged that the demand for the transformation of the monarchy into a republic be pressed immediately by the leadership, that the mass strike be employed as an offensive weapon, and that the party leaders foster an antimilitarist spirit and intensify the class consciousness of the proletariat in international terms.

The validity of this last position was shown when the First World War broke out. There can be little question that the majority of the proletariat did favor war on chauvinistic grounds. In large part, this was due to the fact that the SPD leadership—particularly after Bebel's death in 1913—did not seek to build and then deepen an international proletarian class consciousness within the masses. The primacy that the reformists achieved after 1910 in some sense made the issue of such consciousness a moot point. But the reason for this primacy stems in large part from the division of the radicals that, in turn, divided the SPD into three tendencies. To one side were the reformists like Vollmar, David, Noske, and Ebert, who increasingly espoused support for ruling-class imperialist policies. To another were those like Rosa Luxemburg, Karl Liebknecht, Clara Zetkin, and Franz Mehring, who were bent on a radical republicanism based on the use of the mass strike. Finally, there were the centrists: men like Kautsky, Emanuel Wurm, and Alfred Henke, who in theory sought to maintain the traditional policy of the *Erfurt Program*, but who in reality were moving closer to the Right through the "strategy of attrition." The radical Left was thus bisected, and it emerged politically weaker than ever.

This situation was only exacerbated by the increasing bureaucratization of the party under the stewardship of Friedrich Ebert. Access to the press became more difficult, and after 1912 the Reichstag membership came under the direct control of the party executive, which itself became ever more insulated from the masses while loyalty to the machine increased. This petrification of the party went hand in hand with the SPD's support of bourgeois nationalist aims. And as chauvinism and dreams of imperialist expansion grew, Rosa Luxemburg found herself ever more impotent within the centers of party power. As the war approached, she began an assault on party policy that focused on the question of imperialism and culminated in her major work, *The Accumulation of Capital*, which was published in 1913.

The Theory of Imperialism and the Praxis of War

Interestingly, it was at the point when she was in open conflict with the guardians of Marxist orthodoxy that Rosa Luxemburg made her reassessment of the tradition of Marxist political economy. Roughly speaking, two schools had arisen regarding the future development of capitalism. On the one hand, there were those who believed that capitalism always produces enough purchasing power to absorb an ever-expanding production of goods. From such a perspective, crises occur essentially because of the maldistribution of that purchasing power. On the other hand, there were those who felt that production necessarily outstrips the capitalist market via technological progress. Basically, the foremost followers of Marx in the Second International—Otto Bauer, Bukharin, Lenin, and Rudolf Hilferding—were supporters of the former position, while the liberal A. J. Hobson, Luxemburg's contemporary and the teacher of J. M. Keynes, and Heinrich Cunow took the opposing view. Rosa Luxemburg sided with the second tendency insofar as she believed that, given the extraordinary pace of industrialization around the turn of the century, more goods could be produced faster and cheaper. Following Marx, Luxemburg realized that these goods had to be sold in order for the bourgeoisie to accumulate more investment capital and thus perpetuate the system. But, if this were the case, a terrible situation necessarily arises for the capitalists who appropriate surplus value and who own the goods that are being produced. From Luxemburg's perspective, either the capitalist system in a given country must implode due to the increasing production of unsalable commodities and dead capital or an alternative must exist within the very structure of capitalism. This alternative can only involve the exportation of these goods and capital into precapitalist areas—in short, imperialism. As Marx had already shown, however, the flow of capitalist goods into precapitalist areas would itself eventually transform these primitive societies into industrial ones. Thus, for Luxemburg, the global system of capitalism will necessarily implode in any event, since it will at some point no longer have room to expand. In the meantime, however, there will necessarily be recurrent crises, punctuated by military conflicts over markets and resources.

It is true that Luxemburg did not recognize the possibility that instead of imploding, the capitalist system could intensify exploitation, or the possibility that an artificial bourgeoisie would be created in the precapitalist areas that would cripple the internal development of those areas in relation to the development of the world market. Nevertheless, the essential point of her analysis is that capitalism demands the existence of noncapitalist areas and that imperialism is part of the very structure of capitalism. Consequently, imperialism and capitalism could not be separated in analyzing bourgeois society, as certain social democrats chose to believe. Precisely because imperialism emerges as an immanent necessity of capitalism, the support of militarism and imperialist policies by the SPD actually involved a support of capitalist demands for the perpetuation of the system. Thus, it is perhaps not without a certain irony that the most effective criticism of Rosa Luxemburg's theory was voiced by Marxist theorists of the "Left": Bauer, Hilferding, Bukharin, and later Lenin.

In *The Accumulation of Capital*, theory is once again related to practice, for not only does Rosa Luxemburg's analysis serve to explain the socioeconomic development that would culminate in the First World War, it also serves to attack the entire revisionist trend of the Social Democratic Party. Still, it was in vain. When war did break out, the SPD caved in under bourgeois nationalist pressure and the chauvinism that had arisen within its own ranks. Although, judging from her letters, Rosa Luxemburg seemed to have continually believed that the masses were opposed to the leadership, the fact is that the masses had not been ideologically prepared to counteract the chauvinism of the bourgeoisie, and they succumbed to the war hysteria. Thus, integrated into the existing structure through the reformist policies that it had been pursuing while experiencing the rising tide of nationalism, the SPD voted war appropriations to the government in August 1914.

The SPD, however, had originally counted upon a quick end to the war. As it dragged on, opposition mounted, and in 1915, twenty-two

SPD Reichstag deputies abstained from voting to extend war credits. Of these twenty-two, twenty left the session. It was this group that formed the nucleus of what would become the Independent Social Democratic Party (USPD). The new party was to include people as different as Bernstein, Kautsky, and Zetkin. Thus, it is not surprising that this party should have been torn by conflict from the very start, conflict between those who wanted a radical break and those who wished to recreate the old spirit of the SPD. In fact, the only real unity within the party derived from opposition to the war, and so a year later—in 1916—a minority split from the USPD and formed the Spartacus League.

Rosa Luxemburg herself had little direct involvement in these political machinations, since she had been thrown into jail shortly after the war began and remained there virtually until its end. The despair that she felt with regard to the "Great Betrayal" by the German Socialists extended to the Second International as a whole. The vast majority of her former allies lined up to take sides in the conflict: Jules Guesde entered the French War Cabinet, Eduard Vaillant turned chauvinist, Cunow supported the Germans, and Plekhanov, the allies. The list could go on, and it would be a long one. Almost helplessly, Luxemburg wrote to Camille Huysmans that "the bankruptcy of the International is as complete as it is terrible."

While in jail, however, Luxemburg wrote a work that sharply attacked the degeneration of international socialism, and called for a reckoning with the SPD. This pamphlet, published under the pseudonym "Junius," was entitled *The Crisis of German Social Democracy*. But it was popularly known as the *Junius Brochure*, and it created a sensation. Rosa Luxemburg argued that the continuation of the war would weaken European capitalism, and that the antiwar position must involve a revolutionary attack upon the bourgeoisie by the working class. Indeed, these were the sentiments which Karl Liebknecht expressed in 1916 at the May Day demonstration on Potsdamerplatz in Berlin where he shouted: "Down with the war! "Down with the government!" Afterwards, he was arrested for treason.

It seems from her letters that Rosa Luxemburg thought little of the USPD and was also hesitant about the creation of a Spartacus faction. Still, she ultimately supported Spartacus, since the SPD papers were closed to the Left by 1916, while the party itself was becoming ever more closely aligned with those reactionary militarist groups it had originally opposed. In her view, furthermore, the USPD was composed of many of those veterans of the SPD—like Bernstein,

Kautsky, Wurm, and others—who had led the older party to its present juncture. Moreover, although ideologically to the left of the decayed SPD, many of the Independents could still remain adamantly opposed to the Russian Revolution of 1917, even though the USPD had initially expressed its support of the workers' council movement in Germany. Despite her doubts about its long term success, Rosa Luxemburg saw the Russian Revolution as the only real hope for the European and international proletariat. Indeed, her position is shown in a letter she wrote to Marta Rosenbaum from her prison cell: "Sure Kautsky knows nothing better than to prove statistically that Russian social conditions are not yet ripe for the dictatorship of the proletariat. A worthy 'theorist' of the USPD! He has forgotten that 'statistically' France in 1789 and even in 1793, was even less ripe for the rule of the bourgeoisie."

Her letters from prison, of course, do not mention Spartacus because of the censors. Nevertheless, Rosa Luxemburg tried desperately to stay aware of the changing situation. As the war continued, strikes began to take place, led by the Revolutionary Shop Stewards, who were close to the radical elements in the USPD and Spartacus, and carried through by workers in the more radical unions like the metal workers in Berlin. Meanwhile, the SPD was mounting a slanderous and virulent campaign against Spartacus, and especially against its leaders, Rosa Luxemburg and Karl Liebknecht, after their release from prison in 1918. Deprivation and unrest at home, flagging morale at the front, the disastrous invasion of Russia, and the threat of defeat in the West—all brought the war to a close. In this atmosphere, the bourgeoisie was terrified by the thought of the Russian Revolution spreading to Germany. When the kaiser abdicated his throne, Philipp Scheidemann—an old revisionist and enemy of Rosa Luxemburg's—called for the creation of the republic that would ultimately be led by Ebert and Noske. This seemingly radical demand, however, was not so radical at all, inasmuch as it sought to counter Karl Liebknecht's proclamation of a government to be based on the workers' and soldiers' soviets that were being formed both at the front and at home. It was to this end that Rosa Luxemburg worked during the last months of her life.

Emerging exhausted and emaciated from prison, she immediately began to write articles, make speeches, and help publish *Die Rote Fahne* (*The Red Flag*), while fleeing from one hiding place to another. All this is not to say that she simply supported the revolutionary action of the Berlin proletariat that was inspired by the Spartacists in the wake of the Russian Revolution. Not only was she

unconvinced with regard to the viability of the Spartacist revolutionary project, which was completely disorganized and clearly a
minority movement even among workers, she was also doubtful
about the possibility of creating a communist party from the
Spartacus League. Nevertheless, seeing no alternative, she went along
with both when the Communist Party of Germany (KPD) was formed
in the first days of 1919, and when workers went into the streets in
what came to be known as the Spartacus revolt. Before the Spartacist
leadership had even reached a decision on the possibility of
revolution, groups of workers, perhaps under the influence of agents
provocateurs, invaded the offices of the SPD's newspaper *Vorwärts*.
Immediately, Rosa Luxemburg threw her support behind the
struggle. Her old belief that one must "stay in contact with the
masses" remained with her, and she paid for it with her life. In order
to stem the revolutionary tide, Ebert and Noske entered into
negotiations with the military and its defeated generals, as well as
with the leading industrialists. The result for what would come to be
known as the Weimar Republic was that the old civil service and
judiciary would be retained, private property would not be
expropriated, and the army would serve to secure order. Thus,
capitalism would survive at the very heart of the new republic headed
by socialists; indeed, it was precisely this crucial set of compromises
that would mark the ill-fated "republic without republicans."

Once the deal had been made between the old stalwarts of the
semiabsolutist state and the SPD, the consequences for the
revolutionary Left were a foregone conclusion. The Spartacus revolt
was mercilessly crushed. Rosa Luxemburg and Karl Liebknecht were
murdered at the hands of right-wing soldiers on January 15, 1919,
with at least the tacit consent of Ebert and Noske.

Thus, socialists killed other socialists, helping to set a precedent
that would come to haunt the Left. Out of the piles of dead
revolutionaries, order emerged. Thus, the Weimar Republic, the
object of so much affection by moderates and aesthetes, was built on
blood—only later to drown in it. But order prevailed, at least for a
time. Yet, in her very last article, Rosa Luxemburg could write:
"Order reigns in Berlin! You stupid lackeys! Your 'order' is built on
sand. The revolution will raise itself again with clashes, and to your
horror it will proclaim with the sound of trumpets: 'I was, I am, I
shall be!' "

Rosa was right. The order was built on sand, and the more terrible
alternative in the choice that she had always seen between socialism
and barbarism became a reality. The call to action in the closing lines

of her last article has remained unfulfilled, and this parallels the status of the emancipatory vision that marked Rosa Luxemburg's politics and personality.

Friends

One of the most striking features of Rosa Luxemburg's correspondence is that it shows how very narrow she, a famous figure, kept her circle of intimates. And this was not simply a matter of choice. Though practically every comrade who had ever met Rosa Luxemburg remembered her as "Rosa," she was a difficult and temperamental person. Few friendships remained constant through her lifetime, and it is clear that those who ever became truly close to her do not number more than a handful. Moreover, she often seemed to be arbitrary in choosing both her friends and enemies, and sometimes politics was not even the essential criterion. She respected opponents like Lenin, Jaurès, and to a certain extent, even Bernstein. But she detested the good-natured Kantian-socialist Kurt Eisner. Also, though she thought highly of Parvus, she despised Trotsky and the cynical Karl Radek, who was one of her most gifted students and staunchest supporters in the early years.

Thus, politics was only one element of friendship. Though Rosa Luxemburg's letters are written exclusively to socialists, many of her friends were basically apolitical people who involved themselves with politics only out of loyalty to her. Gertrud Zlottko, Hans Diefenbach, and Mathilde Jacob, who ran such heavy risks smuggling Rosa Luxemburg's letters and manuscripts out of prison, fall into this category, and their own concerns have become a testament to the loyalty that Rosa Luxemburg inspired. Consequently, to view Luxemburg's circle as just another clique in an international socialist movement that was notorious for the cliques it engendered is to miss the point. Although she became acquainted in her youth with subsequent leaders of the SDKPL like Leo Jogiches, Julek Marchlewski, Feliks Dzerzinski, and Adolf Warski, in the larger world of German social democracy and the Second International her close friends were anything but powerful. Indeed, almost self-consciously, Luxemburg always preserved a certain distance from Bebel, Liebknecht, and even Kautsky. Thus, her circle was not one that could protect her from the machinations of other cliques within the movement.

Another point becomes important in this context. In contrast to the brilliant group of Polish organizers and intellectuals, the friends she chose upon entering the international scene were anything but her intellectual equals. Once again, Kautsky was to a certain extent the exception. Yet, even in her letters to him, and especially in her correspondence with Luise Kautsky, Mathilde Jacob, Sonja Lieb-knecht, and Hans Diefenbach, there is little resemblance to Marx's correspondence with his contemporaries or to the letters between Kautsky and Bebel, or Kautsky and Victor Adler for that matter. For Rosa Luxemburg did not generally argue over matters of theory or history with her close friends. In the intellectual realm, she was fully aware of her superiority. In fact, what was probably most important to Rosa Luxemburg in the friends she chose was—beyond any intellectual acumen—a lack of pretentiousness, a warmth, and even a certain naiveté.

The attachments Rosa Luxemburg felt for the members of her little group helped to create a secure private realm for her that stood beyond the political sphere. This circle gave Rosa the opportunity to express her inner needs and feelings with an effusiveness that stands in contrast to the formal role she had to play and, in a certain respect, to the caution she had to exhibit in public.

This private realm was always essential to Rosa Luxemburg. Again and again, she maintained that she was happier in a garden plot than at a party congress. Over and over in her letters to Jogiches she demanded a stable home life. After her death, friends such as Henriette Roland-Holst and Luise Kautsky, for various reasons, sought to show that Rosa Luxemburg was fundamentally an apolitical person. But, as her biographer Peter Nettl correctly stated: "The idea of having to choose between the woman of the red revolution and the woman of the pink window-boxes is ludicrous and arbitrary." There can be little question that Rosa Luxemburg demanded both a secure private life and an active political one—and clearly one served to balance the other. Her intimate circle helped create such a balance. Yet, the security that Rosa Luxemburg was able to find in her circle was to some extent based upon the tyranny she was able to exert. When disagreements did arise, Rosa Luxemburg would brook no opposition. Indeed, what becomes apparent quite often is an almost intolerable arrogance. Thus, after mercilessly attacking Mathilde Wurm, Luxemburg can respond to her friend's reply in the following manner:

> I had to smile: you want to "fight" me. Young lady, I sit tall in the saddle. No one has ever laid me low and I would be curious to know the

one who can do it. But I had to smile for yet another reason: because you do not even want to "fight" me, and also you are more dependent on me politically than you would wish to believe.

In a certain respect, this letter is indicative. Taking all her close friends into account, there was only one person who could consistently stand up to her: Leo Jogiches, her first great love. A man of action about whom still not enough is known, Jogiches always preferred to remain in the background. Secretive and furtive to the point of paranoia, Jogiches was the organizational power behind the SDKPL and later, the Spartacus League. His egoism was legendary, and yet Jogiches was a completely dedicated socialist who used his considerable fortune for the movement without any thought of personal gain or loss.

For the most part, the correspondence between them expresses the conflict for primacy in both the personal and political arenas. Yet their political views were intertwined from the very first, and Rosa Luxemburg always asked his advice on political questions, particularly in the early years. Their emotional intimacy was ended after Jogiches had an affair with another comrade while he was underground. Nevertheless, their working relationship continued until her death, and it was Jogiches who, although once again underground and miserable following the Spartacus insurrection, led the press investigation into the circumstances of her murder. In any event, Rosa Luxemburg's relationship with Leo Jogiches was very different from the ones she had had with Clara Zetkin's son Kostia and Hans Diefenbach.

Rosa Luxemburg had known Clara Zetkin since the Stuttgart Congress of 1898, and though Luxemburg had very little interest in the women's movement and the women's magazine *Gleichheit* (*Equality*), of which Clara Zetkin was the editor, they became lifelong friends. What becomes essential is that Rosa Luxemburg always viewed class—by this she meant the concept derived from the capitalist labor process—as central; in the same way proletarian consciousness transcended national and racial differences, so did it transcend sexual ones as well. Rosa Luxemburg refused to place her own subjective experience of being a woman—or her experience of being a Jew—beyond the fundamental objective contradiction within capitalist society: that between social production and private appropriation. The position of "women" always took second place to the position of the proletariat as a class. If one views Rosa Luxemburg in her historical context and as a follower of Marx, it would have made as little sense to speak of the emancipation of women in capitalist society as it did for Marx to speak of the emancipation of the Jews. Still, the differences between Rosa Luxemburg and Clara Zetkin are not as great as they might initially appear. Although Rosa clearly showed less interest in the women's issue than Clara, even for the latter any discussion about liberating women without proletarian class action would have been unthinkable.

In general, and as usual, Clara Zetkin took a back seat to her friend on intellectual and political matters. She objected strongly, however, to Rosa's brief affair with her young son. Luxemburg viewed Zetkin's stance with outrage as a prime example of hypocrisy. For his part, Kostia Zetkin felt pressure from both sides and so the affair ended quickly. It was after her break with Kostia Zetkin that Rosa Luxemburg formed her last attachment to Hans Diefenbach.

Neither Kostia Zetkin nor Diefenbach had the personal magnetism, or achieved the stature, of Jogiches. Both bowed to her will. Particularly in the case of Diefenbach, whom Rosa Luxemburg quite consciously sought to take in hand, the contrast with Jogiches is striking. Hans Diefenbach, a doctor, appeared to be a decent man, an intellectual dilettante who was uncertain of his future—and who was not particularly worried about it either. Still, Rosa loved him dearly. After his death in 1917 she was overcome with grief. Her letters to him express a lack of self-consciousness and an open equality that is missing in her letters to Jogiches. Yet, her letters to Diefenbach also make clear her desire that he become decisive, that he exert himself intellectually, and that he develop his personal potential to the utmost. In their admonitions, in their anecdotes, in their suggestions, Rosa Luxemburg's letters to him serve a purpose: *Bildung,* that is, cultural education in the broadest sense.

In fact, it is clear that all of Rosa Luxemburg's letters have a purpose behind them. In her early letters, aside from immediate concerns with her own career and party affairs—such as the Bernstein controversy, the mass strike question, and her conflicts with the party executive and the party papers—another element becomes manifest. Thus, in her letters to Jogiches, she quite consciously seeks to convince him of her own independence and also to force him to acknowledge her success within the most prestigious organization of the socialist world. These letters seek to establish her independence and the basis of their personal relationship. But at the same time a process of self-clarification becomes apparent in terms of her own development.

This link between self-clarification and the analysis of her interpersonal relations runs through all her letters. The two are never separate or disjointed. Thus, after coming out of her relationship with Jogiches, Rosa Luxemburg urged her female friends to take a personal stand for independence—particularly when the spouses of these female friends became political enemies, as in the cases of Luise Kautsky and Mathilde Wurm. Clearly, Rosa Luxemburg viewed her own life as an example to be emulated—a notion by which she at once justified herself and sought to develop the character of her friends by forcing them to reflect upon the various influences to which they were subject. This becomes readily apparent in her furious letter to Mathilde Wurm.

> Yes, your letter made me seethe with rage because, despite its brevity, it shows me in every line how very much you are again under the influence of your milieu . . . . (All of) you think that audacity would surely please you, but because of it one can be thrown into the cooler, and one is then of "little use!" Ach!—you miserable little mercenaries. You would be ready enough to put a little bit of "heroism" up for sale—but only "for cash," even if only for three mouldy copper pennies. After all, one must immediately see its "use" on the sales counter. For you people, the simple words of honest and upright men have not been spoken: "Here I stand, I can't do otherwise; God help me!" Luckily, world history up until this point has not been made by people like yourselves. Otherwise, we wouldn't have had a Reformation, and we probably would still be living in the *ancien régime.*

The obvious dynamism of her style carries through most of her letters. Still, for the most part, her early letters are tougher and are written in a more factual vein than the later ones. These are the letters of youth in which she is feeling herself beginning to flex her political and intellectual muscles. The tone changes with the change in her circumstances. Particularly in prison, her letters assume a lyrical power of poetic proportions as her gaze shifts from the infighting within the International to the little world of her confinement: a world of insects, plants, and birds.

The Prisoner

It is easy to forget how drab and debilitating prison life can actually be. Rosa Luxemburg's letters serve as a reminder. In prison, revolt takes on a personal form. True, there are the newspapers, there is the political rage, there is the plotting. But beyond all this there is also the day-to-day life and the protest that must be mounted against the circumstances of confinement. In short, there is the simple demand for sanity and a little life. Thus, Rosa Luxemburg reacts against the drudgery of prison life by looking to the clouds and the multicolored stones in the paved paths on which she walks. She searches for beauty in the cracks of existence, and in response to the boredom of isolation, she watches insects, feeds her titmice, and observes the manifold diversity of nature.

When Rosa Luxemburg emerged from prison in 1918, she was visibly altered; she had withered, and her hair had turned completely white. In prison, she had suffered terribly from stomach problems and from her nerves. Still, Rosa remained active throughout those years. It is true that she wrote little during her confinement: there was the Korolenko translation, and the extraordinary *Anti-Critique*, but little more. Still, she read—geology, animal husbandry, literary criticism, political economy, history, Shakespeare, Goethe, etc.

In truth, Rosa Luxemburg appears as a Renaissance woman from these prison letters: the anti-intellectualism of the pseudo-radical and his flight into nature, as well as the *apparatchik* mentality of Stalinism, are equally foreign to her. Indeed, the popular image of the revolutionary as a dour, sneering, paranoid automaton bears little resemblance to the picture of this spirited woman trying to construct a semblance of life in her tiny cell.

The world remains open to her, and these letters bristle with vitality. The lyricism, which some will discuss with a cynical shrug, allows Rosa Luxemburg to affirm her sense of self, her spontaneity, which was always in danger of being liquidated. At the same time, the repetition of various phrases and incidents is not accidental, for these letters are meant to produce a certain effect.

Many of Rosa Luxemburg's friends, and particularly Sonja Liebknecht, were susceptible to personal depression and political despair. Especially in the now famous *Letters from Prison*, written to Sonja Liebknecht, Rosa Luxemburg sought to dispel this depression by shifting Sonja's focus from the horror of the immediate political reality to the occasional moments of beauty and happiness that continue to exist within the horror.

This is, of course, not to say that Rosa Luxemburg wants to escape the political realm. The possibility of change always exists on the horizon: the objective contradictions of capitalist society do not disappear, and the individual must remain ready to perceive an emerging crisis. For such a perception, however, despair or cynicism are equally useless at best and directly counterrevolutionary at worst. Still, a time of great personal tragedy is not always the moment for doctrinaire and turgid analysis. Thus, Rosa Luxemburg merges the political with the lyrical when she writes: "The psyche of the masses, like the eternal sea always carries all the latent possibilities: the deathly calm and the roaring storm, the lowest cowardice and the wildest heroism. The mass is always that which it *must* be according to the circumstances of the time, and the mass is always at the point of becoming something different than what it appears to be."

In this way, hope emerges—but there are still moments of horror from which Rosa Luxemburg refuses to shy away. In one of her most moving letters to Sonja Liebknecht, Luxemburg describes the anguish of a water buffalo—the slavery to which it is subjected, and the mistreatment it must silently bear at the hands of a sadistic driver. Rosa writes that this episode reflects the entire horror of the war. But there is more: the curt ending makes clear that she and Karl Liebknecht are no different from that tortured buffalo. There is no longer room for silent anguish. At the end of the letter, what was once a passive depression had been transformed into an active anger.

All the later lyrical letters seek to bolster confidence, revive strength, and inspire the will in the face of the political and social degeneration that followed upon the outbreak of the First World War and the "Great Betrayal" by the social democratic movement. In this sense, Rosa Luxemburg comes to incarnate what the philosopher Ernst Bloch has called a "militant optimism." This militant optimism does not simply involve the passive belief that "everything will turn out all right," or a belief in fate, or even an unquestioning belief in the objective "historical" laws of the dialectic. Instead, it demands a consistent engagement to *make* everything turn out all right through struggle. But that is not all, for Rosa Luxemburg does not simply dismiss the personal demand for happiness in the name of this struggle. Her revolt is not only political, but personal as well. A militant hope for change merges with a personal demand—the demand for a measure of happiness in the face of the most brutal oppression. In opposition to the cynicism, pessimism, and despair that is so prevalent following the degeneration of the politics of the sixties, it is precisely this "militant optimism" that makes a view of Rosa Luxemburg's personal life so valuable today.

The Cultural Milieu

It is an implicit assumption of many that radical politics necessarily engenders radical tastes in art. If this is doubtful as a general rule, the division between radical social views and nonradical aesthetics becomes particularly striking in the case of Rosa Luxemburg. Although she was a persistent critic of the Second International and stood politically on the far left, a perception of art results from Rosa Luxemburg's letters that is very much in accordance with the more traditionalist views dominant among the intellectuals of the international social democratic movement.

Those who were more modern favored the naturalistic and the realistic in terms of the formal principles of a work of art. There was, however, also a concern with classicism and romanticism. In short, following the predilections of Marx and Engels, the emphasis was upon the elaboration of what was considered the cultural heritage of the revolutionary bourgeoisie. These aesthetic concerns of the Second International would ultimately serve as a link to the dogmatic policies of the Third International and the emphasis upon socialist realism. Nevertheless, it cannot be forgotten that during these years of the Second International, Marxian cultural criticism was still in its infancy. Indeed, the experimentalist-modernist views that would flower in the twenties with Ernst Bloch, Walter Benjamin, Bertolt Brecht, and even Trotsky, were still virtually unknown to the socialist reading public—as was the concept of "proletarian" culture, at least as it was to be put forward by Stalin and Zhdanov.

The dominant literary figures for the Second International as a whole were Franz Mehring and Georgi Plekhanov. Rosa Luxemburg knew both of them, and thus it is understandable that she should continually refer to Mehring's masterpiece of literary criticism, *The Lessing Legend.* Both Mehring and Plekhanov were socialists whose literary values were derived from the Enlightenment. Both were rationalists, and both were sociological in their approach insofar as art was considered fundamentally in terms of the class relations it mirrored and the pedagogic function it served for the workers. Literature was consequently seen as a tool to both educate the individual and serve the building of class consciousness among the masses. Thus, it is no accident that neither Mehring nor Plekhanov (nor Luxemburg) valued the avant-garde movements—such as Art Nouveau, Fauvism, Futurism, Expressionism, etc.—that were developing around the turn of the century. All these movements unleashed their aesthetic fury upon the classical-rationalist bourgeois past and were, moreover, essentially confined to the bohemian literati until shortly before the outbreak of World War I.

These were the attitudes that fundamentally colored Rosa Luxemburg's aesthetic world view. Two elements were basic to this world view: the pedagogic social content and the expression of the individual's inner experience. Neither alone was enough, and the emphasis that she placed upon one or the other in the particular context was simply that: a matter of emphasis. The social aspect naturally assumed greater primacy in the few aesthetic pieces she wrote for popular consumption. Yet, when she wrote about Romain Rolland's *Jean-Christophe in Paris* in one of her letters, she could say that, despite its progressive political message and naturalist form, "It is not an authentic work of art. I am so inexorably sensitive in these matters that even the most beautiful (political) tendency cannot substitute for God-given genius."

Thus, Rosa Luxemburg was not influenced by the SPD's attempts to create a "popular" workers' culture. Rather, she drew a line between art and propaganda. As becomes clear in her little essay *Tolstoy as a Social Thinker*, the value of the great artist does not lie in the positive propagandist solutions that he holds out for society, but rather in the depth of his criticism of the existent. Consequently, Rosa Luxemburg is quite removed from the Stalinist method of identifying the work of art with the politics it professes and then judging its value. Nevertheless, in the beautiful introduction to her translation of Korolenko's *History of My Contemporary* she can note how the Russian literary tradition "was born out of opposition to the Russian regime, out of the spirit of struggle." She can also criticize Baudelaire, Wedekind, and D'Annunzio for their "egotism" and their "over-saturation with modern culture."

For Rosa Luxemburg, although the experience of art might enrapture the individual, it was to edify him in his personal development and social views as well. Thus, a moralistic element that sometimes verges on the puritanical enters Rosa's observations on art, which is also in accord with the dominant attitudes of the socialists at the turn of the century.

Social democracy saw itself as the wave of the future and as a movement that was preserved from the decadence of bourgeois society. This theme, which Kautsky and others emphasized so consistently, also runs through Rosa Luxemburg's letters, and it is fascinating to see how it influences her aesthetic judgments. Thus, she can claim that everything perverse and decadent is foreign to her. Moreover, in one of her letters to Diefenbach she can cite a lengthy and shallow passage from a review in which a Dr. Morgenstern expounds on Shakespeare's female characters regarding the nobility of their instincts, their freshness, and their lack of corruption. On the other hand, she can criticize Titian for being too elegant, Hölderlin for being "too stately," and even her admired Ricarda Huch for an occasional lack of feminine modesty.

In this sense, it is no wonder either that Rosa Luxemburg should look to Mörike, whose lyrical, often overly sentimental, poetry serves to purify nature. In fact, it becomes obvious that the romantic serves to complement the naturalist-realist world view. The experience of transcendent rapture—which is fundamental to romanticism—is often seen as inimically opposed to a naturalism that brings the individual face to face with the decadence and misery of human interaction in a given system. What unites the two modes, however, is the unmediated character of the subject's relation to his world. For Rosa Luxemburg, the romantic impulse, the concern with nature, and the refinement of the emotions provide a certain insight into the peace and serenity for which she longs. On the other hand, the harsh reality that needs to be overcome becomes clear in the objectivist-realist form.

Rosa Luxemburg never actually links the two aesthetic modes together. In fact, she seems to oscillate back and forth between these two artistic points of view; where, on the one hand, she will demand the subjective emotional experience of reality basic to romanticism, on the other hand she will often call for an objectively realistic quality within an artwork and the comprehension of repression within the objective realm of existence that is fostered by naturalism and realism. The fundamental contradiction between these two views is never reconciled by Rosa Luxemburg. Nevertheless, the very contradiction points up the need for a literature that will attempt to define the liberating possibilities of the future for a subject through an immanent examination of the present in terms of the objective social interactions that shape it. Rosa Luxemburg does not inquire into the question of artistic transcendence. For her, a work continually assumes validity in the present. The sculptures of Rodin strike her for their humanism, their dignity—and she immediately thinks of her fellow member of the International, and opponent, Jaurès. Voltaire: before the war, he had little meaning for her; *Candide*, his "wicked compilation of all human vices," originally struck her as a caricature of the human condition—but there is the war, and thus Voltaire becomes "totally realistic." And Gerhart Hauptmann: the sentimental naturalist par excellence, the author of *The Weavers*, perhaps *the* first great exposition of naturalism with its "soft" socialism. But it is not *The Weavers* that intrigues Rosa Luxemburg. Rather, it is the little known *Emanuel Quint*. When she speaks of the latter work in her letters, she sees her own situation mirrored in the Christ figure of the book. His tragedy is her own: "the tragedy of an individual who preaches to the masses and who feels, at the very moment that the words fall from his lips, that each has become crude and caricatured in the heads of the listeners."

There is hardly a work Rosa Luxemburg praises that is not considered in the context of its immediate relevance. Nevertheless, the immediacy that she prizes is different from the experience of immediacy that has become essential to the avant-garde tradition and that, at present, has become part and parcel of the modern novel: the singular concern with the subject to the exclusion of the external world, the employment of shock, and the existentialist emphasis upon "anguish" as the authentic moment in which reality is laid bare—all go against the grain of Rosa Luxemburg's aesthetic taste.

Indeed, literature meant more than wallowing in a morass of inwardness to Rosa Luxemburg. At the same time, it was not simply a vehicle for an author's contempt for the prevalent forms of social interaction. The latter becomes clear in a discussion of Galsworthy in one of her letters, and it provides a valuable insight into Rosa's own values. Although she attests to the fact that Galsworthy is "brilliant" after reading *The Man of Property*, her opinion changes after reading *Fraternity*. In the latter work, Galsworthy is seen as too "sophisticated," and Rosa likens him to Shaw and Wilde.

There is no question that she is put off by this peculiarly English mode of cynical, civilized, and cultured social criticism. As so often occurs in her letters, what emerges is an observation and not an analysis. Yet, an insight follows that deserves elaboration. What appears with the three authors in question is a type of cynical pessimism that itself marks the ideological decadence of bourgeois culture at the turn of the century. Despite the good humor and the progressive social consciousness—which Rosa Luxemburg fully appreciates—the comedy of manners still leaves the social realm untouched in pointing up hypocrisy. Irony, naturally, is at the center of this form of criticism. And yet, it is precisely this element of ironic cynicism that preserves the status quo, insofar as the author alone achieves exemption from the hypocritical frailties that he reserves for society at large. Since everyone except the author is caught in the mire of hypocrisy, there is no possibility for the social change that could

immanently emerge from the criticism. Thus, a cynical egotism
undermines the social achievement of happiness. This concern with
happiness is part of Rosa Luxemburg's own joie de vivre. Thus, she
can agree with Korolenko's simple statement: "Happiness is
salubrious and elevating to the soul. And I always believe, you know,
that man is rather obliged to be happy."

This is a demand that art puts forward, and it does not mean that art
is simply "an expedient luxury for releasing the feelings of beauty, or
happiness, in beautiful souls," as Luxemburg ironically puts the
matter in her Tolstoy essay. The liberating potential within art is not
there for an elite, but for the masses who must be taught to recognize
it. Art is not passive, but rather becomes part of the social response to
oppression. Much like her perception of nature, Rosa Luxemburg's
literary interests become part of the response to the oppression of her
confinement in the prisons of Germany. Not only was she able to
retain a certain link to social interaction through art, but the emotive
experience became central to her own ability to come to grips with her
imprisonment. Sitting in a tiny cell, she recited her Mörike in the
dark. It wasn't much, but it helped keep the will to liberation alive
through the stimulus to the imagination that these poems produced.

If one were to employ categories, it is clear that Rosa Luxemburg
revelled in what Walter Benjamin would later call the "aura" of a
work of art, particularly when in prison. For her part, however, Rosa
employed no categories: art was the medium for achieving a breadth
of knowledge and an emotive exaltation. Never in these letters does
she seek to reflect upon either the nature of the aesthetic experience or
the epistemological categories that allow for the comprehension of
that experience.

Rosa Luxemburg thought very little of literary criticism. To a
certain extent it made sense. Criticism of this sort was still essentially
the preserve of bohemia—as in the case of Valéry or Mallarmé—while
the university was strongly dominated by Dilthey and the neo-
Kantians. Moreover, Rosa Luxemburg did not in general look to the
complex or the innovative in cultural matters. The names that
consistently appear in her letters are the ones common to the period.
In fact, if there is something striking in these letters regarding the
turn-of-the-century cultural milieu of socialism, it is not the
inclusion of certain names but the omission of certain others. There is
virtually no mention of reactionary, or protofascist, writers like
Barrès who would exert such an enormous influence. At the same
time, writers like Gide or Thomas Mann, who were to fundamentally
influence the cultural production of the future, hardly appear; nor is

there any discussion of painters like Cézanne, Matisse, Klee, or Kandinsky.

These lapses were clearly self-induced; her friend Franz Pfemfert, the editor of the expressionist organ *Die Aktion* (*Action*), would surely have introduced her to the important works of modernism. Nevertheless, Rosa Luxemburg shied away. In one of her letters to Sonja Liebknecht, Rosa responds to the former's statement that she has not kept up with modern developments in the arts. She replies that she had already read Dehmel in 1902 and that she was aware of the work of Arno Holz and Johann Schlaf. But when it comes to two major figures, she can simply state: "I don't understand [Hugo von] Hofmannsthal, and I don't know [Stefan] George. It's true: with all of them, I am a bit frightened by their complete mastery of form, by their poetic means of expression, and their lack of a grand, noble Weltanschauung." From her early, limited flirtation with the avant-garde, Rosa Luxemburg retreated to Mörike and Goethe, to the terrain upon which she and her socialist contemporaries felt secure.

Certain critics and biographers have chosen to regard Rosa Luxemburg's opposition to the avant-garde as somehow precipitating the Marxian theory of realism whose primary exponent was to become Georg Lukács. To emphasize Rosa Luxemburg's role in this regard, however, is to stretch a point. It is not simply a question of her opposing modernism—even Goethe had done that in his time—nor is it a question of her being more tolerant than Lukács in her aesthetic judgments, or more eclectic. What becomes essential is that the categories upon which a Marxian aesthetic can be built are missing in her observations. Unlike Lukács, for example, Rosa Luxemburg never actually describes the concrete content of this "grand, noble Weltanschauung" that is missing in the modernists. Moreover, she does not draw any structural differentiations between writers as different as Galsworthy and Tolstoy, or even Mörike and Goethe.

Rosa Luxemburg does not have a systematic theory of aesthetics. The criteria she uses are generalistic and often even arbitrary; they involve little more than her personal perception of emotional and social needs. Thus, to view Rosa Luxemburg as a real influence on Marxian aesthetics is to do her an injustice. Her aesthetic limitations were the limitations of her age and contemporaries. The theories that would seek to interpret art in terms of its liberating possibilities would have to await the Hegelian revival within Marxism, the degeneration of radical politics following the revolutionary developments after World War I, and, to a certain extent, the displacement of revolution from the political into the cultural realm. For Rosa

Luxemburg, the issue of art was not very complex; thus she could write: "In theoretical work, as in art, I value only the simple, the tranquil and the bold." For her, that was enough.

Rosa Luxemburg for the Present

So, how then is one to assess the legacy of Rosa Luxemburg? Traditional values stemming from the Enlightenment emphasize the notion that politicians and political movements are to be judged by their "success" or "failure," while the importance of the thinker or activist emerges in the relative predominance that his theory has attained within the historical process of "success." Of course, it is clear that Rosa Luxemburg's thought has not achieved the *stature in praxis* that may be attributed to the thought of Lenin, or even Bernstein for that matter. Also, the revolutionary movements that might have retained central elements of her thought are dead—at least for the moment.

Given the prevalence of this historical standpoint among *both dogmatic Marxists and bourgeois political theorists,* Rosa Luxemburg emerges as a courageous, incisive, sincere, and idealistic political activist and thinker. As Lenin expressed it in his obituary, she was an "eagle" who soared above the "chickens." That, however, is where it ends—and that is not enough. Indeed, in a sharply critical letter to Konrad Haenisch, Rosa Luxemburg warns him "never (to) transform political questions into personal, sentimental ones." The fact that Rosa was a warm human being of profound sensitivity, a dedicated socialist, and a woman who died a tragic death is not enough to make her relevant to the present. For there have been countless other dedicated socialists, just as warm and just as sensitive, who have died just as tragically. There must be more involved, but if this dimension is to be uncovered, then perhaps it is necessary to call into question those very assumptions upon which the dominant modes of historical judgments are based.

There is a fundamental problem in viewing history in terms of the successes it has engendered. Truly, Hegel's notion that "the real is rational and the rational is real" comes to be retained in such a view, whether one recognizes himself as indebted to Hegel or not. Two questions must be posed: What about the potential that has not become real? What about the possibilities that have not been actualized? From the traditional perspective, all this comes to be seen as "irrational." Consequently, it is dismissed—but always in the name of the present that has become manifest. In the name of the existent, the relative validity of those emancipatory demands and needs that were expressed both in theory and praxis are brushed aside and termed "impossible to achieve." Of course, since any attempt to achieve them in the present is viewed as "impossible" by definition, a self-fulfilling prophecy results. Under any circumstances, however, these thoughts and events are forgotten as history comes to be judged in terms of its successes alone. Thus, an ideological benefit for the status quo comes to be assured: the present assumes a purity, a primacy, and a truth that separates it from what lies blood-splattered beneath what Hegel—who at least still retained the tragic sense of historical failure—called "the slaughterbench of history." The reason is simple: historical "success" is always judged from the vantage point of the present and on the basis of the validity that is either consciously or unconsciously given to the status quo. This is the reason that both the West and the East can agree to praise Rosa Luxemburg—and then forget her.

The historical continuum that leads to the present is, however, as little sacrosanct as the present itself. Thus, it may become necessary to retrieve the elements of a radicalism whose revolutionary content has not been appropriated by the conventional strategies of success. It is in this context that Rosa Luxemburg assumes her importance.

How often has the cry against "imperialism" or for "anticolonialism" been raised by a nationalist-militarist bourgeois, or even petty bourgeois, elite for so-called revolutionary purposes? And anything can be used in the battle against the oppressor: religion, "the opium of the masses," becomes part of the revolutionary arsenal; tribalism or regional peculiarities, which ultimately further divide the oppressed, assume a wholly positive value; "tradition," precisely that which throws ideological chains on the creation of a liberating future, becomes a source of "cultural identity" as it propagates a terrifying provincialism. Of course, the list can be lengthened, and what becomes evident is that these weapons offered as instruments of liberation become precisely the tools necessary to strengthen the legitimacy of a new national elite.

Yet, in Rosa Luxemburg's *Accumulation of Capital* and *Anti-Critique*, there is the reminder that it is not imperialism alone that must be fought, but rather its progenitor: capitalism. Following Marx, Rosa Luxemburg understood that to be radical is "to go to the root," that is to say, to the actual structural conditions that make imperialism both possible and necessary. In contrast to Lenin, for whom capitalism becomes imperialistic in its final, monopoly phase,

Rosa Luxemburg realized that imperialism was endemic to capitalist expansion from the start. The pure emphasis upon imperialism and anticolonialism obscures the class divisions within the colonized themselves. Thus, it is no wonder that, where nationalism becomes the antiimperialist battle cry, capitalism should emerge once again and even that wars among the oppressed nations should become a commonplace.

It becomes clear from Rosa Luxemburg's letters regarding the Polish question that she already understood that the response to imperialist policies in the name of a simple nationalism—let alone a nationalism decked with religion and other reactionary baggage— necessarily misses the point regarding what is to be opposed. The truth is that Rosa Luxemburg, in her personal views as well as in her theory, makes the Left cognizant of the fact that there can be no compromise regarding what it opposes and no deflection of energies from what it supports. Whether an oppressed group chooses to call its ideology "socialist" or not, "liberating" or not, she recognized that the ideological emphasis upon religion, tradition, sex, or race would only lead to an obfuscation of the actual basis upon which contemporary oppression is grounded: capitalism. As she writes in one of her letters, only when national goals—or any particularist goals—become concomitant "with the solidarity of the proletariat" does the actual potential for liberation from the structural conditions of capitalism arise.

The ability to reflect upon these structural conditions and to judge what will strengthen the "solidarity of the proletariat" without compromising its class consciousness demands the exercise of the critical faculty. This cannot involve judging the present in terms of some abstract ideal. It must rather attempt to clarify and actualize that ideal within the possibilities of the existing situation. In the manifestation of the goal within everyday politics, critical thinking necessarily becomes part of political activity. Thus, Rosa Luxemburg can laud this merger in her letter to Adolf Warski regarding her Polish comrades who did not allow their critical faculties to be swept away by their enthusiasm for the Russian Revolution. Still, the critical faculty must itself be fostered in the masses who are the prime victims of their oppressors' ideology.

From Rosa Luxemburg's life work, it becomes clear that there is no substitute for such activity, which necessitates staying "in contact with the masses" through political organization. Far too much has been made of the overemphasis upon spontaneity in her thought. Rosa Luxemburg always worked through an organization. But this should not be misconstrued as giving solace to the sects that populate the Left. For her, the organization had to be mass-based, socialist, and democratic. Even more, however, in her form of organization the principle had to emerge that "social democracy is not joined to the organization of the proletariat. It is itself the proletariat."

It would be a serious mistake to think that this statement simply avoids the issue of the relation between the masses and the organization. For what becomes apparent from the outset is that there can be no substitute for the masses taking their destiny into their own hands, what Marx called *Selbsttätigkeit*. At the same time, however, Rosa Luxemburg realized that "insofar as the mass must exercise power, it also must learn how to exercise it." Clearly this must be learned through politics, through participating in an organization that is dedicated to increasing the masses' recognition of their own creative powers and their potential for control. Such is the dialectic that informs the relationship between the organization and the mass. Only as the revolutionary consciousness of the masses heightens and then culminates in action does the differentiation between them dissolve in the new forms of social interaction that the masses themselves create.

Of course, the fundamental action by which the masses take charge of their own destiny is, for Rosa Luxemburg, the mass strike. As she writes in a letter to Henriette Roland-Holst, who was to become one of the premier European ultraleftists: "The mass strike should not be considered as a mechanistic remedy for the defense of proletarian rights, but rather as a fundamental revolutionary form." Thus, the mass strike is not to be some particular strike writ large, but rather a complex of actions in which the proletariat gives vent to its creative possibilities. In a letter to the Kautskys in 1906, Luxemburg writes with astonishment that the most important result of the 1905 revolution in Russia occurred when "in all factories, committees elected by the workers have arisen 'on their own' which decide on all matters relating to working conditions, hirings and firings of workers, etc. The employer has actually ceased being the 'master in his own house.' " But in the same letter, and as a recurrent theme in other letters, she complains about the chaos of the organization and the lack of real leadership. Consequently, Rosa is not opposed to organization as such, but rather to any party that refuses to emphasize the self-activity and self-management of the masses. In fact, this is one of the threads that links her critique of the SPD to her later critique of the Bolsheviks in her essay *The Russian Revolution*.

An example from the Russian Revolution of 1905, which is

elaborated in her letters, shows very clearly what Rosa Luxemburg
had in mind in her criticism of organization:

> Recently the management of a factory wanted to punish several
> workers for being very late. The factory committee prevented this;
> whereupon, the factory owner lodged a complaint with the Committee
> of the Social Democratic Party, claiming that the factory committee
> was "not acting in accordance with Social Democratic principles"
> since the Social Democratic Party stands for diligent and honest
> fulfillment of obligations. And so in one case after the other.

This is precisely the type of bureaucratic formalism that incensed
Rosa. For her, the essential element in a working-class party involved
the emphasis upon precisely that radicalization of consciousness and
socialization of knowledge that would undermine the need for
hierarchical leadership to infuse proletarian self-awareness.

In this way, the notion of active self-administration by the masses
emerges at the very center of Rosa Luxemburg's thought. The
proletariat must be pressed to manage itself and engage itself in the
process of fulfilling and creating its own goals. This cannot be done
through distortions, lies, a supposed proletarian infallibility, and
bluster—all of which emerge in the proletarian papers of either the
established communist regimes or our sects here in America. For
Rosa, the proletariat had to know the truth and learn from its
mistakes. Only in this way could the process develop by which the
proletariat would be enabled to enter what she called "the school of
public life" and to create what the contemporary social thinker Oskar
Negt termed "a proletarian public sphere."

What this involves is an emphasis upon self-administration of the
masses by a party whose purpose lies in creating the conditions for its
own disappearance, a party which will carry over and deepen the
theory and radical tradition behind self-administration even in
periods of revolutionary decline. The concern is nothing other than
that the very notion of politics be transformed from one that is
external and irrelevant to the individual to one that is essential to his
own development. Yet, the creation of a public sphere in which the
individual can recognize his own potential for growth demands a new
discussion of the concepts of freedom and responsibility. Freedom
cannot simply remain internal or negative. It must instead become
positive insofar as the individual must assume responsibility—in
common with others—for his destiny and that of the community of
which he is a part. This type of responsibility based on freedom,
however, demands that democracy come to the foreground of

socialism to the same degree that all types of bureaucratic formalism come under attack.

Let there be no mistake: the merger of socialism and democracy does not allow for the right to appropriate the profits produced by the labor of others. This right leaves freedom in the abstract for the majority of the populace. For Rosa Luxemburg, democracy must be extended from the purely formal freedoms of bourgeois representative government to the actual relations of everyday life. But for this to occur, the concrete exploitation of the proletariat in the realm of civil society must be abolished. Thus the bourgeoisie, along with bourgeois relations of production, must be suppressed. In short, the mass must take responsibility and control of the process of production as well as of the process of distributing wealth. Nevertheless, the freedoms that have been developed cannot simply be discarded or abolished by the proletariat; instead, they must be deepened. This is why Rosa Luxemburg can write, in opposition to the Bolsheviks, that

> Freedom only for the supporters of the government, only for the members of one party—however numerous they may be—is no freedom at all. Freedom is always and exclusively freedom for the one who thinks differently. Not because of any fanatical concept of "justice," but because all that is instructive, wholesome, and purifying in political freedom depends on this essential characteristic, and its effectiveness vanishes when "freedom" becomes a special privilege.... The public life of countries with limited freedom is so poverty-stricken, so miserable, so rigid, so unfruitful, precisely because, through the exclusion of democracy, it cuts off the living source of all spiritual riches and progress. (Proof: the year 1905 and the months from February to October, 1917.) There this freedom was political in character; the same thing applies to economic and social life also. The whole mass of the people must take part in it. Otherwise, socialism will be decreed from behind a few desks by a dozen intellectuals.

To put it simply, only through the recognition of democracy in practice—in all spheres of life—does the goal of freedom become manifest. Rosa Luxemburg, of course, supported the Bolshevik revolution, and her remarks can be understood only in terms of this support. For the present, however, what becomes truly essential in Rosa Luxemburg's thought is an insight that has been lost amid the carnage of Stalinism. From her thought it becomes clear that freedom cannot exist in the abstract; rather, it must always mean a freedom for the particular subject in the positive work of expanding the horizon of his possibilities within a nonexploitative society.

In a certain sense, this is precisely what emerges as the revolutionary *telos* once the concept of democracy is viewed in dynamic terms. For Rosa Luxemburg, then, democracy is not confined to one form of government or one static state. Democracy becomes the very purpose of the mass struggle within the socialist context, and yet the democratic progress that has been achieved is not something to be taken for granted. As has been pointed out in the discussion of her debate with Bernstein, Rosa Luxemburg recognizes that democracy is anything but the basic law of historical development. To conservatives and liberals who dote on the relation between capitalism and democracy, Rosa Luxemburg shows that there is no intrinsic relation between capitalism and democracy and that capitalism can coexist with numerous political forms. This, however, only makes the preservation and extension of democratic liberties that much more essential against threats from the Right or groups that foster slogans without content and ideologies without a liberating substance.

For Rosa Luxemburg, true democracy is impossible without socialism. At the same time, however, she warns against allowing any temporary measures to be turned into high points of dogma. In this respect, her criticism of the SPD's "parliamentary cretinism" is not very different from her critique of Bolshevism, where she can take account of expedients necessitated by the historical situation while refusing to see them as established doctrines that might inform any revolutionary strategy. Thus, to be concrete: it is one thing to demand the suffrage or employ electoral strategy in order to propagandize in the positive sense of making clear the proletariat's revolutionary needs; it is quite another when democracy is seen as stopping at a given point or when parliamentarism is turned into an end unto itself.

A new society remains on the agenda that is itself predicated on the conquest of political power by the working class. There is no blueprint. Thus, the new remains indeterminate, open, unstructured, and waiting for the mass action in which its democratic content can become manifest. Yet, this goal must itself become exposed in the concrete actions that the party takes, particularly in the periods between the moments of mass action. Consequently, there can be no simple dichotomy between the tasks of the present and this final goal of the future. Stalinism has shown all too well how the goal can be continually pushed away into an ever-receding future in the name of the immediate tasks of the present, once this split is made.

But such a dichotomy between present and future is not only attributable to Stalinism, for it became a part of reformist social democratic tactics as well. In this context, Rosa Luxemburg's controversy over militarism with the revisionist Max Schippel assumes a basic relevance. At present, the same strains that Schippel played are to be heard: to wit, militarism and the establishment of defense contracts gives employment to the workers. Although this may be true (the question aside whether all this money could be spent in a more productive fashion), as Rosa Luxemburg showed, such a policy only makes the final goal that much more difficult to achieve. And not only that, it deters the workers from recognizing their true international class needs by driving them into an ever closer alliance with those nationalist groups whose interests oppose their own. Thus, any potential for revolutionary consciousness is integrated into the structure of the existent, the strength of which necessarily increases through such reformist action.

Naturally, there can be no program that will guide the working class in the choices it must make in all situations. From Rosa Luxemburg's thought, however, it becomes obvious that an organizational concept based on the actual social conditions of the present must be developed, the purpose of which would be the creation of the critical faculty among the workers themselves. Such an organization cannot be forged by an elite, and its structure must be loose. No one ever claimed that such an organization is the most efficient possible (at least in terms of bourgeois rationality), but one thing is certain: whenever the workers simply hand over their own responsibilities for leadership, they will be misrepresented. Thus, this new organizational form, determined to create the conditions for its own dissolution as it fosters the consciousness of the masses, cannot simply define the goals and needs of the proletariat. The masses must themselves learn to create and determine their goals, their needs, and their structures for the world that they will control.

Democracy becomes its own end where the masses themselves take responsibility for what is produced and how it is to be distributed. But that is only the beginning. As democracy becomes the object of study in "the school of public life," perhaps a cultural renaissance, a many-sidedness, will develop in the lives of the individuals who compose the mass—a many-sidedness and broadness of interest that is itself prefigured in the life of this extraordinary woman, Rosa Luxemburg.

In her politics and life, the other tradition, the forgotten tradition, of Marxism begins. And as the Left starts to make use of that tradition in informing its practice, perhaps it will begin to become really clear what Marx meant when he enigmatically wrote, "the world has long had a dream of something which it only has to conceptualize consciously to possess in actuality. Then it will become evident that there is not simply an empty space between past and future, but rather that it is a matter of *realizing* the thoughts of the past."

The Letters of Rosa Luxemburg

To Leo Jogiches¹

Paris, Sunday, 3:30
[probably 3/25/1894*]

My Dearest!

I was really angry at you and I have a few ugly things with which to reproach you. All this made me so sad that I did not intend to write you until shortly before my departure. But sentiment got the upper hand. Here are my charges: 1) Your letters contain nothing, but I mean absolutely nothing, except *Sprawa Robotnicza*,² criticisms about what I did, and instructions on what I am supposed to do. If you were to tell me indignantly that every letter which you send contains many words of love, I would reply that tender words do not satisfy me and I would sooner dispense with them if, in exchange, I could learn something, anything, of your personal life.

Not a single word! Only our cause binds us, and the tradition of past feelings. That is very painful. It became especially clear to me in my work here. When tired of this work to the point of exhaustion, I let myself go for a while in order to relax. I would let my thoughts wander, and I would feel that nowhere do I have my personal corner, that nowhere can I exist and be myself. In Zurich the same, perhaps even more tedious, editorial work awaits me. I feel, however, just as little desire to stay here as to go back to Zurich. Don't say that I can't bear continuous work, and that I only want to take it easy. Oh no! I can stand twice as much. It only tortures and bores me when, wherever I turn, I find only the *Cause*. Why should others pressure me with it if I, myself, am already thinking about it and concerning myself with it sufficiently?

It makes me impatient that every letter I take into my hands, either from others or from you, always says the same—here an issue, there a brochure, this article and that one. All this would be all right if, at least, *alongside, in spite of everything,* a bit of the human being, the soul, the individual, could be recognized. But for you, outside the *Cause,* there is nothing. During all this time, didn't you gather any impressions, didn't you make any observations which you could share with me?

Perhaps you wish to put these same questions to me? Oh, but on the contrary, with every step, in spite of the *Cause,* I had plenty of impressions and thoughts—only I had no one with whom to share them. With you? Oh, I value myself too highly to do that. It would even be better to share them with [Wladyslaw] Heinrich,³ Mitek

*In the dating of this and other letters, we follow previous editors.

[Hartmann][4] or Adolph [Warski].[5] But, unfortunately, I don't love them and so I have no desire to do this. You are the one I love, and yet . . . but I just said all that. It's not true that now time is of the essence and work is most urgent. In a certain type of relationship you always find something to talk about, and a bit of time to write.

Just look at how typical the following is, and this is my reproach number 2). Let's suppose that now you are simply living for your "cause" and mine. Have you written me one word concerning that Russian affair? What's happening? What's in the press? What's with these Zurich guys? You don't consider it necessary to write a single word. I know that nothing special occurred, but it's to those who are near that one writes even about trivia. You think that it's enough for me to scribble for *Sprawa* and follow your "unpresuming" opinions. That is very characteristic. . . .

Your chivalrous explanation that I should not worry about practical things, since they surely will have been settled without bothering me, can only be given by a person *who does not know me at all.* Such an explanation might suffice for Julek [Marchlewski][6] so that he wouldn't worry since he has weak nerves, but for me such a procedure—even with the addition, "my poor little bird"—is insulting to put it mildly.

Besides all that, there are those frequent and direct remarks: proceed with Adolph like that, behave like this on your visit to [Peter] Lavrov,[7] take this position and that one—all of this, put together, gives one a feeling of great displeasure, fatigue, weariness, and impatience, which I have in those moments when I have the time to reflect. I write you all this, not as if I had any claims on you. I can't ask that you be different than you are. I am writing partly because I still have the stupid habit of saying whatever I feel and on the other hand, partly because I want you to be informed as to how it stands between us. . . .

. . . After all those articles, and that of [Boris] Kritschevski,[8] seven columns remain free on the double sheet. It works out to: 1 column on women, 1-1½ on wages, then there is the political editorial which remains to be written by me. That causes me the most uneasiness because by now the theme has gone flat in my mind. Of course, I will write it anyway. But I want to make it short, about 2-2½ columns. The remaining piece will be a little article on the preparations for May 1 abroad,[9] in which I will go into only 3 factors: the English have moved the celebration to May 1; the Germans have agreed to celebrate it; the French have all united to celebrate the day. For the first time, all the parties will celebrate May Day together. In this way the issue will be full and rich in variety.

As far as sightseeing in Paris is concerned—I hesitate to go anywhere because the mad racket and the crowds only make me faint and bring on migraines. After a half-hour stay in the *Bon Marché*, I could barely make it to the street. The celebration of the anniversary of the Commune went miserably. [Paul] Lafargue,[10] Paula Mink,[11] [Alexandre] Zévaes,[12] [René] Chauvin[13] and a few others spoke. All the speeches were insipid, especially Lafargue's. [Jules] Guesde[14] wasn't there, although he had promised to come. There weren't more than 200 people. . . .

Notes

[1]Leo Jogiches (1867-1919): In some letters, Jogiches is addressed by the pet name Dziodzio. He was Rosa Luxemburg's lover, friend, and political collaborator. Known for his organizational abilities, Jogiches was one of the founders of the SDKPL and later of the Spartacus League. One month after Luxemburg and Karl Liebknecht were killed in the Spartacus rebellion, Jogiches was killed by right-wing troops.

[2]*The Workers Cause*, founded in Paris in 1893, was the central organ of the SDKPL.

[3]Wladyslaw Heinrich (1869-1957): A friend of Rosa's from her university days in Zurich, Heinrich was a member of the SDKPL in the 1890s. Later he was to become a prominent Polish educator, philosopher, and psychologist.

[4]Mieczyslaw Hartmann (1869-1893): Another student friend of Luxemburg's, he committed suicide.

[5]Adolf Warzawski-Warski (1868-1937): One of the founding members of the SDKPL and later of the Polish Communist Party. A school friend of Rosa Luxemburg's, Warski became an editor of *Sprawa Robotnicza*, and after the Russian Revolution entered Lenin's inner circle. Purged by Stalin in 1937, he was rehabilitated in 1956.

[6]Julian Marchlewski (1866-1925): Another one of the founders of the SDKPL. From 1906 on, Marchlewski became one of the most prominent members of the left wing of the SPD. He was also instrumental in the founding of the Spartacus League, the German Communist Party, and the Third International.

[7]Peter Lavrov (1823-1900): Probably the leading theoretician of the Russian *narodniki* and an initial supporter of Warski's.

[8]Boris N. Kritschevski (1866-1919): A militant since the late 1880s, Kritschevski was one of the premier Russian social democratic writers and organizers. An editor of *Sprawa*, he was also the Paris correspondent for *Vorwärts*. With Jogiches, he was instrumental in setting up the socialist publishing network and in disseminating socialist material in Eastern Europe.

[9]May Day: A pet issue of Rosa Luxemburg's. May 1 has become the day marking the solidarity of the working class. It was initiated in Chicago in 1886.

[10]Paul Lafargue (1842-1911): One of the leaders of French socialism, he was also a member of the First International and active in the Paris Commune. Marx's son-in-law, Lafargue, a mulatto and native of Haiti, is perhaps best known for his essay "In Defense of Laziness."

[11]Paula Mink-Mekerska Bogdanowiczowa (1840-1901): Member of the Parti Ouvrier Français (POF), she was active in the First International and in émigré Polish circles. She also took part in the Paris Commune.

[12]Alexandre Zévaes (1873-1955): A historian of French socialism and the syndicalist movement, he was twice voted a parliamentary deputy. In 1902, he broke his ties to the socialist movement.

[13]René Chauvin: a member of the POF.

[14]Jules Guesde (1845-1922): Probably the leading "orthodox" Marxist among French socialists. A member of the left of the POF in the Dreyfus affair, Guesde—like Mehring in the German party—argued that the conflict was between bourgeois forces and thus took the position "neither the one nor the other." In World War I, he became a chauvinist and a minister without portfolio in the war cabinet.

To the Editors of Neue Zeit[1]

Zurich, March 5, 1896

To the editors of *Neue Zeit*:

I am also sending you a rather long article on the nationalist currents in the Polish Socialist movement. The topic—as I hope you will see for yourselves from the article—is decidedly a timely one. The change in the position of the Polish socialists in Germany and Austria, which was already prepared far in advance, in my opinion can lead to the secession of the Galician Party from the Austrian Social Democratic Party. This could mirror what has already taken place in Germany. As an initial consequence, the change has already brought forth the decision of the Galician Party concerning the next May Day Celebration, which is of great practical importance. All this lends a purely practical character to the analysis of this topic. In fact, its implications extend far beyond the limits of the Polish Movement itself, since—even without taking into account the immediate significance of the Polish movement for the German and Austrian comrades—the entire nationalist movement taking place among Polish socialists is trying to endow itself with a Marxist appearance, mainly through the sympathetic reaction of the German Social Democratic Party. On the other hand, the Polish Socialists are seeking to win the sympathies of other western European socialists by publishing a particular journal, which is being printed in London, entitled *Official Bulletin of the Polish Socialist Party.*

Treating this question appears to be especially important due to the fact that the representatives of the nationalist-socialist viewpoint will—as they themselves write in the Allemanist[2] *Le Parti Ouvrier*— advise the International Congress in London to adopt a resolution which sanctions the demands of the proletariat as to the restoration of the Polish state. This will pave the way for the inclusion of this measure into the practical program of the Polish parties.

Should you decide to publish the article, the earlier you publish it, the more practical significance it will have, especially in view of the Austrian Social Democrats who will concern themselves with the question of the May Day celebration and other problems touched upon in the article.

Most respectfully,
Rosa Luxemburg

Since the German language is a foreign tongue to me, it is quite possible that an incorrect expression may have crept in here or there. Therefore, I politely ask you to correct my essay in this respect, should it be necessary.

Notes

[1]*Die Neue Zeit* was founded in 1883 by Karl Kautsky. The first true theoretical organ of Marxism, it also remained the most prestigious for the duration of the Second International.

[2]Jean Alleman (1843-1935): Proudhonist leader of the Parti Ouvrier Socialiste Révolutionnaire.

To Robert Seidel[1]

Berlin, August 15, 1898

Dear Friend,

In your review of my *Industrial Development of Poland*, you say: "The birth of industry in Russian Poland is no doubt due to the initiative and the efforts of the government. That is what Luxemburg herself says, and thus, once and for all, she refutes the erroneous opinion that the economic factors are the 'motors' (here you are quoting an expression taken from my introduction), i.e., the sole and single forces of development, that determine political life and political forms. That sort of historical materialism is erroneous, and we have to abandon it."

Since I do not want to take responsibility for having refuted myself and also thereby create a completely erroneous interpretation of historical materialism, permit me a few words of reply. You forget one thing: If the government (that is, the political factor as you are conceiving of it here) had also taken the initiative in the industrial development of Poland, the reason was that a purely "economic" phenomenon in its turn had forced it to take this initiative—the deficit in the state treasury, created by the decline and the low yield in agriculture. Hence, no matter where you encounter the political factor, in its effects on economic life, after painstaking analysis you will discover that it, in turn, is based on an economic condition. After that, even in its effects, the political influence is tied to its given economic base.

Proof: Half a century ago, the same efforts of the Polish government to create industry in Poland, a country with a feudal and barter economy, ended in a lamentable fiasco. So, while no doubt the economic and the political factors are always taking turns in affecting the social development, in the last instance, the economic factor is the essential and decisive one; and that is why I have called it the "motor" of social life.

But as to the "erroneous interpretation of materialism," according to which the economic factors supposedly were the only basis of development, I am convinced that it has only a mythical existence in your imagination. Materialists who assert that economic development rushes headlong, like an autonomous locomotive on the tracks of history, and that politics, ideology, etc., are content to toddle behind like forsaken, passive freight wagons—you won't find even a trace of such a conception, not even in the most backward Russian provinces (and, as you know, in this respect they are very talented in Russia; on request they will prepare for you such a gruel of old and new materialists that you will feel all topsy-turvy). If ever you should find such a prodigy, have him exhibited in the waxworks.

Notes

[1]Robert Seidel (1850-1933): A German émigré to Switzerland, Seidel was an editor of *The Workers' Voice*, which was the organ of the Swiss Social Democratic Party, and a writer of popular works, songs, and poems. Rosa was an intimate of his family.

To Leo Jogiches

[Berlin] Saturday morning
9/24/1898

Dziodzio,

The events follow one another so rapidly that I can't keep up with giving you information about them. Point number one: I have decided to come forward at the convention as soon as possible, on the questions of tactics and opportunism, and advance a resolution. I couldn't do that if I had not previously appeared in the press. It was too late for the N[*eue*] Z[*eit*]. That's why I sat myself down for two days and wrote a series of articles of 107 pages for the L[*eipziger*] V[*olkszeitung*]. Because of the lack of time, they weren't copied out, when I sent them off.

[Bruno] Schönlank[1] has fallen into a terrible frenzy. There will be seven articles.[2] I sent you the first three. Schönlank considers this a "masterstroke" and a "masterpiece of dialectic." The article has already attracted attention. In Leipzig they're saying that I got a raw deal. Perhaps you will think that I suffered a loss since it won't be in the *Neue Zeit*. Nonsense! 1) There will a continuation of the debate in the *Neue Zeit* because Ede [Bernstein][3] always takes his stand there after the Party Convention. Naturally the same goes for me even though Schönlank has already stipulated in advance that I will write for him. 2) What's most important: the articles so impressed Schönlank that afterwards he wants to publish them as a brochure. Naturally, I made it clear to him in advance that I would want to work them over for this purpose, expand them, and add a general introduction on the meaning of opportunism inside the Party, etc. After these articles, I can boldly come forward with a speech—so long as the "old boys" don't smother the debate.

Intermezzo: right in the first article, I left out a page in the middle (I had left it at home). But Schönlank, the ass, didn't notice the gap despite the most careful editing. As I read it, I thought I would have a heart attack. I immediately telegraphed Leipzig. They answered that I was mistaken. I telegraphed a second time—they answered that I should come and make the corrections. At the same time, I received another telegram from Dresden: *Most important, come immediately.* I went there and at the train station Julek [Marchlewski] told me that I should try for the job of editor-in-chief of the *Sächsische Arbeiter-Zeitung*[4] edited by Parvus!! Naturally, it was Parvus' idea. Still, [Hermann] Wallfisch[5] and others from there are very happy about it, and they urgently asked me to accept. What pleases them particularly is the chance of my stepping forward with public speeches. At present, I am the only "revolutionary" candidate. Opposing candidates: [Max] Schippel[6]—opportunist; Georg Gradnauer[7]—a nothing, and [Georg] Ledebour[8]—a weathervane! . . .

Just this moment, I received a telegram with the final answer of the Dresden Party Press Commission, to which I, in turn, have to wire my final answer, about which I will likewise inform you by telegram. I have decided to accept. Parvus and Julek naturally committed themselves to write as much as possible. Besides, from the start, I will have other coworkers who did not want to write for Parvus: e.g. [Franz] Mehring[9] whom, with the help of Schönlank (they are close friends), I will immediately collar. Today, after it is finalized, I will go to Dresden to take over the editorial offices, since the Fat One [Parvus—trans.] and Julek must decamp tomorrow! And right after the Party Convention, I will take over the editorship for good.[10] They want me to start immediately because they don't have anyone, but I'll lead them by the nose. Perhaps next week I'll go to the Leipzig editorial offices for a few days to look at the technical end. This is the project of Frau Schönlank, who has already grown very fond of me (*nota bene*: it was she who told me that her husband had told her that my work was like "the genuine Marx at his best" . . . and naturally she wants me to live with them, which I probably won't). Schönlank is already thinking with glee of the looks on those faces at Beuthstrasse and Katzbachstrasse.

Your R.

Notes

[1]Bruno Schönlank (1858-1901): Editor of the *Leipziger Volkszeitung*, and member of the Reichstag.

[2]The articles under discussion were published serially in the *Leipziger Volkszeitung* and constituted her attack upon Eduard Bernstein in the "revisionism debate." These articles would later be turned into her pamphlet *Social Reform or Revolution*.

[3]Eduard Bernstein (1850-1932): Friend and literary executor of Engels' estate. An editor of *Die Neue Zeit*, Bernstein sparked the revisionist controversy in 1898 with a set of articles that have been translated under the English title *Evolutionary Socialism*. His theories were officially condemned at the party's Dresden Convention in 1903. A pacifist in World War I, Bernstein was a consistent opponent of national chauvinism. He was also a founder of the Independent Social Democratic Party (USPD) that split from the SPD while the war was in progress. After the USPD dissolved in 1920, he reentered the SPD.

[4]Alexander Helphand—Parvus (1869-1924): One of the key figures in Second International social democracy. Always on the left wing of the party, Parvus developed the Marxist notion of the mass strike and worked with

Trotsky on the theory of "permanent revolution." Increasingly disenchanted with the bureaucratization of the SPD, he left the party and became a nationalist during the First World War. It was Parvus who funneled German money to the Bolsheviks and who organized the famous train ride of socialist leaders from Switzerland to Russia.

[5]Hermann Wallfisch (1862-?): A social democratic organizer in Dresden, he was the administrative coordinator of the *Sächsische Arbeiter-Zeitung.*

[6]Max Schippel (1859-1928): One of the leaders of the right wing of the SPD, Schippel was an editor of the weekly *Sozialdemokrat* and an editor of the prestigious revisionist organ *Sozialistische Monatshefte.*

[7]Georg Gradnauer was an important social democratic functionary from 1898 to 1906.

[8]Georg Ledebour (1850-1947): A centrist deputy to the Reichstag, Ledebour became one of the founders of the USPD. An editor of *Vorwärts,* he was also an editor of the *Sächsische Arbeiter-Zeitung.*

[9]Franz Mehring (1846-1919): Another key figure of German social democracy. A supporter of Rosa Luxemburg, though their friendship was stormy at times: a publicist and a leading literary critic, as well as an historian; a founder of the Spartacus League and the German Communist Party. His most famous work in English is his biography of Karl Marx, on which Rosa Luxemburg collaborated.

[10]After Schönlank's death, Rosa assumed coeditorship of the *Leipziger Volkszeitung* with Mehring.

To Leo Jogiches

[Postcard]
Berlin 9/25/98

Just this moment, my dearest, I returned from Dresden for the second time, and I sent you a telegram saying that I have taken over the editorial offices. I have so much work to do that a longer letter is out of the question: tomorrow I must meet with [Franz] Mehring, [Arthur] Stadthagen,[1] [Max] Schippel, etc., in order to commission articles. For me they will write all right, and I will at once take them all in hand. Then too, if possible, this week I must hold a meeting in Dresden in order to present myself to the masses. At the same time, I must prepare two speeches for Stuttgart, and perhaps as early as the day after tomorrow, stop by the editorial offices.

The articles in the *Leipziger Volkszeitung* are creating a sensation.[2] Parvus wired me his congratulations and [Clara] Zetkin[3] wrote a letter to [Bruno] Schönlank with hymns of praise to "the

Leo Jogiches. (Courtesy Dietz Verlag)

valiant Rosa who beats that flour-bag [Eduard] Bernstein so fiercely that the thick powder dust rises into the air and the periwigs of the Bernstein school are blown from their heads because they can no longer be powdered."

These articles have also influenced the Press Commission who voted me in unanimously (it has seventeen members). At the beginning [August Wilhelm] Kaden[4] screamed: "What? Petticoat politics?" But everyone laughed at him and, afterwards, he himself said: "Yes, her articles on the Orient[5] really were excellent"—when [Jean] Jaurès[6] received my work he said: "Ah, that's by Rosa Luxemburg" and put it in his briefcase immediately. [Ignaz] Urbach[7] spoke with him, and Jaurès promised that, as soon as he had the time, he would write an article for me. But I will at once write him a letter from Dresden with a request for an article on the Dreyfus affair[8] for the *Sächsische Arbeiter-Zeitung.* I will also corral [Robert] Seidel for the Swiss section.

I'm in a hurry!

Your

R.

Notes

[1]Arthur Stadthagen (1857-1917): A longtime friend of Luxemburg's, Stadthagen was a lawyer, member of the Reichstag, and editor of *Vorwärts.*

[2]The reference is to the articles attacking Bernstein in the revisionist debate.

[3]Clara Zetkin (1857-1933): One of Rosa's very closest friends and a leader of the German women's movement. She stood with Rosa on the left wing of the movement and was one of the founders of the German Communist Party.

[4]August Wilhelm Kaden (1850-1913): A leader of the SPD organization in Dresden, Kaden also ran the party publishing house which put out the *Sächsische Arbeiter-Zeitung.* He was a Reichstag representative from 1893 until his death.

[5]The reference is to Rosa's debate with Wilhelm Leibknecht on the national question that emerged in her article "Oriental Politics in *Vorwärts.*"

[6]Jean Jaurès (1859-1914): Not a Marxist, Jaurès was one of the leaders of the French socialists and the Second International. On the right wing of the party, he was one of the major antimilitarist exponents in Europe and was assassinated on the eve of World War I.

[7]Ignaz Urbach: Originally a supporter of the PPS, Urbach came closer and closer to the SDKPL. He lived in Paris for most of his life.

[8]The Dreyfus affair was one of the most sensational cases in European history. In 1894, Dreyfus, who was a Jewish officer of the French General Staff, was falsely accused of treason and banished to Devil's Island. The struggle for vindication split French society between republicans and

monarchist militarist opponents of the Third Republic. With the help of the writer Emile Zola, Georges Clemenceau and others, Dreyfus was finally cleared in 1906. Jaurès was one of his warmest supporters, in contrast to Guesde (See letter of 3/25/1894, note 14, p. 58). Luxemburg never wrote about the case; she apparently sided with the reformist Jaurès.

To August Bebel[1]

Dresden 10/31/1898

Editor of the *Sächsische Arbeiter-Zeitung* and *Volksfreund*

Esteemed Comrade!

I am very grateful for the information which has served to orient me regarding the state of things. It was of course clear to me that [Eduard] Bernstein's argumentation is no longer based on our Party program. But it is very painful to think that we have to abandon all hope for him. Yet, I am amazed that—if you viewed the matter this way—you and Comrade [Karl] Kautsky[2] did not want me to use the favorable mood created by the Party Congress to launch an immediate and energetic debate, but instead suggested to Bernstein that he write a brochure, which will only drag out the whole discussion. Anyway, I believe that by publishing [Georgi] Plekhanov's[3] letter, I and the others have acted correctly in the sense of the situation as you characterized it in your letter. If Bernstein is really lost to us, then the party must accept the fact—no matter how painful it might be—that he be considered like [Gustav] Schmoller[4] or any other social reformer.

As for the further discussion, I don't even know at the moment whether I will be able to carry it on in the *S[ächsische] A[rbeiter-Zeitung]*. My colleagues, on the one hand, and Gradnauer, on the other, are urging me to enter a conflict in which I can very easily see myself being forced to resign the editorship. In the meeting of the Press Commission, which will take place on Wednesday, and in which the issue will be decided, I will state my terms: complete freedom in continuing the discussion on tactics. The relations on our editorial board are very disagreeable and, despite the greatest efforts on my part to bring about harmony and mutual understanding, the demagoguery and fault-finding continue. . . .

With best regards,

R. Luxemburg

Notes

[1]August Bebel (1840-1913): A central figure in the development of

European socialism. Among the founders of both the SPD and the Second International, Bebel was a friend of both Marx and Engels. As a member of the Reichstag, he went to prison for treason for opposing the Franco-Prussian War and the subsequent annexation of Alsace-Lorraine. Essentially, Bebel was the political leader of the SPD until his death.

[2]Karl Kautsky (1854-1938): Editor of *Die Neue Zeit* and leading theoretician of the Second International. An early member of the radical faction of the SPD, he became a centrist after his break with Rosa Luxemburg. (*Centrism* may be defined by his famous distinction: "The SPD is a revolutionary party, but not a party that makes revolution.") He helped found the USPD, only to rejoin the SPD in 1922. His best-known works in English include his popularization of *The Erfurt Program*, which is translated as *The Class Struggle*, and *The Dictatorship of the Proletariat*, in which he explains his opposition to the Bolsheviks.

[3]Georgi Plekhanov (1856-1918): One of the founders of Russian Marxism whose influence extended to Lenin himself. As an editor of *Iskra* (*The Spark*), he opposed Bernstein's revisionism but sided with the Mensheviks after Lenin's split in 1902. During the war, he emerged as a patriot and later opposed the Bolshevik government. His best-known works in English are *The Monist View of History* and *The Fundamentals of Marxism*.

[4]Gustav Schmoller (1838-1917): An economic and social historian, Schmoller was a member of the SPD and then split from it; he was known as a "socialist of the lectern."

To August Bebel

Dresden 11/7/1898

Esteemed Comrade!

I prefer to reply *directly* to your letter, a copy of which reached me through Comrade [Bruno] Schönlank. I consider it beneath my dignity to go into issues of "Moral slaps in the face," "Unbelievable tactlessness," etc.

Regarding the issue itself: [Hermann] Wallfisch was able to inform you in "a most objective manner" of some facts, but not of the general situation of the editorial board and the mood that prevailed in the Press Commission. Ever since Parvus' time, the relations within the editorial board have been so disrupted and untenable that, sooner or later, a clash was bound to occur. Especially since my colleagues were on edge after the long conflict with Parvus, they were determined to make use of the change in editors and take complete control of the paper. In this they gained the support of the Press Commission, which had been intimidated by the attacks upon the vulgar tone of the paper. For my part, I consider it wrong to confine myself—like Parvus—to writing tactical and polemical articles while leaving the rest of the newspaper to God's wisdom. I considered it my first duty, next to the discussion of tactical matters, to uplift and improve the general state of the neglected paper. Thus, I got involved in other departments, which caused new frictions with my colleagues. . . .

You are of the opinion that the Commission gave in to me in all essential points. In fact, they turned down all my proposals and requests. They supported my colleagues on the editorial board right down the line. Had I returned to the editorship—given the present relations on the editorial board and the present mood of the Commission—I would immediately have had to give up all my independence. Formally, it involved only correcting the paper's "tone." In fact, soon I would not have been able to publish my articles nor—very important—those of Parvus.

I said to myself: If that is the Commission's standpoint, then there is nothing for me to do on the editorial board; then everything is already lost. If, however, the Commission means to give me the necessary latitude, they can still tell me after my resignation. Please note: ten times I repeated in the meeting that my resignation was forced upon me, that no other way remained open to me. They smiled and took it as an empty threat like the gestures which Parvus used to make.

One more point to advise you about the situation as it stands at the moment. The members of the editorial board are negotiating with [Georg] Ledebour, who said he would gladly assume the editorship on any terms. As for me, some members of the Commission have privately tried to persuade me to assume the editor's chair once again. I answered that this is out of the question unless I have (1) the right to accept the articles written by outsiders (I am thinking, above all, of Parvus who has made my editorship a condition of his contributing anything); (2) complete freedom to write under my own name should the editorial board disagree with this or that article. In tomorrow's meeting, the Commission will have the chance to state formally whether they will persist in their strange viewpoint or not.

I hope that these facts will prove to you that you have been a bit hasty in giving your verdict on my course of action.

With best regards,
R. Luxemburg

To Leo Jogiches

[Berlin]
12/3/98

I was at Mehring's yesterday, and I came home with the sad conviction that I have no choice but to sit down and write a "great work." Exactly like Kautsky, Mehring immediately asked me: "Are you writing a major work?" And he was so serious that I felt that I simply had to begin working on one. There's nothing to be done— apparently I have the appearance of someone who should write a great work, and I have no choice but to fulfill this general expectation. (Perhaps you can tell me what I am to write this great work about.)

Dearest, if you dispense me from giving you a detailed report on my visit with Bebel and Kautsky, in exchange I will tell you more about my talk with Mehring, which is much more interesting. 1) He told me several times that I had edited the *Sächsische Arbeiter-Zeitung* very well, much better than Parvus. "One saw that the paper was really being edited," also that the *Sächsische Arbeiter-Zeitung* was, in general, edited best during my tenure. He also said this to Kautsky. 2) He (and it appears the other "old boys" as well) is only considering Ledebour as a temporary replacement as editor. They are absolutely certain that I will come back to Dresden, and that I will then exercise a dictatorship. They discussed it with such exhilarating certainty that I was really amazed. 3) When Bernstein's name came up, [Mehring] told me: "You really thrashed him in the *Leipziger Volkszeitung*. It did my heart good." . . .

The interesting piece of news which I promised you is this: the police have been watching me for a few weeks. During the last few days, two spies were at the janitor's day and night dogging my footsteps. The janitor, a former comrade, secretly informed me. When I got sick and tired of it, I went straight to the police, to a Herr Lieutenant, and laid my cards on the table. I told him that if this didn't stop, I would go to the top and cause a stink. Of course, the lieutenant pretended that he didn't know anything about it, and that it wasn't so, but in fact the spies disappeared on the second day. Mehring advised me, should they reappear, to put a notice in *Vorwärts*—and that then they would creep away. . . .

Your R

To Leo Jogiches

Berlin 1/3/1899

Dziodzio!

Just this moment I received Karl Kautsky's *Agrarian Question* from Leipzig,[1] and a letter from Schönlank in which he informed me that Mehring, who was supposed to write a review of the book, had written him that he couldn't and had advised him to write it himself. Naturally, poor Schönlank doesn't have the self-confidence to write it and besides, he doesn't have the time. So, he asked me to extricate him from this fix and to take on Karl Kautsky along with Bernstein in the review. For, as Dietz said to him in his letter,[2] Ede's [Bernstein's] book will appear in two to three weeks and so, in the meantime, I might be able to write it up in a pinch.

The awkward thing is that, as you know, I still don't know anything about the agrarian question, and so I do not have a starting point for criticism; but the starting point can emerge from reading. Also, it's a shame about the time which will be lost, since up to now I have been meaning to dedicate the entire two to three weeks to preparing for Ede. But, on the other hand, it is 1) a prestigious assignment for me since certainly, except for Parvus and me, no one in the entire Party can say anything about the issue which can be taken the least bit seriously,[3] and the Party is certainly waiting for a hint regarding what position it should take on the book. 2) I really must help out Schönlank. He has no one else, and it is an important matter. This is no simple review, but rather involves taking a stand and, as you know, on the agrarian question, he does not have a clear conscience[4] and therefore is scared to step forward himself. This is a question of orientation in terms of the program, and that it why it is important for me to step forward in the *Leipziger Volkszeitung*. By the way, it's not settled yet! Schönlank writes that he told Mehring firmly to fulfill his obligation. But should Mehring, in spite of that, refuse again, then Schönlank will telegraph me.

Anyway, now I entreat you to send me immediately 1) the volume of *Neue Zeit* containing Parvus' series on the "Agrarian Crisis." 2) the volume containing Engels' articles on the French agrarian program. 3) the package of newspapers which we saved, with the discussion of the agrarian program. I don't have it here, so it must be in Zurich. 4) Write me whatever you can think of that might be appropriate. 5) the minutes of the German convention where the issue of the agrarian program was discussed.

It's understood that under no circumstances will I put aside the work on Ede even for a day. At best, for a change, I will work on both these things, which, in fact, might animate me a bit since the brooding about Ede sometimes tires me quite a bit. I am working efficiently these days. My leg is better. Today the doctor was here again and bandaged it. Tomorrow I'm definitely going out. I embrace and kiss you.

Your Rosa

Notes

[1]Kautsky wrote his *Agrarfrage* in 1898, in which he shifted his original position. The debate over the agrarian issue began in 1894 at the Frankfurt party congress, and the importance of the agrarian issue was that it would later merge with the revisionist debate. In 1894, the position put forward by Kautsky and Max Schippel prevailed; they essentially argued that agriculture had different laws of development than those which govern industry. Still, this position did not support any strengthening of private property. Nevertheless, in his work of 1898, Kautsky took the position that modern agriculture is indeed a capitalist economic formation.

[2]Joseph Dietz (1843-1922): Founder of the SPD publishing house. Dietz was also a Reichstag deputy.

[3]This is an interesting assertion, since those who really were involved in the agrarian question were mostly reformists like Eduard David. Indeed, the agrarian issue was perhaps the weakest plank in the entire left Marxist platform.

[4]In 1894, Schönlank had suggested collaboration with the bourgeoisie on agrarian matters.

To Leo Jogiches

Berlin 1/9/1899

Dearest Dziodzio,

. . . Now help me—and fast—to solve the following little problem. With the development of capitalism, contradictions develop and therewith both the economic system of capitalism, and the capitalist state, become untenable. The latter—that is to say, capitalist politics—leads likewise to a collapse. An illustration from praxis: in international politics, 5 or 6 years ago, Constantinople played a central role around which the entire international struggle turned. But, since here the conquest of a purely strategic point was directly involved, over the last 10 years a policy of stabilizing the integrity of Turkey has emerged in view of maintaining the balance of power. Thus, the Constantinople issue has arrived at dead center, the development of international relations has gotten stuck there.

Around 1895, a basic change occurred: the Japanese war opened the Chinese doors and European politics, driven by capitalist and state interests, intruded into Asia. Constantinople moved into the background. Here the conflict between states, and with it the development of politics, had an extended field before it: the conquest and partition of all Asia became the goal which European politics pursued. An extremely quick dismemberment of China followed. At present, Persia and Afghanistan too have been attacked by Russia and England. From that, the European antagonisms in Africa have received new impulses; there, too, the struggle is breaking out with new force (Fashoda, Delegoa, Madagascar).

It's clear that the dismemberment of Asia and Africa is the final limit beyond which European politics no longer has room to unfold. There follows then another such squeeze as has just occurred in the Eastern question, and the European powers will have no choice other than throwing themselves on one another, until the *period of the final crisis sets in within politics* . . . etc. etc.[1]

Well, you understand the wonderful prospects which this affords. Consider this and, if you have something to add, write me immediately—*and I do mean immediately*. At first this occurred to me as a theme for a beautiful lead article entitled "Shifts in World Politics" but then, instead, I decided to incorporate it organically into my paper on Ede [Bernstein] in order not simply to speak in abstractions, but rather to point to concrete facts.

So much for the time being, my dearest. I am working very hard on Ede; you are mistaken in regard to "English Eyeglasses"—the way I am working it through, it is a very basic part of the argument. For I am slowly coming to the conclusion that in England, where the very first unfolding of capitalism took place, the ossification of capitalism will also first set in, and that this process of ossification has already begun. I have plenty of proof. This shows the conclusions which Ede draws from England in a very peculiar light: turned upside down.

I have been depressed since yesterday and that's why I can't write more. I send you a kiss from my heart, my dearest. Write, don't wait for me. When I am feeling just a bit better, I will write you again.

Your
R.

Notes

[1]The beginnings of what would become one of her central theses in *The Accumulation of Capital* is already to be found here.

To Leo Jogiches

Berlin, Sunday 1/22/1899

My dear Dziodzio:

I have been waiting quite some time for the extensive letter which you promised, but when I received this non-extensive one, I lost the desire to reply for a few days, and now I am writing with difficulty.

To me, your entire stance in regard to the "Russian Revolution"[1] is, as I already told you in Zurich, incomprehensible and odious. Eventually, one must admit that all this criticizing, all this fault-finding without seeking to make things better oneself is senseless. Already in Zurich, I disliked the kicks in the pants which you kept inflicting on every Russian who wished to get close to you. One can boycott or "punish" a few people, or a group, but not an entire movement! Your entire behavior is more suited to an "embittered schlemiel" like [Boris] Kritschewski than to a forceful, upright individual.

I am not writing you all this because of your remarks concerning my intention to collaborate with the Russian Revolution. This means nothing to me: while I do not agree with your views, the whole thing has too little significance for it to be worth getting into a strident argument with you. I personally don't give a damn about the Russian Revolution. I thought that in *some* way, contact would be useful to *you*. But *surely* only in the event that you really wish somehow to participate. Your gibberish that they do not turn to you is, as you yourself must have seen while writing, completely laughable. For, as a matter of principle, you have mocked anyone who has approached you at any time—as you said yourself. How are they then to approach you?

Forgive me that I write all this to you. Perhaps it will embarrass you, and make you angry but, this once, I must tell you the truth. Think about it, and you'll see that I am right. It's almost beneath your niveau to take a stance such as the one you have stubbornly taken for the last few years. That is unworthy of a man who cuts a great figure. I would rather, if only out of spite, praise what the others do than carp at everything without attempting to make it better. I repeat once again so that there won't be any misunderstandings between us later: I do not write you any of this in order to justify my taking part in this whole "revolution." For it means as little to me as a fifth leg would mean to a dog. I write you simply and solely because of your own relation to just this "revolution."

Notes

[1]The reference is to an organization of Russian social democrats who had formed an émigré circle.

To Leo Jogiches

Berlin 3/2/1899

My dearest one!

Your lovely letters have been a great source of strength these days, for in general I don't feel particularly well. I sleep all day and can neither work, think, nor write a letter. I go around like a mindless little animal.

I wonder why; getting exhausted to such an extent just writing those 4 articles should be declared a felony. And at this moment, I am writing you with the greatest effort, for after every two words I forget what I meant to say.

Do you know what occurred to me last night? That I might possibly end up mentally ill, for I have been feeling very strange for a long time (as far back as last summer). I never told you about this or wrote you. I have such feelings of mental fogginess. I am thinking and feeling everything as if through absorbent cotton. Then too, sometimes in the middle of the most intensive mental labor, a train of thought breaks off in such a way that I must exert myself to remember what on earth I was thinking about. Also I suffer continually now from loss of memory and mental drowsiness. Imagine that I never remember when I wrote you last or what about; then, after I send the letter off, whether I wrote the address, etc. It only amazes me that I can think so aggressively and fast while writing those Schippel articles. But enough of that, let's get to the point.

Your critical remarks (that is, actually your one, most important, remark) to my polemic with Max Schippel pleased me enormously because I was once again convinced that I can completely rely on my own critical faculties. When I sent off the reply I said to myself: You overstepped yourself, kitten, and strayed from the path. Instead of undertaking something against opportunism, I allowed myself to be carried away by my beloved economics and entered the jungle of theory. Then I opened your letter and read the same thing, word for word.

Now you will ask me why I didn't write better, even though I knew this. I can only tell you that I am admiring myself for being able to write this well under the circumstances. Imagine, I had to write this reply in the space of four hours in the presence of [Bruno] Schönlank! I thought I would go mad. . . . Everyone is enthusiastic about my articles, and shocked that Schippel could write such nonsense. Today, Schönlank came by to report on the "impressions." Above all he spoke with August [Bebel]. A[ugust] said: "The articles are brilliant, I endorse them word for word. The tone is refined and irreproachable. That the faction concealed its decision is of course idiotic. The question must come before the convention. But . . . " About the "but" which concerns him more than me—later . . .

To Leo Jogiches

Berlin 3/3/1899

My dearest,

Now you can see what's happened to my mind. I wrote you yesterday about Bebel's "but" and I forgot to explain it later. Here now, the "but" . . . He went on: "*Vorwärts*[1] remains silent because of the "Old Man" (Liebknecht)—besides, you know that Gradnauer is actually a follower of Schippel's. The provincial press will remain silent because, it does not dare speak; we, for our part, are of different opinions on all the more important points. When you see all this, you get depressed yourself and lose the desire to fight."

In a word, all this talk had only one meaning: Bebel himself has become senile, and no longer holds the reins in his hands. He is happy when the others fight, but he has neither the energy nor the fire to initiate it himself. Singer himself was never of great importance. K[arl] K[autsky], as you see, confines himself to theory. In short, when you look around, the Party looks damn bad—completely headless as the Ruthenians say. No one leads it, no one shoulders the responsibility.

Of the pitifully few people who are courageous and up-right, Parvus—the devil knows why—has turned to writing for the stupid *W[elt] P[olitik]* instead of writing for the *S[ächsische] A[rbeiter-Zeitung]* as he should be doing. (Obviously, like Seidel, he means to show the Party that nothing can be done without him.) Because of a stupid trifle, Mehring, that ass, has abandoned the *L[eipziger] V[olkszeitung]*. Only K[arl] K[autsky] and I remain at our posts.

It is a situation in which a person in my position, with energy and in good health, can do a great deal. So, for example, I ought to hold a few meetings, one after the other, on the theme of "Militarism and the Militia" in order to set the masses in motion and egg on Bebel and the other old goats. But, but—my health! Miserable! . . .

A thousand kisses,
Your R

Notes

[1]*Vorwärts* was the "central organ" of the SPD, a daily that appeared in Berlin.

To Leo Jogiches

[Berlin]
5/1/1899
Dziodzio!

Thanks for yesterday's special-delivery letter. It pleased me greatly, since I sat all alone in the empty house all day—waiting for your [brother] Jozio. Anyway, I had no place to go; it was raining, and I wasn't feeling well at all. Unexpectedly, the mailman rang and brought me the news from you for which I have been waiting the last few days. . . .

You ask whether the speeches for the Party Convention have been assigned. I believe I already told you that Bebel will discuss Bernstein—it's not yet known who will speak about militarism. The other items have nothing to do with us.

Your advice "to attempt to give a speech at any cost" is truly childish. It amazes me that you still keep serving up such inappropriate counsel, and that in such an important matter. Do you seriously believe that there is even the remotest chance for someone to be entrusted with a speech who has only been in the movement for a year, whose presence has only been established through a few articles—even if they are excellent? Someone who does not belong to the clan, who avails herself of no one's protection except for her own elbows? Someone who is not only greatly feared by her enemies (Auer & Co.)[1] but also, in their heart of hearts, by her allies—Bebel, K[arl] K[autsky], Singer[2] etc? Someone who gives them the feeling that it might be best to put her off for as long as possible, because she might quickly surpass them? Don't you understand any of this? To get the chance to speak without their consent—there is no way to do this for it is clearly they who are pulling the strings behind the scenes.

But I contemplate all this with the deepest calm; I knew in

advance that everything would develop as it has, and I know also that in a year or two no intrigue, no fear or envy, will prevent me from achieving one of the premier places in the Party. Certainly the situation at the present moment—Bernstein—is an exception. Still, you seem to think, once again, that the navel of the world is right here and that, if action is not taken now—everything is lost. That is nonsense. The Party only now (over the last two years) has been entering the whirlpool of ever more difficult tasks, ever more dangerous situations. There will be thousands upon thousands of occasions to show, in daily combat, its strength and indispensability.

At that, I do not have the slightest intention of limiting myself to criticism. On the contrary, I have the intention and desire of actively pushing, not individuals, but the movement as a whole, to re-examine the whole of our positive work, to point to new forms of agitation and praxis—if they can be found, and I don't doubt they can—to fight tedium and sloth, etc. In a word, I wish to be a continual spur for the movement—what Parvus was at the beginning and unfortunately carried on well for only a few months. At any rate, I have the same unshakable belief that Parvus had, that one can do a great deal within the movement, do it daily and for many years to come.

All of our present time is extraordinarily critical. But the fact that there is no one who can take the Party by the collar is shown in the problem of the Landtag elections, in which, unfortunately, I got involved too late. But, year by year, there will be hundreds of issues like this one. If you only take the issues of tariffs, foreign affairs, and craft unions—already you have three untapped opportunities. And then there is the oral and written agitation which, petrified in old forms, affects practically no one any longer and which must be directed into new channels; new life must be injected into press, meetings and brochures.

I write you all this in haste and not in any special order, to show you that I am not without a plan and not without ideas while looking at what is happening all over and, second, to remind you that the world does not stop with Bernstein and Hannover. I do not agree with the view that it is foolish to be an idealist in the German movement.[3] To begin with, there are idealists here too—above all, a huge number of the most simple agitators from the working masses and, further-more, even in the leadership, e.g., Bebel. Secondly, the whole matter doesn't concern me because the ultimate principle to which I sub-scribed during all of my Polish-German revolutionary praxis is to al-ways remain true to oneself without regard for the surroundings and the others. I am and will remain an idealist in the German as well as the Polish movement.

Naturally, that does not mean that I will play the role of an obedient donkey who works for others. Very definitely, I want to strive, and I will strive, for the most influential place in the movement, and that does not in the least contradict my idealism since I will not employ methods other than the use of my own "talent"— insofar as I possess it. . . .

Already I must close for today. I kiss you tenderly.

Your Rosa

Notes

[1]Ignaz Auer (1846-1907): One of the earliest members of the SPD, secretary of the party from 1875, and many times a Reichstag deputy, Auer became a leading reformist in accordance with the dominant tendency of the social democratic organization in Bavaria.

[2]Paul Singer (1844-1911): Founder of *Vorwärts*. He became a centrist and was active in the International Bureau of the Second International. He was also a Reichstag deputy.

[3]The letters of Jogiches have not been preserved; but passages like this in Rosa's letters reveal fundamental differences of outlook between the two lovers.

To Arthur Stadthagen

Friedenau, Wielandstrasse 23
[Probably December 1899]

Most esteemed friend!

Thanks so much for the copies of *The Torch*,[1] which I am reading with the greatest interest. They are really written with talent: vigorous, lively, and rich in content.

That affair with the detective was more harmless than I thought: the person only confided to my landlady that I had an editorial position in Leipzig(!) but had to relinquish it since I was expelled from Saxony(!).

Merry Christmas to you, too. On the 25th I am leaving to campaign in Upper Silesia. I will stay there until the 1st of January. So, at any rate, we will not see each other again in this century (according to governmental decree). Also, for that reason—Happy New Year!

With best regards,
Your
Rosa Luxemburg

Notes

[1]The reference here is to Karl Kraus' weekly *Die Fackel* (*The Torch*), which was published in Vienna. It was unrivalled in its criticism of contemporary politics, manners, and especially the press.

To Karl and Luise Kautsky

12/30/1899

My dear friends!

I am sending you affectionate greetings from the boundary between civilization and barbarism. My compatriots are quite happy that I am here and so am I. The trip was very useful: after all, a word in Polish is much more effective than the alien German word.

Our [Dr. August] Winter[1] is very nice and a most decent comrade. One little thing is quite characteristic of his spouse: after her first visit with me she wrote him from Berlin: "Rosa Luxemburg is quite human." Yesterday, in their naïve way, the comrades here confessed that they had imagined me to be quite different: big and fat! . . . We have only two public meetings, but every night in between—in my honor—they hold their "beer parties," now in Kattowitz, now in Zabor, etc. Although (unlike Ballestram's crack) the workers here don't drink champagne from beer mugs, Ballestram's producers of surplus value are being filled with the Holy Spirit of S[ocial] D[emocracy].

Seriously, such private discussions have an even more stimulating effect on people than a public speech. They are very emotional people like all Poles and the personal touch is important. Everywhere I must recount where I went to University and what I studied, how old I am, where I get my income, what my family is like, etc., etc. It is all simultaneously funny and touching. Some of the miners come straight from the job, all black from the coal. Tomorrow is the last meeting on my present trip (I am leaving on the 1st), the last in this beer-hall and in this century.

So, Happy New Year! Best wishes to the whole Kautsky clan and all three generations.

Your
Rosa

Notes

[1]Dr. August Winter (1866-1907): A founder of the SPD organization in

Upper Silesia, which was populated with many Polish workers, and an opponent of the PPS.

To Leo Jogiches

[Berlin-Friedenau]
3/29/1900

My dearest!

I was so tired when I returned from Posen; it is only today that I find myself able to lift my pen.

I will reply to your letter very briefly. At first, after reading it, I felt the desire—as in earlier times—to tell from my side the whole story of my stay, the reason for my abrupt departure, etc. But I recalled that I have been doing this steadily for eight years without success, and so I gave up. I will only write you about what affects future projects, facts, etc.

Your letter makes it clear to me; it is not for certain reasons which I cannot guess, but rather because of a lack of real will that you put off moving to Berlin. To my way of thinking there is simply a lack of inner courage in maintaining a marital relationship[1] merely from a distance, or through brief visits, when one does not simultaneously see the basis for a lasting relationship.

In that connection, the question of Berlin as a permanent residence is of no importance. If you feel no inner urge to move to Berlin, then there is no basis for our living together as we did in earlier times, even if only temporarily like in Zurich—in fact, not even for our corresponding in the tone of earlier times. For me to go to Zurich, as you write, for the one purpose: to awaken in you the desire to move to Berlin—that is a strange suggestion; I simply can't understand that you don't see this yourself.

Perhaps this, too, is incomprehensible to you. But I can't explain it to you. I can only assure you that I will never again set foot in Zurich, and that I will never go anywhere else to meet you. . . . How soon you will feel the final impulse—if you ever feel it at all—to settle down here at my side is completely your concern, a concern in which I cannot and will not get involved in any way, not even by writing letters.

As regards my health, I will inform you in case of serious illness; as regards my lack of finances, I will also turn to you in an emergency. (By the way, this month I have managed to earn nearly half of my livelihood due to a return trip from Zurich on the 15th, as well as a trip to Posen. If you can, enclose about 50 marks so I have them on the first.) There is then only this final remark: my decision not to write you until my arrival here was and is neither an act of revenge nor a boycott as you believe. It is the simple determination to finally break out of this vicious cycle of paradoxes in which I have been turning for so long.

Your
Rosa

Notes

[1]It was very rare in those days that a woman would refer by that term to the kind of extramarital relationship Rosa had with Jogiches. That she did throws significant light on her attitude toward feminism.

To Leo Jogiches

[Berlin-Friedenau]
4/24/1900

My dear Dziodzio!

Your letter came at precisely the right time, just when the thought was ceaselessly plaguing me how this mess between us would finally be straightened out. In order to explain my state of mind and my recent actions, I will tell you only briefly that through the past months, but especially during my stay in Zurich, I came to the conclusion that you . . . had ceased to love me, that perhaps you had even taken up with someone else and that, at any rate, I had stopped being for you the person who could make your life happy—as far as that is at all possible.

The thought immediately became clear during a night which I spent on [Clara] Zetkin's sofa and in which I could not fall asleep due to the stream of thoughts. Suddenly it presented itself to me unquestioningly and clearly. In the light of this fact, your hesitation to come to Berlin and your whole behavior of late became understandable. Then my heart grew lighter, like that of a person who has finally found a simple and clear answer to every question— even if it is the most painful answer—after endless riddles, complications, confusions and mix-ups.

I immediately decided to act in a way that would make the separation easier for you; that is to say, above all break off the correspondence and not form new bonds with my letters, nor influence your mood. In so doing, I told myself: Here the question will be decided. If he loves me and wants to live with me, then he will come—if not, he will use the break-off of our correspondence and slowly wean himself of me; the relationship will "dissolve" of its own.

And so I began to live here in complete loneliness thinking that I am alone and always will be. I grew a bit cold, but also proud. And whenever I, without meaning to, began to foster new plans and hopes, when I saw how other people lived with one another, how nice life was in the spring, whenever it occurred to me that you would find no one with whom you could live quite as well as with me, it took only one simple thought: By now he is already living a different life, or— you can't give *him* anything. This thought was enough to banish all reveries and turn me back to work with my teeth set.

Your letter somehow indicates that—that I was mistaken (it seems that I cannot get myself to express certain things), that our relationship still has a basis and that there is hope for the future. But are you certain? Do you really know what is going on in your heart? And if everything is all right don't debate with me about what happened and how it happened. Only write when and how we can settle it. . . .

To Karl and Luise Kautsky

Friedenau, July 13, 1900

Thanks for the charming post card. So, in this magnificent weather you are having a wonderful time, and all is for the best in the best of all possible worlds.

I am enclosing [Franz] Mehring's reply, which I received today, and from which you will learn the odyssey of my article.[1] I found myself in a quaint situation: no answer from M[ehring], so definitely I could not send [the article] to [Heinrich] Cunow[2]; but neither could I notify Cunow that he could not count on me for this *Neue Zeit* issue since I don't have his address (I had failed to write it down.) Nor could I ask you for it, dear Karl, because, believe it or not, I didn't have your address either until your post card arrived. I have an abominable head (cat's head we call it in Poland) for names, addresses, and similar details.

Now the thing has been cleared up and is O.K. As you see, Mehring agrees with *you* as to the inopportune nature of the article, which confirms the intention I already had after I talked with you: I'll leave the article to the gnawing criticism of—well let's say, considering the season, of the moths.[3] All I had wanted was Mehring's *opinion*. However, I admit my tactical error only as far as the political moment is concerned, not regarding parliamentary cretinism within the Party itself, which you denied.

But under that radiant July sun, in nature's green, fragrant, shady temple (i.e., the woods on your post card) and listening to the peaceful murmur of the eternal sea, should you have to read, or think, or debate "parliamentary cretinism?" I'll spare you that.

And so let's talk of the sea. Do you think, while it rustles at your feet, of that pretty legend of a blind Greek singer who played his lyre on the shore of the sea and took its rustling for the murmurings of the people? And how, when he had finished his most beautiful song and failed to hear any applause, he bitterly complained of the crowd's ingratitude and, in bitter dismay, hurled his lyre far away to dash it to pieces? And how it was caught by the wave of the sea, which, lovingly rocking it, carried it further and further away? Are you remembering that?

And do you have fancies, over there, as if the entire sea smelled of freshly baked cake, a baked fata morgana, as that fisherman on Helgoland sensed it?[4]

I think that the most overwhelming sensation when facing the sea, the eternal, immutable loftily indifferent sea, must be feeling our own nothingness. I had this same feeling when I saw the Rhine Falls in Switzerland. Their unceasing roar, never abating for a second, going on day and night and outlasting centuries, imbued me with a horrible feeling of annihilation. I got home quite crushed. And even now, whenever I pass there and, from the train window, see the dreadful spectacle, the foam, the white, boiling watery cavern, when I hear the deafening roar, my heart feels strangled, and something inside me says: That is the enemy.

You are surprised? Certainly it is the enemy—the enemy of human vanity which has been thinking that it is something and now all of a sudden collapses into being nothing.

By the way, there is a similar effect in a philosophy which like Ben Akiba[5] says of everything that happens: *"It has always been that way,"* "Things will turn out all right by themselves," etc.; man with all his ability, his will, his knowledge seems so superfluous. . . . That is why I hate this sort of philosophy, my dear Charlemagne,[6] and insist that we should rather throw ourselves into the Rhine Falls and go down in them like a nutshell than sagely nod our heads and let them go rushing the way they have rushed in our forefathers' time and will go on rushing after our time.[7]

Notes

[1]It is unclear which article is involved; if she is referring to a published article, it is probably "The First Fruits of National Intolerance," which appeared in June in the *Leipziger Volkszeitung*.

[2]Heinrich Cunow (1862-1936): A historian, sociologist, and ethnographer, Cunow took part in the battle against revisionism and later became a social patriot in the First World War and a supporter of Philipp Scheidemann. He also served as editor of *Die Neue Zeit* from 1917-23.

[3]The reference is to an expression used by Marx and Engels. After finishing *The German Ideology*, they chose not to publish it and left the manuscript "to the gnawing of the mice."

[4]The reference here is to Heinrich Heine (1797-1856), one of Germany's greatest and most political poets. Among his most famous works is the poem *A Winter Fairy Tale*.

[5]Joseph Ben Akiba (seventeenth century): A rabbi, also a leading talmudist and kabbalist. Ben Akiba was also a character in a play by Karl Gutzkow.

[6]Charlemagne was a nickname for Kautsky, who was tall in stature.

[7]Already, early in their friendship, one of the major issues that will later divide Kautsky and Luxemburg emerges. Kautsky's well-known objectivist theory of Marxism will be opposed to Rosa Luxemburg's emphasis upon the subjective activity of the masses.

To Karl and Luise Kautsky

[Undated. Probably Friedenau,
about 8/9/1900]

My dearest ones,

You have probably discovered your error by now.[1] I had sent you a telegram regarding [Wilhelm] Liebknecht's death.[2] The purpose was to enable you to arrange your departure so that Karl, at least, would be present at the funeral. It will take place on Sunday at 12 o'clock. At the same time you will also see Clara [Zetkin]. By the way, I haven't spoken to her yet either. . . .

The Old Man's death has deeply shaken me. Now all the trivia disappear and I see only—be that as it may—the old man's sturdy, generous figure. Ah, my friends, things around us are beginning to crumble. The *moral* loss resulting from L[iebknecht]'s death is greater than you would perhaps initially care to think. The old generation passes on, and there remains—God have mercy. . . . Not long ago, when I was at the offices of *Vorwärts* (I wrote you about it), the Old Man suddenly whispered to me as I was leaving: "I will always do whatever I can for you. I had quite seriously proposed you for editor, and I would have been happy to have you. In any event, if you have a thunderous article, give it to me for *Vorwärts*; it really will have a greater effect there than in the *L[eipziger] V[olkszeitung]*." I promised him that I would, and, in closing, he extended a hearty invitation: he and his wife would very much enjoy seeing me.

It is a little thing, but it does me good to know that I took leave of him in peace. We talked with him, and [Paul] Singer as well, about questions concerning the provincial assembly in Mainz; more about this when we can talk.

Now, who will take his place at *Vorwärts*? I think that [Franz] Mehring would really be the most suitable! Whoever it may be, the change will be a significant one. The poor old man—he died just barely in time to retain his fame. . . .

I kiss you affectionately! Let me know when you are coming; I am looking forward to it.

Your Rosa

Notes

[1]Liebknecht was referred to as *Der Alte* (literally, the "Old Man," but also the equivalent of "The Boss"), but when Rosa Luxemburg cabled "The Old Man died," the Kautskys had assumed that Rosa Luxemburg's father had died and had expressed their condolences.

[2]Wilhelm Liebknecht (1826-1900): A friend of both Marx and Engels, Liebknecht participated in the revolutions of 1848 and became instrumental in the formation of the SPD and the Second International.

To Karl Kautsky

Friedenau 10/3/1901

Dear Karl,

Naturally, I will forego my declaration published in *Neue Zeit*.[1] Permit me now to add a few words of explanation.

If I were amongst those who choose to safeguard their own rights and interests at any cost—and these are a legion in our party, or rather that's the way they all are—then I would naturally insist upon the publication of my article; especially since you admit that you, as the editor-in-chief, have an obligation to me in this instance. But, while admitting this obligation, you simultaneously point a revolver of friendly admonitions and entreaties at my chest to make me forego the

August Bebel. (Courtesy Dietz Verlag)

Wilhelm Liebknecht. (Courtesy Dietz Verlag)

Eduard Bernstein. (Courtesy International Institute of Social History, Amsterdam)

use of your obligation and my rights. Well, insisting on my rights disgusts me when one grants them with such wailing and gnashing of teeth; also, when at every word of defense one ties my hands so that I have to "defend myself" in this matter, and when on top of all that, one tries to bully me into renouncing my rights.

You have achieved what you wanted—I release you from your obligations to me in this instance. But, to all appearances, you are still making the same mistake. You still seem to believe, in all seriousness, that you were acting solely out of friendship and in *my* own interest. Allow me to eradicate this self-deception. *As a friend,* you should have told me something like this: "I absolutely advise you to protect your honor as a writer at any cost. Greater men and writers, whose reputations have been established for decades, like Marx and Engels, wrote whole brochures, waged entire ink-wars whenever anyone dared accuse them of the slightest 'misrepresentation.' All the more must you, as a very controversial young writer demand the most meticulous satisfaction in such an instance." Surely as a *friend,* this is what you should have said.

The friend, however, allowed himself to be completely ruled by the editor-in-chief of the *Neue Zeit* and, since the Party Convention, the latter has only one wish: he wants to be left in peace, he wants to show that the *Neue Zeit,* after its recent drubbing, has learned how to behave and keep its mouth shut. And that's why even the simple right of any *Neue Zeit* contributor to protect her most important interests and defend herself against public slander may be sacrificed. Thus, someone who works for the *Neue Zeit*—and who does neither the least nor the worst work at that—must swallow the public accusation of "misrepresentation" so that "quiet will reign in the treetops."[2]

That's how the matter stands, my friend. And now, with affectionate greetings, your

Rosa

Notes

[1] The reference is to the response that Rosa wished to make in regard to the Lübeck Congress of 1901. At this conference, she attacked Bernstein—which she had been enlisted to do by the party executive. After she left the conference, she was attacked for the vociferousness of her polemic—even by members of the executive, despite the fact that they had enlisted her in the first place.

[2] The reference is to one of Goethe's best-known lyrical poems.

To Leo Jogiches

[Berlin-Friedenau]
2/11/1902

Dear Dziodzio!

. . . Naturally, as usual, I had a few funny episodes on my trip. After the meeting in Reichenbach—in every city, after the meeting, I must sit with the comrades in a more private setting until 2 a.m. which, by the way, I don't regret in the least!—one of the local big shots said, after he had looked me over for quite some time: "Well, you couldn't be more than 27 years old. And I thought you were around 42." But why?—I asked in amazement. "Well, there was that picture in the *Süddeutscher Postillon.*"[1]

You can imagine how I laughed. It turned out that, in their naiveté, they had taken the picture for my actual portrait and that each had solemnly kept a copy.

After the meeting in Meerane (Saxony), on the other hand, I was formally interpellated on the woman's question and on marriage. A splendid young weaver, Hoffman, is zealously studying this question. He has read Bebel,[2] Lili Braun[3] and *Gleichheit*[4] and is carrying on a bitter argument with the older village comrades, who keep maintaining that "a woman's place is in the home," and that we must seek the abolition of factory work for women. When I agreed with Hoffman, what a triumph! "There, you see," he cried, "the voice of authority has spoken for me!"

Answering one of the older men who called it a disgrace that pregnant women should have to scurry around in the factory in the midst of young men, Hoffman cried out: "Those are mistaken moralistic notions! Can you imagine if our Luxemburg were pregnant today while giving her lecture? Then I would like her even better!"

At this unexpected declaration, I almost exploded with laughter. But they took it all so seriously that I had to bite my lips.

Anyway, I must make an effort to be pregnant the next time I go to Reichenbach. Do you hear? After the farewells (at two o'clock in the morning), this young fellow held me a moment longer so that I might answer an important question: Should he get married, even though present-day marriage is a perverse arrangement? Luckily I answered that he should get married, which pleased him greatly, since, as the whispers and laughter of the others, and later his own confession brought out, he was just getting ready to be married—and it's high

time too, since his fiancée is exactly in that condition which he likes
so very much. . . .
    I embrace you.

Your R

Notes

    [1]They had seen a caricature that appeared in the Munich biweekly,
Süddeutscher Postillon, which was an SPD publication edited by Eduard
Fuchs.
    [2]Bebel's classic, *Women Under Socialism.*
    [3]Lily Braun (1865-1916): Active in the women's and the youth movements,
her best-known work is *Memoirs of a Socialist.*
    [4]*Gleichheit (Equality)* was the women's paper of the SPD, edited by
Clara Zetkin.

To Franz Mehring

Berlin 9/27/1902

    . . . I consider the way in which you have mutilated my article on
Poland—without writing me a single word about it, or leaving me
free to decide on its publication—as a deliberate provocation which is
but one link in a whole chain of slights. You yourself could have
realized that these tactics would necessarily force me to resign from
my work on the *L[eipziger] V[olkszeitung].* Well I draw the
consequences, and suspend my collaboration. . . .

To August Bebel

10/11/1902

Dear Comrade!
    Although I do not want to take up your precious time with trifles
now—before the beginning of the session—still I feel that I must
write you a few lines in response to your friendly letter.
    It's really important to me that you do not harbor the mistaken
assumption that I am inclined to draw myself back into a corner and
sulk, or isolate myself by blindly striking out left and right. If I were at
all inclined to sulk, I truly would have had ample opportunity to do
so—starting from the first moment of my appearance in the German
movement, from the Stuttgart Party Convention. Despite the strange

reception which I—like other non-German "outsider" comrades— received, and that not just from the opportunists, I have not passed up any chance to stick my neck out. It never occurred to me, quite apart from any question of sulking, to withdraw into the corner of scientific study, which is so much more agreeable and quiet!

Also, I can assure you that I do not let blind passion guide me. Even in the case of the article about Poland, I was quite prepared to receive a sharp rejoinder from you, and probably to hear much that would be personally unpleasant.[1] Still, I decided that, despite all of this, on the merits I would carry my point and that the public debates would be useful to our cause in any event. . . .

Since last June, Lensch[2] has been pushing me out of the *Leipziger Volkszeitung* step by step. If I have committed any sin, it was perhaps my almost bovine patience, through which I let myself be pushed out gradually due to considerations for personal friendships instead of resigning right away. All this, however, confidentially, and only to vindicate myself to you.

With best regards,
R. Luxemburg

Notes

[1]The leadership of the SPD was slowly growing disgusted with the continuous conflict between the two Polish parties and began to be more and more contemptuous of these *Polendebatten*.

[2]Paul Lensch (1873-1928): Initially a member of the left wing of the SPD, Lensch moved ever further right until, at the outbreak of World War I, he became a social patriot. The shift right continued after the war when he became an editor for Hugo Stinnes, the industrialist and press magnate.

To Karl and Luise Kautsky

[Undated. Probably Zwickau Prison, 1904]

Dear Carolus,

. . . Well, so now you have other battles to fight! That makes me very happy, for it shows how acutely those dear little people felt the weight of our victory in Amsterdam.[1] As I view the situation, they want to take their revenge in Bremen—and indeed, that will be spoiled for them. This is why it annoys me that you should envy me my cell! I don't doubt that you will knock Kurt [Eisner],[2] Georg [Gradnauer] & Co. squarely on their so-called heads. But you must do it with joy and gusto, and not as if it were a troublesome intermezzo.

For the public always senses the mood of the combatants, and the joy of battle gives the polemic a clear sound and a moral superiority.

From what I see, you are now, to be sure, completely alone; August [Bebel] will certainly remain in the Lord's vineyard until the end point is reached, and dearest Arthur [Stadthagen] and Paul [Singer] are, as you put it, "elegiacal." Why, thunder and lightning should strike them seven fathoms deep into the ground if they can be "elegiacal" after such a convention—between two battles, when one should be happy to be alive.

After all, Karl, this present "brawl" is not the type of forced skirmish, carried out in a grey atmosphere of indifference, such as those which you had to fight so often in the last few years. Now again, the interest of the masses is aroused; I can feel it here right through the prison walls. And, then too, don't forget that the International is watching us intently—or, I should say watching you people—since the starting point of the whole controversy is, after all, Amsterdam. I write all this to you, not to "egg you on"; I am not quite that tactless. Rather I wish to raise your spirits for your polemic, or at least transmit my exuberance to you since I haven't much use for that commodity here in No. 7.

You know, I have reflected on Amsterdam a good deal, on the general state of the international movement and the prospects for our Marxism in the International; I have so much to say to you about it, but that must wait. For me, the moral is that we have an enormous amount to *do* and, above all, to *study*. I mean this in terms of the movement in the different countries. I have a feeling that we ("Germans"), if only through our mere understanding of the actual movement in other countries, are already gaining influence and preeminence internationally. On the other hand, I have a feeling that merely through our drawing closer to the International, we are strengthening our position (strictly speaking) within the German movement. In a word, I'm very happy with life.

With your letter, please enclose your articles—but as clippings. I am certain that Clara [Zetkin] is with the two of us. For both you and her there are hot days ahead in Bremen. Come to an understanding quickly; one can rely on her. I would so very much like to get a letter from her. Apropos the fourth volume:[3] just when will it appear? You see, I would like to review it; a number of thoughts about the subject are swarming around in my head.

Now, to you, dearest Luise, or rather now to you only since of course the entire letter is for you as well. Often, you understand my mood better and more quickly (if there is anything to "understand").

There was so much I meant to write, and yet I must be so brief! Well, only this much: Your letters put me in the sunniest frame of mind; a thousand thanks for every word! You give me such a vivid picture of your surroundings! Send my most affectionate greetings to Holland. Write often, but only when you want to—don't force yourself. I kiss you all, and the boys. Regards to Granny.

Your Rosa

Notes

[1]Amsterdam Congress of 1904: Rosa attended with a double mandate from the SDKPL and Germany. Fundamentally, the issue under debate was the demand for unity under Marxist principles. The German position was an attack on the split within the French party. Rosa's main opponent was Jean Jaurès. Interestingly enough, when Jaurès spoke, it became evident that there was no one in support of his position who could translate his speech. At that point, Rosa jumped up and reproduced his moving speech into an equally moving German. Jaurès thanked her profusely and publicly. It must have been painful for her to translate phrases such as: "Have you Germans, with all your revolutionary class consciousness and Marxist principles, produced a single law?" That she had learned something from Jaurès is apparent in the following letter, which is recommended to neo-Marxist sectarians.

[2]Kurt Eisner (1867-1919): A Kantian socialist who opposed the mass strike strategy vociferously, he was consistently antimilitarist and participated in the founding of the USPD. Imprisoned in 1918, Eisner was freed and became the premier of the Bavarian Republic until he was assassinated in the streets on February 21, 1919.

[3]Refers to the "fourth" volume of *Das Kapital* as Engels termed it. Kautsky was the editor of the manuscript, which was entitled *Theories of Surplus Value*.

To Henriette Roland-Holst[1]

[Berlin?]
12/17/1904

. . . I would like to talk to you about the "race problem" in the Social Democratic movement, and I'd like even better to discuss our present general situation. The role which this supposed orthodox "radicalism" has been playing so far does not delight me at all. Attacking each of the opportunist imbecilities and submitting it to a garrulous exegesis is not a job that would satisfy me. On the contrary, this sort of activity is so unbearable to me that in such cases I prefer to remain silent.

I also admire the perseverance of quite a few of our radical friends who endlessly find it necessary to bring the stray lamb, the Party, back into the safe fold of "firmness of principles" without realizing that these negative proceedings will not get us ahead even one step. And for a revolutionary movement, not moving forward means retreating. There is only one way for us radically to fight opportunism: we ourselves must move ahead, *develop* our tactics, *reinforce* the revolutionary side of the movement. In any case, opportunism is a swamp plant which develops rapidly and abundantly in the stagnant waters of the movement: in a strong and fresh current, it dies all of itself.

Moving ahead is, here in Germany, one of our most critical and urgent needs! How few are those who sense that need! Some exhaust themselves in guerrilla warfare against the opportunists; others believe that if (in elections and in their organizations) their number grows mechanically and automatically, that this in itself is progress. They forget that quantity has to transform itself into quality, that a party of three million cannot content itself with automatically repeating the gestures of a half million member party.[2] I don't have to tell you, of all people, that I envisage neither a "sudden descent into the street" nor some haphazard adventure. But all our work must assume a different, more profound tone; the consciousness of our strength must grow and . . . and well, we'll discuss that some day, otherwise my letter will turn into an editorial. Does all this occur to you, too? Actually, this is not just a German problem, it is an international problem. The Amsterdam Congress has made it very clear to me. But German Social Democracy must give the signal and show the direction. . . .

Your Rosa

Notes

[1]Henriette Roland-Holst (1867-1952): Leader, with Anton Pannekoek, of the Dutch left-wing socialists. An activist in the international women's movement, she opposed the war and in 1919 became one of the founders of the Dutch communist party. After leaving the communist party for good in 1927, she moved closer to the workers' council movement and the anarchists. An author of assorted literary, political, and sociological writings, Henriette Roland-Holst also wrote a biography of Rosa Luxemburg.

[2]In 1903, the SPD polled 3.5 million votes, which constituted an enormous triumph for the party. "Quantity into quality," of course, refers to one of the "three laws of dialectics" that Engels mentions in *Anti-Dühring*, a socialist best-seller.

To Henry Hubert Van Kohl

Berlin-Friedenau, March 1, 1905

Dear Friend Van Kohl: .

I suppose the Dutch party, too will follow the example of all the other parties and raise funds for the victims of Czarism. In addition, there may be in your country, as in France, committees of bourgeois "philanthropists" that raise funds for this purpose.[1] If so, may I urge you 1) to give me the addresses of the policymaking people on these committees; 2) to fraternally intervene and induce the committees to allot at least half of the funds raised—particularly of the funds raised by the Party—to the Social Democrats of Russian Poland.[2] We have had a momentous strike, the likes of which the world has never seen (135,000 workers!)—all the more impressive since they have no right whatsoever to organize; there are no strike funds, no true trade unions. They are risking their lives all the time—in a period of frightful depression, where the masses have been starving for months!

This heroism of the masses deserves all possible help, and I warmly urge you to take up the matter so that we get at least half of the funds for the Polish workers, who by now are in the forefront of the fight.

Any monies may be sent to me or directly to the Committee of the Social Democrats in Cracow. . . . Both the Treasurer and the Polish party paper will acknowledge the receipts.

Thanking you in advance on behalf of our fighting workers and hoping to hear from you soon,

Cordially yours,

Notes

[1]After reports on the Petersburg "Bloody Sunday," European social democratic parties and trade unions appealed for donations and called mass meetings. In Paris, "Friends of the Russian People," an association headed by (among others) Anatole France and Georges Clemenceau, was founded to protest the imprisonment of Maxim Gorky.

[2]Actually only 15 percent of the donated funds was allotted to the Polish social democrats. On a few occasions, Rosa Luxemburg was able through her connections to increase this rate.

To Henriette Roland-Holst

July 3, 1905

Dear Henriette:

I hasten to answer your question. Never in the entire history of the Party have I come across an interpretation of a resolution like the one you described.[1] The German Social Democratic Party has always followed the opposite course: When it decides, for instance, that Liberal candidates are to be supported, this automatically means that supporting the other candidate is *prohibited.*

More generally speaking, the individual liberty of party members in regard to supporting opponent candidates seems monstrous to me; it clashes with the Social-Democratic organizational concept. To be sure, once in a while the German party may, as it did in Württemberg, give election districts a free hand regarding the Liberals (*Volkspartei*) who are too despicable to be endorsed across the board and yet in some districts may be preferable to the other reactionaries. However, such an assessment cannot be left to the individuals; it should be left up to the Party organization of the election district.

In contrast, giving party members carte blanche is a well-known policy of the *bourgeois* parties and a well-known mask for cowardly treason. Whenever the German Liberals wish to support a reactionary against a Social Democrat in an election, they rely on this laissez-faire gimmick. Only rarely on those occasions, and in so many words, do they recommend that their followers support the reactionary; instead, they cover themselves by "leaving the decision to each individual's discretion." This never fails to serve as a license to support—either passively or actively—the Social Democrat's opponent.

As to my plan for a trip to beautiful Holland, you guessed it: Nothing will come of it. I cannot get away from here. But I feel splendid in my work, for the revolution is growing according to expectations; it is a great joy to watch, understand, and help this development. You mention "hoping and worrying"; but only a mere observer, and an observer devoid of understanding at that, like for instance the *Vörwarts* people or the Russian Liberals, could feel that way. People such as we cooperate cheerfully and the intellectual work involved—analyzing the revolutionary progress—is perhaps even more highly gratifying than practical work. Our masses today truly crave enlightenment—crave class-consciousness; I call myself happy to be able to contribute at least a tiny little grain to appease this hunger for culture. The only pity is that you, all of you, cannot take a direct part, cannot write for the proletarians in Russia and Poland: Language is still a hellish obstacle for the International. If I had my way, all fresh spirits of all countries would be busy using all their united strength for the Russian Revolution; they would direct a torrent of good pamphlets that way. Then things would come to a head fast! Instead, you have to fritter away your precious forces on idiotic parliamentary elections, etc. What a shame!

I shall venture to give you my humble opinion on your book[2] in

Die Neue Zeit. So far, I am afraid I have been too busy to do the article, precisely because of the work for the Russian-Polish workers.

Many fond greetings and kisses from your Rosa

Notes

[1]Before the 1905 runoff elections, the congress of the Dutch party had decided to support only those Liberal candidates who were committed to the introduction of universal suffrage. The party executive, however, "interpreted" this resolution as allowing the individual party member to decide whether to be guided by the anticlerical rather than by the suffrage issue.

[2]Henriette Roland-Holst's *General Strike and Social Democracy,* which appeared in 1905.

To Arthur Stadthagen

[On *Die Neue Zeit* stationery.
Undated letter. Probably Friedenau, 1905]

Dear Arthur!

You have probably read in tonight's [*Berliner*] *Tageblatt* that [Jean] Jaurès has been invited by the editors of *Vorwärts* to come to a meeting in Berlin on the 9th. Well, once again, Mr. [Kurt] Eisner and Mr. [Georg] Gradnauer have executed a characteristic coup, and that "in the name of the Berlin socialists"—as reported by *Humanité*.[1]

We two Friedenau people feel unanimously that one must compensate for this intrigue by at least inviting [Jules] Guesde and Vaillant[2] to the same meeting. Especially in their foreign policy, but also in their entire point of view, they are closer to the Berlin people than Juarès with his pothouse politics. By the way, particularly in the Morocco affair,[3] Jaurès is definitely feeding the blind clamoring of the semi-official press through his interminable editorials.

Well, if you are of the same opinion, then immediately explain the situation to the Berlin people and propose that they invite both Guesde and Vaillant. (They should write them in French.) Also, the Berlin people must promise to pay the travel expenses since the two of them are not as rich as Jaurès. Let me know as soon as you have accomplished something.

Best regards,
Your Rosa

Agreeing completely, and considering this extremely important.

Best regards,
Kautsky

Notes

[1]*L'Humanité* was founded in 1890 and became the organ of the SFIO. Now it is the official paper of the French Communist Party.

[2]Eduard Vaillant (1840-1915): Took part in the Paris Commune. He was originally a disciple of Blanqui and then became one of the founders of the French Socialist Party. An antimilitarist for many years, he supported the French government in the First World War.

[3]Morocco was a continual point of crisis among the great powers in the years before the First World War. The first Morocco crisis took place in 1905, and the second broke out in 1911.

To Karl and Luise Kautsky

[Undated. Probably the summer of 1905]
Dearest Carolus,

Enclosed is Lenin's prattle,[1] the last lines of which concern you. I consider it necessary that you prepare a few words of correction for Camille Huysmans[2] so that he can inform the Bureau; at your convenience, you might mention that my article was not in favor of decentralization. That, however, is unimportant. . . .

The family has experienced a calamity. Puck fell down the stairs and broke a paw. Hence: anxiety, the doctor, poultices, sleepless nights, etc. It's already getting better, but every other minute the rascal is gnawing through its bandage, and even the carpet beater doesn't help. Oh yes, do write me when you expect to return. Many kisses to everyone.

Your Rosa

Notes

[1]The reference is to the Russian organizational debate in which Lenin emphasized the role of the vanguard party which Rosa Luxemburg opposed.

[2]Camille Huysmans (1871-1968): A leading figure in the Belgian Workers' Party, he was secretary of the International Socialist Bureau from 1905 to 1922. He later became president of the Council of Ministers from 1946-47.

To Henriette Roland-Holst

Friedenau 10/2/1905
My dear Henriette,

I hasten to respond to your questions, but even more I wish to joyously salute the second edition of your book. I am in complete agreement with you that Bebel's resolution deals with the question of the mass strike in a one-sided manner and abounds with platitudes. When we spoke at Jena, some of us decided to combat it in the [floor—trans.] discussion by emphasizing that the mass strike should not be considered as a mechanistic remedy for the defense of political rights, but rather as a fundamental revolutionary form. But Bebel's speech has changed the orientation considerably and the attitude of the opportunists (Heine, etc.)[1] has changed it even more. On several occasions, those of us on the "far left" have found ourselves on the same side as Bebel—despite the important differences between us—in fighting against the opportunists.

To intervene directly in the discussion at Jena against Bebel's resolution would have been a tactical mistake on our part. It was much more important to show where we stood in solidarity with Bebel than to give his resolution a revolutionary taint. In the discussion, the mass strike was considered as a form of struggle for the revolutionary masses even by Bebel—though perhaps he was unaware of it. The spectre of the revolution clearly dominated the whole of the debate and the congress. The opportunists themselves have attested to the fact by playing Cassandra for us insofar as they put themselves on guard against the inevitable consequences of the new tactic—the violent revolution. The result was such that it fully satisfied our *tactical* plans. The resolutions of the congress have never had any purpose other than to exhaust a question on the theoretical level and to formulate it definitively for all occasions. . . .

Rosa

Notes

[1]Wolfgang Heine (1861-1944): One of the most prominent followers of Bernstein. In 1890, Heine became a Reichstag deputy and, in 1893, an editor of *Vorwärts*. In 1916, he joined the USPD.

To Leo Jogiches

[Berlin-Friedenau]
10/6/1905

Dearest!

Today I will finally write extensively and mail my letter in time so that I won't have to go running into the city at night. Yesterday I received a letter from Bebel with the following text: (Unfortunately, I must copy it out for you, since you will surely be unable

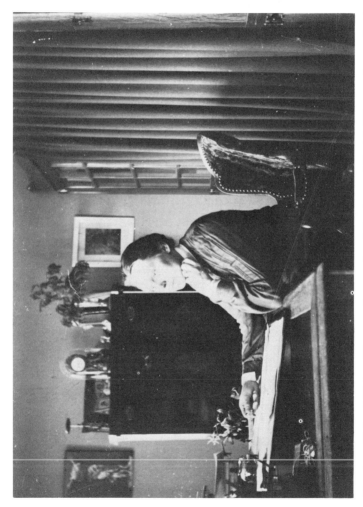

Henriette Roland-Holst. (Courtesy International Institute of Social History, Amsterdam)

to decipher it).

"May I ask you whether you would be willing to write 2 lead articles per week, on a regular basis, for *Vorwärts* if the proper quarters should ask for your collaboration?

"I take it for granted that you will not be bound either by dates, or by themes. Depending on the circumstances, the articles should treat economic or political themes. Either you or the editorial board will pick the themes; the editorial board will request an article on such and such a theme and will then have to accept the article unless press law considerations apply. Should it have objections to the contents, the Executive and the Press Commission must be informed immediately. The articles are to be presented as editorials unless from time to time you wish to sign one.

"Naturally you will be appropriately paid for the articles. Where possible, the articles should not run over two columns—by way of exception an important theme can be dealt with in other sections. I would ask you to give me your reaction as soon as possible."

As you can see, it's a marriage proposal in the best of form. In themselves the conditions are superb: especially protection by the Executive. . . . However, the letter really puts me in a difficult situation. I know the counter-arguments very well and there is no need to repeat them. On the other hand, the situation is as follows: after all the rumpus over *Vorwärts,* to some extent this move would involve turning to our Left with the recommendation that we build a cabinet.

Although, strictly speaking, I never overtly took the least part in these quarrels, thanks to Jena,[1] I figure once again as the driving spirit of the Left; a refusal—precisely on my part—would mean: There you have it! These people only have big mouths to cause a stink, but when it comes to doing better, then they skedaddle!

Besides it would be a particularly grievous blow and casus belli for August [Bebel]. Naturally, he is the one who is promoting this whole reform, who is anxious to reorganize *Vorwärts* in accordance with our wishes, and who took it into his head that I can handle the job! To refuse him would mean thwarting all his plans, and leaving Eisner and Co. the field without a fight.

In a word, the situation is worse than embarrassing. Since I was given until today to give an answer (after lunch, there is to be a meeting of the Executive with the Press Commission regarding the "great reform"), I went to Karl Kautsky last night in order to ask his advice. At present (for certain reasons) he is more furious than ever at *Vorwärts* and August. In spite of that, he immediately said that "to decline is utterly impossible." So we worked out the following plan: to come to an arrangement immediately with [Heinrich] Cunow and right off to form an offensive-defensive alliance with him and Ströbel[2] (and possibly with the entire Left) with the reciprocal obligation that, in the event of a clash with the Editorial Board or the Executive over my articles, not only I alone but our entire Left would walk out on *Vorwärts* in solidarity. With that, the Editorial Board will blow up, and then Eisner and Co. will assuredly be thrown out since *Vorwärts* cannot exist without Cunow.

This morning we both went to see Cunow; he gleefully agreed and is eagerly awaiting a chance for a showdown. As you should know, this man has been so furious at Eisner and Co. lately that in all seriousness he had meant to withdraw from *Vorwärts*—but with me on the board the whole thing would take on quite a different significance. (By the way, before Jena, at the last meeting of the Press Commission and the Editorial Board, Cunow and Eisner came to blows. Cunow threw himself at Eisner, grabbed him by the throat, pushed him against the wall, and was ready to belt him when the others pulled him away. Still, Eisner is now as *sweet* as can be to Cunow and keeps buttonholing him.)

On the basis of this, I wrote Bebel explaining that, from the outset, I did not believe in the success of such an artificial reform and that nothing will change as long as E[isner], G[radnauer], and W[etzker][3] are on the Board. In order to show good will on the part of our left wing, however, I would go along with B[ebel]'s proposal on condition that first a permanent majority of leftists on the Editorial Board be guaranteed.

This is how I tackled the situation and, although you are certainly making a face, you will have to agree—after thinking it over—that I had no choice! (By the way, this job will place me in an influential position in the very center of the Party—especially in view of the amazing fondness that August [Bebel] has lately shown for me.) . . . I have had great pleasure with my own scribbling, and I can feel the spiritual spark leaping into my fist. I try to write in such a way that one can tell the author from ten paces away. Cunow is already rubbing his hands with glee at the thought of the faces on the "right wing" when they see such articles appearing in the *central organ*.

Just a bit about me personally. You are mistaken, sweetheart! My mind is not constantly on the Polish work. Unfortunately, just the opposite. Jena has again turned me "inside out" in this respect to the point where I sometimes doubt whether anyone is doing anything at all, since I always feel so cut off from everything. But, although my thoughts are completely on the German work, I still want to keep track of at least the most important aspects of our work, and I ask you not to be so childish, and not forcibly to isolate me from the work in Poland by not informing me of anything. Sweetheart—just don't ever apply your kill-or-cure remedies to me again, eh? When I assure you that a few informative reports on the state of activity can't do me any harm, but rather are a necessity, then you can rest assured that this is the case. . . .

                                                                              R

Notes

[1]The annual SPD congress held in Jena. Rosa Luxemburg pushed through the "mass strike resolution," which made the mass strike part of the official tactical arsenal of the SPD to the dismay of the trade union delegates.

[2]Henrich Ströbel (1869-1945): A German social democrat who took an internationalist position at the outset of the First World War, he later turned into a social chauvinist and split from Luxemburg and Mehring. At the turn of the century he was an important force in *Vorwärts*.

[3]Heinrich Wetzker (1861-?): A member of the editorial board of the *Sächsische Arbeiter-Zeitung*.

To Leo Jogiches

                                                      [Berlin-Friedenau 10/26/1905]
Dearest:
    I enclose my piece on "Self-Administration."[1] When I received the telegram, I thought over your remarks carefully, and found one of them very pertinent: namely, that we cannot base self-administration on cultural interests. Here, too, we must above all take into account not the "economic peculiarity"—as you put it inexactly—but rather the *class struggle* which is becoming ever more localized in character (due to the decentralization of capital). That is why I have tried to make corrections! "Historical and economic peculiarity" is mechanically repeated by the *Iskra*[2] people (Mensheviks)[3] after the bourgeois politicians, the way children imitate grown-ups—that only proves their lack of a critical faculty; we are under no obligation to accept their theories. This type of formulation is good enough for Trubetzkoi[4] and Struve.[5] We are the party of class struggle, and not of "historical laws."
    As to the other remarks, I stand by my exposition:
1) I give first priority to the abolition of special privileges and to equal

rights for all nationalities; self-administration is only a detail and a consequence. That is precisely the crucial point which differentiates us from the PPS, etc. and their notion of autonomy. For us, the starting point is the general interest—that the solidarity sought within national identity equal the solidarity of the proletariat. For the PPS, the starting point is—Polish peculiarity, while for other nationalities, inverting their autonomy notion, they derive magnanimous pipe dreams based on "federalistic maxims" like "Do not do unto another what you would not have him do unto you," "Each is master in his own house," "Unleash the elemental forces." We must hold on to our logical proposal in our agitation too, and, among other things, I will try to develop it in a brochure or an article about autonomy.

2) That is why I will not title my paper "Self-Administration" as you suggest, but rather "Institutions of the State which, etc.," as we proposed to the Muscovites as an item in the general program and on national autonomy. Remember that we, as Social Democrats, although active on the spot, in contrast to the PPS, still are not a localized particular party, but a splinter of a national party, which is why our program must maintain its basic national character in all points.

Well, I suppose that I have impressed you with these enlightening insights, eh?

Your Rosa

P.S. As to the title, a few doubts come to mind: the "assurance to all nationalities" is a pious wish rather than a programmatic formulation of a demand. In the program, one should demand specific, concrete institutions or laws. From this viewpoint, that formulation of ours which we proposed to the Muscovites (State Institutes) seems to me to be equally inappropriate now. Speaking concretely, what shall we now demand for all of them? I suggest "civic equality of rights for all nationalities residing in the Russian state, with the guarantee of linguistic and cultural freedom, especially in the schools, and territorial self-government for Poland and Lithuania."

Notes

[1] The article appeared in Polish and was translated as "A Commentary to the Social Democratic Program of the Kingdoms of Poland and Lithuania."

[2] *Iskra* (*The Spark*) was founded in 1900, and its editorial board included Lenin, Plekhanov, Martov, Axelrod, Zasulich, and Potresov. In 1903,

however, after the split within Russian social democracy, Lenin left the editorial board, and *Iskra* subsequently became the central organ of the Mensheviks.

³Menshevik means a member of a minority. At the London Conference of the Russian Social Democratic Labor Party in 1903, Lenin's group—though a minority within the movement as a whole—emerged through parliamentary skill as the majority and thus assumed the title of the Bolsheviki ("Majoritarians"). The fundamental cause of the split was conflict over the question of revolutionary organization.

⁴Sergei Trubetzkoi (1862-1905): A professor of philosophy and rector of Moscow University, he presented Czar Nicholas II with a list of liberal demands.

⁵Peter Struve (1870-1944): The outstanding example of "legal Marxism" in the 1890s, he later became a leader of the Constitutional Democrats, opposed the October Revolution, supported the counterrevolutionaries in the civil war, and then emigrated.

To Leo Jogiches

[Berlin-Friedenau 11/3/1905,
according to the content]

Dearest!

I have received all the telegrams and, this very moment, your special-delivery letter.

You ask why I don't write and what I'm doing. Well, "What can I tell you?" I feel wretched. As you correctly remarked, *Vorwärts* is rapidly sinking to the level of the *Sächsische Arbeiter-Zeitung* and the worst is that I am the only one who is aware of it (in part Karl Kautsky is, too).

The Editorial Board consists of asses, and pompous ones at that. "Journalists"—not a one! Moreover, Eisner and Co. are engaged in a vicious polemic against us in the press, along with the whole pack of revisionists—and the response is given by either August [Bebel](!), or Cunow and his crowd (!!!). And I can only concern myself with Russia, write a lead article now and then, give good advice, and propose initiatives which then fall to pieces in their execution so horribly that I could tear out my hair. . . .

And I don't see any way out because there aren't any *people*. On top of all that, I am dead tired and can barely crawl about. Driving to the editorial offices at 4 o'clock every day, returning at 9, and the palavers with this gang tire me indescribably. Then too, I get up at 8 o'clock in the morning (since I hear the maid) and walk around in a daze, since I can't fall asleep nights due to my distress. In a word—it's just great. The activities of our people at home delight me. Unfortunately, due to lack of space, I can't repeat much in *Vorwärts*. I did not praise the Russian Socialists alone, but rather the Social Democrats in the whole realm, that is to say, our tactics in regard to the Duma—in case you read it carefully.

Heartfelt regards.

R.

To Karl and Luise Kautsky

[Postcard from Warsaw,
postmarked Saturday, 12/18/05 (Russian calendar).]
Saturday

My dearest ones!

Last night, I arrived safely on an unheated and unlit train which was under military escort. Due to fear of "surprises," it proceeded at a grandmother's pace. The city is as quiet as the grave: general strike, soldiers wherever you look. The work is going well; today I begin.

Many affectionate greetings,
Your Rosa

To Karl and Luise Kautsky

[Picture postcard from Illowo (East Prussia).
Postmarked Friday at noon 12/29/05]

My dearest ones,

Here I sit, to be sure not "moulding men"[1] but rather eating schnitzel and potatoes. I spent the whole night on the slow train between Alexandrowo and Thorn, and I'm dog tired. I am waiting here for the train to Mlawa. What's next—is still unclear. No hope of a horse cart until Sunday because of Shabbes.[2] But instead, a train is to leave today for Warsaw—under military escort! In the latter case, you can picture for yourselves the tragi-comic aspects of the situation. The whole train is to be occupied by the military—and amongst them, probably the only *remaining* civilian passenger: myself. . . .

This joke of history can, however, easily become a serious matter should there happen to be a *rencontre* along the way with striking railway men. Let's hope I won't be received in W[arsaw] with Brownings!

Many kisses!

R

Notes

[1]An allusion to Goethe's poem "Prometheus." Considering that Rosa Luxemburg is on her way to participate in the Russian Revolution, the joke is half serious.

[2]It is probable either that Rosa was in Jewish territory or that Jews held the horse cart concession in Illowo. Since, according to Jewish law, one is not allowed to travel on Saturdays, this surely caused the delay.

To Karl and Luise Kautsky

[Warsaw]

1/2/06

My dearest ones,

This letter will be brief, since I have very little time. Up to the present, I have been trying to orient myself on the state of our work and the general situation; now, I am throwing myself into work. To characterize the situation in two words (but this is only for you): the general strike has just about failed, most of all in St. Petersburg, where the railway workers took no initiative at all to carry it through. (Deutsch's[1] information was, therefore, unreliable.) Everywhere, there is a mood of uncertainty and waiting. The cause of all this, however, is the simple fact that the general strike, used alone, has played out its role. Now, only a direct, all-encompassing fight in the streets can bring about a resolution. Yet, for this, we must work toward the right moment. This state of waiting could continue for a while unless some "accident"—a new manifesto or something like that—should cause a sudden and spontaneous eruption.

In general, the work is going well and the mood is a good one, only one must explain to the masses *why* the present strike has run its course without achieving any visible "results."—The organization is growing greatly everywhere and yet, at the same time, it is in a sorry state since everything is in flux. The chaos is at its worst in St. Petersburg. In Moscow, it's much better and the strategy there has brought the general strategy forward to a new stage.—Leadership from Petersburg is out of the question, for the viewpoints of these people are so parochial that it's laughable. (By the way, this also appears in Deutsch's line of argument, in which he demands material aid for Petersburg *alone*. As I had to confess later, this was most unwise even from their own standpoint. The revolution can never triumph in St. Petersburg alone; now it can only triumph in the country as a whole.) . . .

Dearest [Luise—trans.], it is very nice here. Every day, two or three people in the city are stabbed to death by soldiers and arrests occur daily. But, aside from that, it's quite jolly. Despite martial law, we are publishing our *Sztandar* daily and it is sold on the streets! As soon as martial law is abolished, *Trybuna*, the daily paper, will legally appear once again. At present, the daily printing of *Sztandar* must be carried out by force, with revolver in hand, in the bourgeois print shops. The meetings too will immediately begin to take place as soon as martial law is lifted, then you shall hear from me. Here it's bitter cold and one only travels by sled.

I must close. Many kisses to you both, and to the boys. Affectionate greetings to Granny, Hans, Mehring, Singer, and to my colleagues. Write me *at once* how everything is going with you, and what is happening in general, how things stand at *V*[*orwärts*] and whether August [Bebel] has been scolding. Address ordinary letters to Goldenberg, with an envelope for me inside.

Affectionately,
Your R.

Notes

[1]Lev Deutsch (1858-1941): An organizer of the Emancipation of Labor group founded in 1883, he became a Menshevik in 1903, and in 1918 removed himself from political activity.

To Karl and Luise Kautsky

[Warsaw]
1/11/06

My dearest ones,

Thanks very much for your two (alas! so very short) letters, which I awaited with impatience. I did not send you a telegram since M[archlewski] was just then supposed to be leaving for Berlin. His journey, however, as often happens, was delayed for several days. I hope he has delivered my greetings to you and asked you to send me the things I requested as registered commercial papers; that way, everything can be easily sent in two envelopes. Here, we have received

V[orwärts] once (two copies of the "red" issue), but since then—nothing! The gods and the cossacks may know the reasons for this. I am most impatiently awaiting Mehring's article, since it is holding up the publication of Karl's work! Is it possible that M hasn't even written it yet? I am writing him at the same time; you work on him as well, Luise.

During the last few days, a member of the OK [the Mensheviks] was here. I squeezed all sorts of information out of him regarding the situation and I will make use of it for *V[orwärts]*. Aside from this, I have the laudable intention of writing regularly for the *Neue Zeit* from here, and that more in terms of casting light on the events (a purpose to which *V[orwärts]* is not suited). If only one had a little more time!

By the way, I learned from the Muscovite that Parvus has given up both the chairmanship and his seat on the council of delegates after he found himself in the minority in the course of the last general strike. The question involved how to inject new life into the abortive strike. Parvus suggested following the example of Moscow: that an armed uprising be proclaimed in order to save the situation. Everyone agreed with the idea, but the majority was convinced of its impracticality under the existing circumstances. Parvus explained that he fully realized that he had overestimated his knowledge of the conditions and that, above all, he wished to learn more about it. Therefore, he resigned in order to dedicate himself to his newspaper, which has had a colossal success. By the way, at the moment *not a single* Social Democratic newspaper is appearing in the whole of Russia. It's the same with all the democratic papers, and in fact, even the most colorless and reactionary ones are banned. (You know from M that, in spite of it all, our *Sztandar* appears daily and is sold in the streets.)

At the moment, the situation is as follows: On the one hand it is generally felt that the coming phase of the struggle will be that of armed *rencontres*. I have learned a great deal about Moscow, and the most encouraging things imaginable. (I will write you as soon as I receive entirely exact and reliable information.) For the present, suffice it to say that in Moscow one can probably record a victory rather than a defeat. The entire infantry was inactive along with the cossacks! Only cavalry and artillery are still "capable of fighting." Losses on the revolutionary side were minimal, and the whole, enormous sacrifice was borne by—the bourgeoisie: that is, those who were completely uninvolved, because the soldiers simply fired blindly and destroyed private houses. The result: the whole bourgeoisie is furious and in a state of revolt! It is giving large amounts of money for arming the workers. Hardly one of the leading revolutionaries perished in Moscow. But, right from the start, all of the S-Rs[1] came to grief at a "closed" conference. The whole fight was conducted by the S-D.[2] On the other hand, elections and a duma are on the agenda. You know of the despicable suffrage law. In addition, martial law will not be lifted for the election period! It would seem that taking part in the elections under such circumstances should be even more strictly ruled out than during the Bulygin duma.[3] Well, there you have it: the S-D in Petersburg has decided to take part in the elections using another crazy, artificial plan: All people, no matter what their rank (there are *four* grades of voting in the provinces!!) are to vote, but on the basis of a universal (non-existent) suffrage. Furthermore, only the electors, up to the highest levels, are to be elected. They, however, are not to elect representatives to the duma, but rather take over the governmental power in the provinces. The devil take it! I can't even repeat such bosh. That is what constitutes the *Iskra* faction's "victory" over the Lenin faction—of which they are very proud. Unfortunately, I couldn't get to Petersburg in time, otherwise, I would have spoiled their "victory." Now we, the other "peoples," are in a ridiculous position. Concretely, this artificial plan will naturally fall apart in practice since in the very first rush to election meetings a general confusion is bound to arise through which the entire electoral campaign will be transformed into direct struggle. But, out of consideration for our solidarity with Petersburg, it wouldn't do to offer a separate and different solution. Still, we can't be a party to such nonsense. So, I guess that after all we will probably keep on simply declining to participate in the elections on the grounds of the four-class system and the continuation of martial law.

In a few weeks, I will be going to St. Petersburg. Early in February, the two factions will hold their first joint constituent party convention. Naturally, I want to be there. Moreover, it occurs to me that it would be advisable for the SPD to be represented at this convention in order to strengthen the connection between the German party and the revolution. This would also have a beneficial effect on the factions and on the possible frictions between them. Inasmuch as no one in Germany will go to Petersburg under existing conditions, and since no one knows any Russian, the Executive Committee might possibly commission me to represent Germany. I will be there anyway, so the Committee would incur no expenses. If you, dear Karl, agree with this, then please talk to the Fathers about it, since I don't care to; I wouldn't want them to think that I have a personal stake in the matter. But you would have to take care of it very soon since the date has not been set as yet and it can easily be moved up.

While here, I have already written a brochure about the general situation and the things to do, which is being printed. Aside from this, a *German* weekly and *trade union* weekly are to be started this week. I am, therefore, anxiously awaiting the *Korrespondenzblatt*[4] and other trade union papers (Austrian).

Personally, I am not as well as I would like. I feel somewhat weak physically, but it's getting better. I see my brothers and sister once a week. They complain about my neglect a great deal, but I just don't have time! What are you all doing, my dearest ones? What are you writing now, Carolus? How is dear [Emanuel] Wurm?[5] How is it going with *V*[*orwärts*]? Has Block[6] been hired yet? How are Granny and the boys? In the midst of the commotion, here, I constantly think of all of you, my dear Lulu. Please do write me soon. With a thousand kisses, and regards to all.

Your R.

Notes

[1]The Socialist Revolutionaries were organized in 1901 to represent the interests of the peasantry. Nevertheless, they were not a homogeneous organization. The group split in October 1917 when the left wing formed a coalition with the Bolsheviks. This group then left the government over the Treaty of Brest-Litovsk.

[2]The reference is to the Social Democrats.

[3]Alexander Bulygin (1851-1919): czarist minister of the interior in 1905, who was instructed to convene the first Duma in that same year. The voters were divided into four classes, according to income, and each class elected the same number of electors, who then elected the deputies.

[4]The *Korrespondenzblatt* was the central organ of the German Trade Unions.

[5]See letter of 7/8/1906, note 1, p. 118.

[6]Hans Block was a friend of Rosa Luxemburg's and an editor of *Vorwärts*. Later, Rosa broke with him.

To Karl and Luise Kautsky

[2/5/1906]

My most beloved ones,

You have not heard from me for quite some time and, probably, you are angry with me—and rightly so! But, in my defense, I can cite the unending commotion and the "uncertainty of existence" which we are constantly suffering here. I can't go into detail very well here, but the main thing is: tremendous difficulties with the print shops, daily arrests, and the threat of shooting for those arrested. Two of our comrades had this Sword of Damocles hanging over them for days on end; it appears, however, that matters will rest there.

In spite of it all, the work is progressing briskly. Great meetings are taking place in the factories, handbills are written and printed almost every day and, with no end of trouble, the newspaper is published almost daily.

Just now, a little conference took place in Finland, in which all the parties participated.[1] It was a new variety of the "bloc" idea, and naturally, it came to nothing. Still, one at least had the opportunity of gaining a clearer view of what is happening in Petersburg. Unfortunately, the picture which one gets seems to make a veritable mockery of the most recent reports from Petersburg in the *L[eipziger]* *V[olkszeitung]*. There's indescribable chaos within the organization, quarreling among the factions in spite of all the unifications, and general depression. Let's keep this between us.

But don't take it too badly. As soon as there is another fresh wave of events, the people there will come forward with more strength and vigor. It is only a pity that they still waver so much and find so little steadfastness in their *own* minds. The family gathering will take place somewhat later than intended; at any rate, thanks for the greetings from the Elders, and I shall pass them on in due time.

The sore point at the moment, in Petersburg, as well as for us, is the colossal unemployment which causes indescribable misery. Actually, I meant to give only a few lines of introduction concerning the conditions in order to come to that which, at the moment, interests me the most. I see, however, that in this letter, too, "events" again threaten to engulf me.

So, I will make a bold move and finally emerge as a *"Mensch"* with the question: How are you, dearest Lulu? Carolus did, indeed, write me a few times reassuringly, for which I am thankful. Still, worry constantly gnawed at me in the midst of commotion, even though I didn't get around to writing. What suddenly became the matter with you? To this day I don't know. It surely must have been something abominable, if it had such lengthy aftereffects. Do you go out yet? Are you very weak? Look here, during all those years I was with you, you were always in good health and spirits. Hardly do I move out into the world—and suddenly you fall seriously ill!

How many times did I think to myself during my work

here: Were I there, how I should like to sit by your side for a few hours every day and be your devoted nurse! Now, I hope, you are no longer in need of nursing. If you are up to it, do write me a few lines as a token; it would give me enormous pleasure!

The rest of you are well, I hope. It vexes me quite a bit that the youngsters haven't written me yet. We don't receive *V*[*orwärts*] at all, and the *L*[*eipziger*] *V*[*olkszeitung*] only at very irregular intervals. As for me, the coming days will decide whether I will go from here to Petersburg for a short time or whether I shall first go home—to you— for two months. Of course, for me personally there is only one thing that draws me there: seeing you. For otherwise, to tell the truth, I loathe returning to the treadmill and the arguments with Peus and Rexhäuser.[2]

Taking up the thread once again: unemployment—that is the open wound of the revolution! And no means of putting a stop to it! At the same time, however, a quiet heroism and a feeling of class solidarity are developing among the masses which I would very much like to show to the dear Germans. Workers everywhere are, by themselves, reaching agreements whereby, for instance, the employed give up one day's wages every week for the unemployed. Or, where employment is reduced to four days a week, there they arrange it in such a way that no one is laid off, but that everyone works a few hours less per week. All this is done as a matter of course, with such simplicity and smoothness that the Party is informed of it only in passing. In fact, the feeling of solidarity and brotherhood with the Russian workers is so strongly developed that you can't help but be amazed even though you have personally worked for its development. And then too, an interesting result of the revolution: in all factories, committees, elected by the workers, have arisen "on their own," which decide on all matters relating to working conditions, hirings and firings of workers, etc. The employer has actually ceased being "the master in his own house." A curious little example: recently the management of a factory wanted to punish several workers for being very late. The factory committee prevented this; whereupon the factory owner lodged a complaint with the Committee of the Social Democratic Party, claiming that the factory committee was "not acting in accordance with Social Democratic principles" since the Social Democratic Party stands for diligent and honest fulfillment of obligations! And so in one case after the other.

Naturally, this will all be very different after the revolution and the reestablishment of "normal conditions." But the present situation will not pass without leaving its mark. Meanwhile, the work which the revolution has accomplished is enormous—the deepening of class antagonism, the sharpening and clarification of social relations. And abroad, all this goes unappreciated! They think that the struggle has ceased, because it has been deepened. And, at the same time, the organization advances indefatigably. In spite of martial law, trade unions are industriously being developed by the Social Democrats—and quite properly: with printed membership cards, stamps, bylaws, regular membership meetings, etc. The work is being carried out just as if political freedom were already a reality. And the police is, of course, powerless against this movement of the masses. In Lodz, for example, we have 6,000 enrolled members in the Social Democratic Union of Textile Workers! Here in Warsaw: 700 masons, 600 bakers, and so forth. On the other hand, in Petersburg, work has supposedly gone "underground," which is also why it has come to a standstill. There they are absolutely unable to bring out a paper or even hand out flyers. I wish I were already there in order to explore all of this. . . .

Your
R.

Notes

[1]The Kuokkala Conference, where she first spent time with Lenin and came to know him. They had only met once previously in Munich in 1901.

[2]Peus and Rexhäuser were revisionist trade union opponents of Rosa Luxemburg.

To Karl and Luise Kautsky

[Obviously from Warsaw Prison.
Received 3/13/06]

My best beloved ones,

On Sunday the 4th, in the evening, fate caught up with me: I was arrested. My passport had already been stamped for the return, and I was just on the point of leaving. Well, we'll have to make the best of it. I hope that you won't take the matter too much to heart. Long live the Re . . . ! and all it will bring. To a certain extent, in fact, I would rather be sitting here than—arguing with Peus. They found me in a somewhat awkward situation, but pay it no mind.

Here I am, sitting in City Hall, where the "politicals," the common crooks, and the mentally unbalanced are jammed together. My cell, which is a jewel in this setting in normal times (an ordinary single cell for one person), contains 14 guests, luckily all of them politicals. Next door to us, on either side, is a large double cell. In each, there are about 30 people pell-mell. But, as I have been told, these are really conditions which approach paradise since formerly 60 people were cooped up in one cell. They slept in shifts during the night, changing shifts every few hours, while the others went "strolling." At present, we all sleep like kings on boards, diagonally, packed next to each other like herrings, and we manage nicely— insofar as we are not disturbed by some additional music; like yesterday, for example, when we were joined by a new colleague, a raving-mad Jewess, who made a number of politicals burst out into fits of sobbing, and who kept us busy for 24 hours with her shrieking and her running about in all the cells. Today we are finally rid of her and have only three quiet "myschuggene"[1] with us.

Walks in the courtyard are unheard of here. Instead, during the day, the cells are thrown open and one can spend the whole day walking about in the corridors in order to bustle about among prostitutes, hear their delightful little songs and proverbs, and enjoy the odor of the ⊖⊖⟶ [2] which are likewise wide open. All this, however, is merely to characterize the conditions and not my mood, which is as excellent as ever. For the time being, I am still assuming my false identity—but that won't last long; they don't believe me.

Taken as a whole, the situation is serious, but after all, we are living in agitated times where "whatever exists deserves to perish."[3] That's why I don't believe at all in long-term letters of credit or bonds. So, be of good cheer and thumb your noses at everything. On the whole, while I was alive our work has gone superbly. I am proud of that; ours was the only oasis in all of Russia where, despite the storm and stress, the work and the struggle continued as energetically and advanced as merrily as during the time of the very freest of "constitutions." Amongst other things, the notion of resistance, which will be the model for future times throughout Russia, is our work.

As regards my health, I am quite well. Soon, they will probably transfer me to a different prison, since my case is a serious one. I will then let you know.

How are you, my dearest ones? What are you, the boys, Granny and Hans, doing? Give friend Franciscus[4] my most affectionate greetings. I hope that, thanks to the firm [Hans] Block, things are again going well at *V[orwärts]*.

                                                                        Your Anna

Notes

  [1]Yiddish for someone who is crazy.
  [2]The symbol is for the toilet.
  [3]The reference is to Goethe's *Faust*, Part I.
  [4]A nickname for Franz Mehring.

To Karl and Luise Kautsky

[From Warsaw Prison.
Received 3/15/06]

Dearest Karl,

Only a few lines. I am well; will be transferred to another prison either today or tomorrow. Now, only one more request: the correspondent of the *L[eipziger] V[olkszeitung]* is also in jail here. Mr. Otto Engelmann from Berlin.[1] (Of course you know him. He is the blond gentleman who lived on Kranachstrasse for quite some time.) Now, in case the editors of the *L[eipziger] V[olkszeitung]* should be asked whether this is true, they should confirm that he actually went to Warsaw several months ago as their correspondent. (In case the same inquiry should be made under another name, they should confirm it in any event.) I have already received news from my family, and I regret very much that they are making such a tragedy out of my case and inconveniencing all of you. I am perfectly calm. My friends absolutely insist that I telegraph Witte,[2] and that I write the German Consul here. I wouldn't think of it! These gentlemen can wait a long time before a Social Democrat asks them for protection and justice. Long live the revolution! Be happy and of good cheer, otherwise I will be seriously angry with you. The work outside is going well. I have already read some new issues of the paper. Hurrah!

Yours with all my heart
Rosa

Write your letters directly to me. In a few days, you can address them to: Pawlak Prison, Ozielna Street, Warsaw, for the political prisoner so-and-so.

Notes

  [1]Alias used by Leo Jogiches.
  [2]Sergei Witte (1849-1915): The Russian prime minister from 1905-06 who crushed the revolution of 1905.

To Emanuel Wurm[1]

Warsaw 7/8/1906

Dear, esteemed Comrade,

Many thanks for your nice lines. I am unable to answer your question regarding the charges against me since, up to this moment, I have not received word of them myself. The state's prosecutor told me himself that he—along with the police—is still in doubt as to which charge should be raised against me. I have been set free under 3,000 rubles bond with the proviso that I not leave Warsaw under penalty of forfeiting bail.

Your advice regarding a vacation is exactly what I received from the friends I have here.[2] Yet, I was, and at this moment I still am, hesitant for various reasons, some of which I mentioned above, some of which must remain unmentioned. At any rate, over the next few days, I will reach a final decision, and naturally I will inform you just as soon as I am beyond good and evil.

For your efforts in regard to the affidavit of the Police Presidium—just as in this entire affair—my heartfelt thanks. To be sure, I am physically pretty feeble and, as they tell me, I look quite yellow. Still I feel so fresh and excited about work that I hope soon to forget all about my "yellowness" and debility. The general situation is excellent, the conditions grow ever sharper and powerfully drive themselves to an acute resolution. I find everything much better than I had expected, and that makes me cheerful and happy.

With best regards to you and your dear wife,

Your

R

Notes

[1]Emanuel Wurm (1857-1920): A chemist by profession, Wurm joined the SPD in the 1880s. A teacher at the party school, he was originally on the left wing of the party, but later followed Kautsky and took a more centrist position. He was also a member of the Reichstag and, for a time, coeditor of *Die Neue Zeit*.

[2]"Vacation"—a hint to jump bail.

To Emanuel and Mathilde Wurm

[Warsaw]
7/18/1906

Dear Emmo and Tilde![1]

Heartiest thanks for your detailed report. Finally I know what is

happening in the world. Your earlier letters, like those from the
K[autsky]'s, were lost and it appears that my own address is the best.
From what you wrote, among other things, I learned for the first time
of Luise's mishap, and you can imagine how shocked I was even if
only *post festum!*

As for me, I am on the point of leaving this hospitable domain,
and as soon as I am *au bon port*, I will send you news and my address. I
am burning with the desire to work—that is, to write. Among other
things, I will joyfully intervene in the debate about the general strike.
Just be patient for a few days until I have a firm roof over my head and
better working conditions. Here, this running around to the police,
the public prosecutor's office, and to similar pleasant institutions
never comes to an end.

The most recent "little tiff" in the Party makes me laugh—
forgive me, but it makes me laugh quite diabolically! Oh, those
world-shaking incidents between Lindenstrasse and Engelufer[2]
which unleash a tempest! . . . . How funny such a "tempest" looks
from here! . . . . Here, the period in which we are living appears
glorious; that is to say, I call glorious a time which raises no end of
problems, powerful problems, which stimulates thoughts, which
inspires "Critique, Irony and Deeper Meaning,"[3] which stirs
passions and which—above all—is a fruitful, pregnant time, which
from hour to hour gives birth and with every birth comes forth even
"more pregnant" than before. At that, it does not give birth to dead
mice, let alone dead gnats as in Berlin, but rather all sorts of colossal
things such as: huge crimes (vide the government), huge disgraces
(vide the Duma), huge stupidities (vide Plekhanov & Co.), etc. In
advance, I tremble with delight at the thought of designing a prettily
sketched picture of all those enormities—naturally, above all, in the
Neue Zeit. So reserve the appropriate huge amount of space.

As to your kind proposal to provide me with newspapers, the
N[eue] Z[eit], etc., I will make full use of it, once I have moved into the
new domicile. Sending anything here is useless. I was heartily
pleased, dearest Emmo, to hear of the complete improvement in your
health. Just keep on being well, and don't work too hard. Above all,
don't allow yourself to be depressed by anything. The revolution is
grand; everything else is rubbish! With many affectionate regards to
you both, also to Arthur [Stadthagen],

I remain your

Rosa

Notes

[1]Mathilde Wurm (1874-1935): A close friend of Rosa's, Mathilde Wurm
served as a Reischstag deputy for the USPD.

²The locations of the party and trade union headquarters respectively.
³Alludes to the somewhat similar title of a play by Christian Grabbe.

To Franz Mehring

Kuokkala [Finland]
Aug. 22, 1906

Dear and honored friend,

For a long time I have been feeling a need to send you and your wife my most affectionate regards, and also to ask you to send me some books. But only since last week have I been sufficiently well to send you my address, and to muster the courage to write a letter. For a whole month after my release, I had been held on a leash by those dear authorities who let me flounder about while trying to nail me. Then in Petersburg, the first time I met with the Russian friends, I almost fell again into the hands of the police; and here again, in Kuokkala, some fishy characters followed me, right from the railway station, all the time I was looking for accommodations. However, here on Finnish soil I find myself in what is called a "constitutional state," and I can scoff at that sort of guardian angel.

Well, here I am submerged in work up to my neck. You can imagine how much I have to catch up with: in Russian the entire duma period (brochures, newspapers, reports); in German, our most recent "Party crisis," *Vorwärts, Neue Zeit*, etc. Unfortunately, I lack the *Leipziger Volkszeitung*; only in Warsaw, where a good many people appreciate it, was I able to see some issues. Thanks to [Emanuel] Wurm I received and read the report of the Holy *Feme*.¹ Before one reads it, one has to take a deep breath so as not to suffocate in this stifling atmosphere of narrow-minded stupidity. But the "crisis" will seem very salutary to me if in Mannheim they know how properly to utilize it for a general process.

You must have learned from Kautsky that I visited our friend Parvus in his prison. As always, he is vigorous and adventurous. We had a long chat; he sends brotherly greetings to all his friends in Germany. We hope that he will soon be able to come back. By now I have gotten so used to the revolutionary milieu that I become anguished when I imagine myself immersed again in the humdrum German routine and quiet; down there I fear I cannot endure long. Perhaps you would then go on a little escapade to Warsaw with me— how about it? . . .

Notes

¹*Die heilige Feme* was a medieval kangaroo court. She compares the party executive's verdict to that of an arbitrary court. See next letter.

To Clara Zetkin

March 20, 1907

. . . The appeal of the Party Executive has had the same effect on me as it had upon you—that says it all. Since my return from Russia, I have felt rather isolated here. I feel the pettiness and indecisiveness which reigns in our party more brutally and more painfully than ever before. But I do not get as angry as you about it, because it has already become clear to me—shockingly clear—that neither people nor things can be changed until the whole situation has been completely changed. And even then—after cold reflection—I have come to the conclusion that we must count upon the inevitable *resistance* of those people, should we wish to inspire the masses.

The situation is simple: August [Bebel] and still more all the others have given themselves over to parliamentarism without reservation. Whenever events take a turn which goes beyond the limits of parliamentarism, they are lost. No, they are worse than lost, for they seek to lead it all back into parliamentary channels. This is why they furiously attack as an "enemy of the people" any movement or individual who wishes to go further. The masses, and still more the great mass of comrades, in the bottom of their hearts have had enough of this parliamentarism. I have the feeling that a breath of fresh air in our tactics would be greeted with cries of joy. But, still they submit to the heel of the old authorities and, what's more, to the upper strata of opportunist editors, deputies and trade union leaders.

Our task actually consists simply in protesting against the stagnation brought on by these authorities as vigorously as possible. In such actions, according to circumstances, we will find ourselves opposing the opportunists as well as the Party Executive and August. As long as it was a question of defending themselves against Bernstein and friends, August & Co. accepted our help and assistance with pleasure—because they were shaking in their shoes. But, when it comes to any *offensive* action against opportunists, then the veterans stand with Ede [Bernstein], Vollmar¹ and David,² against us. This is how I see the situation. And now to what is essential: keep your chin up and stay calm. The tasks are many and I calculate that it should

Rosa Luxemburg with Clara Zetkin. (Courtesy Dietz Verlag)

take many years to complete them.

Rosa

Notes

[1]Georg Vollmar (1850-1922): One of the very earliest reformists and a leader of the Bavarian social democratic contingent.

[2]Eduard David (1863-1930): A leading socialist supporter of imperialist policies and right-wing member of the SPD, David was a staunch chauvinist during the war. He became a minister without portfolio and later first president of the National Assembly in 1919.

To the Latvian Social Democrats

Berlin, September 11, 1908

Dear Comrades,

It was with a deep feeling of joy that I learned you are publishing a jubilee issue of your Party paper which, unfortunately, I will be unable to read since I don't know the language. In this difficult time, our task is to prevent the proletarian organizations in Poland, in the Latvian areas and the whole state from disintegrating and, at the same time, untiringly continue to disseminate political consciousness in the masses. The publication of a Party paper holds a greater significance for Social Democrats at this time than during the revolution when many other means were at our disposal to create an impression upon the masses.

I believe that, notwithstanding these exceptionally difficult times, none of us have reason to lose courage. It is true that, for the most part, our organizations have been shattered and stand exhausted. Reaction rages, counterrevolution exults. But doesn't all this go to prove that the manifold Russian liberal bourgeoisie is not able either to protect the given order from ruin or to create a new, up-to-date legal or political order?

The Moscow proletariat, during its first revolutionary offensive, was beaten in armed battle and was forced to retreat. Notwithstanding the flood of fiery speeches in the first Duma, and notwithstanding the parliamentary scene, the revolution was crushed. The first Duma was already suspended in the air. Like the first, so the second, and even more the third "Parliament" have merely helped absolutism to strengthen itself under a constitutional veneer. And so, after three years of the most difficult attempts, we find ourselves faced once again with the Gordian knot: neither the liberal bourgeoisie nor its artificial unification with the revolutionary proletariat can actualize the task of the Russian revolution. Only the independent activity of the proletariat as class, supported by the revolutionary movement of the peasants, will be able to destroy absolutism and introduce political freedom into Russia. This is the most irrefutable and most important lesson from the history of revolutionary development. And if this is the case, then the renewal of revolutionary action by the proletariat—be it sooner or later—is a historical necessity.

For us, the general situation is not hopeless; it gives us hope for a new struggle, for new victories, but also for new trials and new sacrifices. One thing we have learned: to bear everything bravely and courageously, and we have learned this mainly from the Latvian comrades. And with that, I hope to see you soon on the battlefield "at Philippi."[1]

With most affectionate wishes for your jubilee and a strong clasp of the hand.

Notes

[1]Refers to *Julius Caesar*, IV/3 (a very popular quote in Germany).

To Karl and Luise Kautsky

[Undated postcard. Levanto:
postmarked 6/11/09]

Dearest Lulu:

Today the package of books arrived (the stamps had been prudently removed so that I cannot determine the date of the postmark). Many thanks.

Now I hasten to ask you once again to send me the little extract from [Gustav] Schmoller's article on political economy in the *Hand-wörterbuch*. You see, you sent me an excerpt which was different from the one I need. I didn't want his definition of political economy, but rather that passage in which he explains why political economy as a science arose only in the 18th century (namely, due to the needs of governments based on modern centralized bureaucracy). Be so good as to send me the excerpt, but this time in a *letter!*

I will write you a more detailed letter today or tomorrow. In the meantime, this postcard is only to reassure you in regard to the fate of the books. Well, Lavoisier was right:[1] nothing is ever lost from the materia of the world, it's only that it sometimes moves damned slowly. Affectionate greetings to all of you. In haste,

Your R.

Notes

[1]Antoine Lavoisier (1743-1794): French scientist who virtually founded modern chemistry. He refuted the phlogistic theory and also wrote essays on political economy. Lavoisier was killed during the reign of terror.

To Leo Jogiches

[Quarten: probably beginning of August, 1909]

. . . The uproar over my first foray was completely superfluous. The view that anarchism is the ideology of the lumpenproletariat was, if I am not mistaken, already expressed by Plekhanov in his German brochures.[1] And, in fact, even as careful a "thinker" as Kautsky agreed with me completely and suggested that I preach these views in the *Neue Zeit* (which is naturally out of the question). In judging the essence of a theory or a politics, it is utterly unimportant who carries it out. Thus, the argument concerning Stirner,[2] Lagardelle,[3] and the syndicalists, completely missed the point.

I am still up to my ears in the work on "Autonomy." One must arrange it in such a way that the article does not come out on the first, but if possible on the third printer's sheet. As it is, I am having a hard time writing the article, and to hurry would be less than useful. . . .

By the way, Kautsky is preparing an article for the *Neue Zeit* on the occasion of the visit of Samuel Gompers,[4] the President of the American Federation of Labor. This upstanding gentleman, who is a scoundrel of the first order, was even celebrated by *Humanité*, and he will appear in Germany. Julek [Marchlewski] or [Karl] Radek[5] should perhaps write something about him for *Przeglad Socjaldemokratyczny*. A knowledge of American conditions would be necessary. To this end, I am writing to [Morris] Hillquit[6] requesting a response by telegram whether he will write something.

I also wrote to some people abroad: [Gustav] Bang,[7] [Louis] Boudin,[8] and [Friedrich] Austerlitz.[9] [Emil] Vandervelde[10] would certainly write something immediately, but I must first send him the agrarian theses of Lenin, [Pyotor] Maslow,[11] and Julek so that he can have some particulars to which he can refer. I have been asking for these theses for the longest time. Without them, I cannot ask him. . . .

Notes

[1]The reference is to Plekhanov's *Anarchism and Socialism,* published in Berlin in 1894.

[2]Max Stirner (1806-1856): Bourgeois anarchist philosopher, he was ridiculed as "Saint Max" by Marx in *The German Ideology.* His most famous work is entitled *The Ego and His Own.*

[3]Hubert Lagardelle (1875-1914): French anarcho-syndicalist and editor of *Le Mouvement Socialiste.*

[4]Samuel Gompers (1850-1924): President of the AFL for close to forty years, Gompers was instrumental in quelling radical forces within the American trade union movement and emphasized that the position of American trade unions should be to seek economic benefits and not organize politically in terms of a party.

[5]Karl Radek (1885-1939): He stood on the left wing of the Polish and German movements. A supporter of Lenin after the Russian Revolution, Radek was instrumental in the formation of the German Communist Party. Returning to Russia, he became a supporter of Trotsky and the Left Opposition until Trotsky was banished to Turkey. He then gave his support to Stalin and became his advisor on European and Chinese affairs. He was purged by Stalin in 1937 and then executed in 1939 after confessing to treason in the Moscow trials.

[6]Morris Hillquit (1869-1933): A founder of the American Socialist Party that opposed entry into the First World War and that also opposed the Bolsheviks.

[7]Gustav Bang was a Danish socialist.

[8]Louis Boudin: A well-known American socialist and a prominent publicist.

[9]Friedrich Austerlitz (1862-1931): One of the most prominent leaders of Austrian social democracy. Austerlitz was a parliamentary deputy and editor of the *Arbeiterzeitung.* Originally a supporter of Austria in the First World War, in 1916 he became a pacifist. From 1919 until his death he served on the Austrian National Council.

[10]Emil Vandervelde (1866-1938): A leader of the Belgian Workers' Party and later a president of the Second International and prime minister.

[11]Pyotor Maslow (1867-1946): A Russian social democrat who supported the Mensheviks, an expert on the agrarian question, and a chauvinist during the First World War, he opposed the Bolshevik Revolution.

To Leo Jogiches

[Quarten. Probably 8/10/1909]
It is difficult for me to judge just how much of a danger the Bolsheviks now present to the integrity of the Party and how much

they are giving themselves airs as the bosses; difficult to decide.[1] If they will anyway, merely through our abstentions in the voting, remain a minority in the Central Committee, I don't understand the sense of withdrawing from the central institutions instead of working against them from within.

In general, the idea of an open war with the Bolsheviks does not seem feasible for us: 1) They will attack us in their Russian papers— we'll shoot back in Polish and the Russian Party will neither see it nor hear it. 2) They are very agile with the pen, and they are able to spawn their endless, slipshod articles, brochures, and whole volumes, while we have 1½ miserable writers, hardly enough for the most pressing current needs of *Przeglad Socjaldemokratyczny*. 3) And this to me seems the most important reason: a break between us and the Bolsheviks would considerably heighten the chaos in the Party; the real winners would be the Mensheviks, who present the most dangerous disease for the Party, especially for us, since they are the protectors of the PPS and, in their heart of hearts, our bitterest enemies.

I assume that the inclination to declare war on the Bolsheviks is principally the result of their Tartar Marxism getting on people's nerves, which calls forth the psychological need to set limits to their arrogance. But I think that political considerations rather advocate working against them from within the central institutions (Central Committee and the central organ) as long as circumstances will allow.

Kautsky will accept an article for the *Neue Zeit* without any argument, it must only be written adroitly. In my opinion one can write such an article without officially breaking with the Bolsheviks as long as one conveys a *friendly criticism*.

Regarding the Bolsheviks, I need some information as quickly as possible. Gorky[2] and Bogdanov[3] have invited me to give some lectures at their school on Capri. Since they will bear the expense, I would like to make use of the opportunity to go there for a week or two. But I don't know to what extent this will collide with party politics in view of the enmities between the Capri colony and Lenin. I think, however, that the Party in general and I, as a private individual, can say to hell with it. In any case, I await your reply so that I can inform Bogdanov.

Notes

[1]Through the good offices of the International, the differences within Russian social democracy were temporarily patched up and a joint central

committee was formed. Bolsheviks, Mensheviks, Poles, and (Jewish) Bundists were all permitted to designate members. The SDKPL thus seemed in a position to tip the scales of power. The whole arrangement, however, broke down in 1913.

[2]Maxim Gorky (1868-1939): One of the most famous Russian realist writers, his autobiography and novel *The Mother* remain classics. A social democrat who was one of Lenin's friends, Gorky still opposed the Russian Revolution, though later he gave it his critical support. At first opposed to Stalin, he ended his public criticism in the 1930s.

[3]Alexander Bogdanov-Malinowski was—off and on—an associate of Lenin's and a party functionary.

To Leo Jogiches[1]

[Berlin-Friedenau, 1908 or 09]

Yesterday, after the talk, I was so upset that I was unable to sleep half the night, and today I am unable to work. I don't know how many times I have asked, but I must ask again, that one[2] take care of business by mail so that I have peace and quiet in my little corner. I don't need the room, and I won't step over its threshold. When someone comes to see me, we crowd each other in the bedroom simply in order not to use this room. After all, I must be able to live in my own apartment and not like in a hotel in which one can come and go without my consent.[3] I don't have the strength to bear this situation any longer. I have asked so often that it be stopped; all through the summer, I gallivanted around outside the house simply in order not to have to see the goings-on—and now it's the same all over again. . . . This can't go on! I do what I can for *Przeglad Socjaldemokratyczny* and *Czerwony Sztandar*; I am prepared to act as a replacement in the editorial offices as far as it becomes necessary. But I want to have my own corner all for myself! If I cannot have that, I would rather give up the whole apartment, including the maid, and take a furnished room somewhere so that I know that I am at home and not in a hotel. I ask for an answer whether this is to go on so that I can determine what to do with myself.

Notes

[1]The letter was apparently written after Rosa Luxemburg's break with Jogiches. He was, apparently, still using her apartment for party purposes.

[2]*Sic!* She writes "one" in order to avoid using the familiar "thou" form.

[3]Jogiches still had the key to her apartment.

To Leo Jogiches

[Berlin. Between February and March, 1910]
[Karl] Liebknecht's[1] stance is like always: a jump to the right, a jump to the left. In the Prussian *Landtag*, he announced the mass strike. In the City Council he was against our proposal, "A Protest against the Ban on the Treptow Meeting,"[2] since he said we proceeded in an illegal fashion by not heeding this ban. . . .

[Arthur] Stadthagen was here two weeks ago. When I spoke with him, he was convinced that a mass strike was impossible; now he wants to bawl out his *Vorwärts* colleagues for rejecting my article (I purposely offered it to them) in view of the fact that the entire press has printed it.

[Heinrich] Cunow is very radical. But this same Cunow and the whole editorial staff are simply lackeys of the Prussian Executive Committee and the Party Executive. The latter, in turn, in the last analysis is led by the nose by the General Commission [of the Trade Unions].

It was [Karl] Legien[3] who recently pushed through the decree muzzling the press, and threatened them because of my article. That is the situation. But the whole thing couldn't matter less since the mood throughout the country is splendid as never before, and Berlin will have to move forward under pressure from the provinces. One must not try to apply leverage in Berlin. This "head" will follow all right, once one gives a few kicks to the backside.

By the way, and as a closely guarded secret (for example one should tell Julek [Marchlewski] absolutely nothing about it): the Berlin people have asked me whether I would accept a mandate from election districts for the International Congress—a demonstration against the Executive.

Notes

[1]Karl Liebknecht (1871-1919): Liebknecht is usually mentioned in one breath with Rosa Luxemburg. Rosa was especially close to Karl's wife Sonja, who did not have much of a role in politics. Two of Wilhelm Liebknecht's three sons were active politically. Theodore became the leader of the USPD after 1921; Karl, a lawyer by profession, was a member of the left wing of the SPD from his entry into the party. In 1907, Karl Liebknecht was imprisoned for treason for his *Militarism and Anti-Militarism*. A Reichstag deputy, he was the first to break SPD discipline and vote against the granting of war appropriations to the government in 1915. Liebknecht participated in the founding of the Spartacus League, and became a hero of the masses—on a par with Rosa Luxemburg and even Lenin and Trotsky—for his consistent and

courageous antiwar activity. He was murdered with Rosa Luxemburg during the Spartacus rebellion.

[2]The Treptow Meadow—outside Berlin—was the usual place for the May Day rally.

[3]Karl Legien (1861-1920): Secretary general of the German trade union movement and an outspoken revisionist who supported the war, he was a major force within the party. After Bebel's death in 1913 and the rise to power of Friedrich Ebert, Legien became one of the virtual rulers of the party. Interestingly enough, though he vociferously opposed Rosa Luxemburg on the mass strike issue, he was one of the leaders of the general strike that caused the collapse of the Kapp Putsch, which threatened the Weimar Republic from the right in 1920.

To Clara Zetkin

3/7/1910

My dearest little Clara,

First of all, many, many thanks for the magnificent presents (even though I am very sincerely angry that you think of celebrating such a trifle,[1] on the same occasion I pass Kostia[2] a cake of soap each time).

How much I wished for Mistral's[3] works I told you myself; but just as much I felt like reading Keller,[4] whom ultimately I can no longer ignore. On my very birthday, I read *Spiegel das Kätzchen*, which amused me greatly.

Now something else: Yesterday's demonstration was very confused, not well coordinated, and without clear orientation; but on the whole, it had a good effect and constitutes a step forward. Of course, the masses, as soon as they see police horses and drawn sabres, beat it without a moment's thought (the three of us, with your son and little Rosenfeld, stood our ground every time, without retreating an inch, and naturally the cops didn't dare touch us); but everything can be learned, including not to run away. At any rate, among the masses the wish to demonstrate and the rage against the police has grown; hereafter there certainly will be demonstrations, whether or not the leadership gives the signal.

Another bit of news: I wrote an article on the Mass Strike and the Republic. First I offered it to the *Vorwärts*, which rejected it on the pretext that the Party Executive and the Action Committee have ordered the Editorial Board not to publish anything about the mass strike; at the same time, I was told confidentially that just then the Executive was in negotiation with the trade union executive about the mass strike.

I then gave the article to the *Neue Zeit*. But Kautsky got terribly cold feet and implored me to cut out above all the passage on the republic,[5] that this was a completely new subject of agitation, that I had no right to expose the Party to immeasurable perils, etc. Since I had no choice, and since, for all practical purposes, the mass strike idea seemed more important, I gave in and killed the republic passage. The article was already at the printer's, with an editorial note: "We are submitting the viewpoints developed herein to our readers' discussion."(!)

Notes

[1] Rosa's birthday.

[2] Kostia Zetkin was Clara's son and a lover of Rosa Luxemburg's.

[3] Frederick Mistral (1830-1914): French poet, whose best-known work is the autobiographical *The Islands of Gold*.

[4] Gottfried Keller (1819-1890): Swiss novelist, a realist and humanist, his major work is *Der grüne Heinrich*. *Spiegel das Kätzchen* is a novella.

[5] The reference is to the motion that Rosa Luxemburg sought to put forward in agitational activities. Rosa saw this as a fundamental step toward radicalization. As becomes clear, Kautsky drew back from this in the face of a mounting tide of reaction in Germany, and this proved one of the fundamental reasons for the break between them.

To Luise Kautsky

3/17/1910

Dearest Lulu,

At present, I am living so feverishly that I simply don't get around to writing to you, although I have had a strong urge to write. Well, from the "theatre of war": the article which Karl [Kautsky] turned down has been worked over.[1] It is better (clearer and sharper) and it has already come out in the *Dortmunder Arbeiterzeitung* (Konrad Haenisch).[2] The Leipzig and Bremen people have already reprinted it and I hope that others will do the same.

Day before yesterday, on Tuesday the 15th, forty-eight evening meetings were arranged with the clear intention of preventing some type of action for tomorrow the 18th. As speakers, all sorts of fourth- and fifth-rate types, most of them union officials! Besides that, *Vorwärts* had already come out with an editorial prohibiting street demonstrations after the meeting. At school,[3] on the 12th, I learned that they were a speaker short. I accepted immediately and, that night, gave a speech in the fourth electoral district. The meeting was packed to the point of suffocation (around 1½ thousand). The mood was superb. I unsheathed my sword, and this met with stormy applause. Hans [Diefenbach],[4] Gertrud [Zlottko],[5] Kostia [Zetkin] and [Gustav] Eckstein[6] had come along; the latter has—since yesterday—switched to my point of view, as he told me.

Yesterday, by telephone, I received an urgent summons from Berlin—and one from Essen by mail—to speak at meetings on the mass strike. I am considering whether I should quit the school and move into the country to fan the fires everywhere. I'll send you my article. . . . Write soon. I miss you so!

I kiss you in haste.

Your,
Rosa

Notes

[1] Rosa Luxemburg's article, "What Next?"

[2] Konrad Haenisch (1876-1925): A writer for many social democratic papers, he was on the left wing of the SPD before the war and then became a chauvinist.

[3] The reference is to the party school that was set up in 1906 and that Rosa Luxemburg joined as a teacher in 1907.

[4] Hans Diefenbach (1884-1919): Became the man closest to Rosa Luxemburg after the break-up of her relationships with Jogiches and Kostia Zetkin. A physician, he was killed in World War I.

[5] Gertrud Zlottko, her maid.

[6] Gustav Eckstein (1875-1916): A collaborator on *Die Neue Zeit*, an Austrian social democrat, and a follower of Kautsky's.

To Luise Kautsky

[Undated postcard, postmarked Dortmund 4/13/10]
Dearest Lulu,

Everything is going well, eight meetings behind me and six still to come. Everywhere I find the comrades in unconditional and enthusiastic agreement. People shrug their shoulders at Karl's article:[1] I observed this particularly in Kiel, Bremen, Dortmund, and with [Wilhelm] Dittman in Solingen. The funniest part is that, as Clara writes me, the district secretary Wasner (!) at a public meeting expressed his astonishment regarding Karl's behavior in the sharpest language.

By the way, I knew immediately that I would not get the galleys.[2]
For as long as he can, Karl means to make it impossible for me to
respond: moreover, it is not "Wurm's way," as you surmise, to have
the article appear in two issues, but rather Karl's own way to the same
purpose. Tell him that I fully know how to assess the loyalty and
friendship involved in these little expediencies, but that with his
courageous stab in the back he has really gotten himself into scalding
hot water.—How are you? How is my Mimi?[3] Do write me a line here
in care of Haenisch (Dresdner Strasse 16). I will be here until the 16th
and travel around from here.

A kiss and a greeting to you and the boys.

Your
Rosa

Notes

[1]Kautsky's response to Rosa Luxemburg's "What Next?"

[2]The reference is to Rosa Luxemburg's "Ermattung oder Kampf?" ("Attrition or Struggle?").

[3]Mimi is Rosa's cat. She will play a prominent part in future letters.

To Leo Jogiches

[Aeschi, ca. 7/10/1910]

The *Dortmunder* [*Arbeiter Zeitung*] did not accept my article on
the Baden people (Haenisch is taking a vacation!) and sent it to
Bremen, but the devil knows whether they will take it![1] And it means
so much to me that it be printed! It would really deal K[arl] K[autsky]
and the whole clique a pretty blow. Also the devil only knows
what will happen to my reply to Mehring in the *Leipziger
Volkszeitung*; they haven't answered the telegram which I sent
on Saturday.

K[arl] K[autsky] has naturally fabricated these "falsified
quotations." Today I sent him a *correction* with material that is
deadly for him. From Berlin, they write me that he is no longer in his
right mind on account of my article. "With every word his head grows
more flushed, he slams his fist on the table and loses every remnant of
journalistic propriety and common sense." Obviously, he has noticed
what has been happening to him. In case of a refusal from K[arl]
K[autsky], I will immediately go to Berlin in order to pressure him
with the Executive's help (it's like going to the devil's mother in order
to complain about her son) since under the libel laws I have a claim

against his accusations.

I have only sent the corrections with proof. To hit him with brickbats at this time would be highly inappropriate. In our Party, one cannot be too victorious; for that no one would forgive. Even now the German principle is revenging itself upon me: "Woe to the Victorious!" Especially since it would be little fun for either the radicals or the Party as a whole to see K[arl] K[autsky] finished off. By the way, [Konrad] Haenisch sent me his "heartfelt congratulations on the magnificent articles in the *Neue Zeit*" which he says have "guessed his innermost thoughts."

In a week I will return again to Berlin since Munio[2] is coming on the 20th to introduce his wife and three children.

Notes

[1]Her article "The Baden Budget Vote" was published in the *Bremer Bürger-Zeitung* in August 1910. The reformist social democrats in Baden had voted for the state budget—a breach of the "not a penny for this system" principle; the party executive, however, was loath to censure the breach.

[2]Rosa Luxemburg's brother.

To Leo Jogiches

[Berlin 7/20 or 21/1910]

Both articles enclosed.[1] As to their length, I don't think that they exceed the assignment. I shortened the article on the trade unions by cutting about two pages. If something else seems expendable, it can also be cut. There will probably be no grounds for reworking it, since I rewrote the article as best I could; in fact, I wrote the articles on the union twice. The present version has, for the most part, been copied directly from the letter since I felt more secure with this formulation than with my own as I don't feel too familiar with the subject.

The *N[eue] Z[eit]* came; it carries a long editorial note in which K[arl] K[autsky] prints the explanation he proposed to me, and charges me with putting "my concerns" above the interests of the Party. I will emphatically answer this in a footnote to the second article (I already have the proofs). Now I must certainly write an article on the Baden people in order to shut Kautsky's mouth. I will definitely write on Saturday, but I request now to be left alone with regard to correcting trivia in the article for [*Czerwony*] *Sztandar*, otherwise I won't be able to write the article on the Baden people.

If it must be shorter, then one can cut the last page of the Copenhagen article—about the Women and Youth Conference—and only mention it briefly.

Notes

[1] Two articles, written in Polish, on the trade union question.

To Konrad Haenisch

[Undated. Undoubtedly Summer 1910]

Dear Comrade Haenisch!

Enclosed are two lead articles whose publication, particularly in your paper, would please me very much.

To put it briefly, the situation is as follows: the Party Executive and the General Commission [of the Trade Unions] have already considered the mass strike issue. After long discussions, the issue ran aground due to the resistance of the General Commission. In view of this, the Party Executive naturally believes it must strike sail, and it would love to forbid even a discussion of the mass strike! That is why I consider it urgent and necessary to carry the discussion to the broadest masses of the Party. The masses themselves should decide, but it is our duty to present them with the pros and cons of the argument. Therefore, I am counting on you to support me and publish the articles immediately. When they are printed, please send me a few copies. I hope that the articles will be reprinted.

Best regards
Your
Rosa Luxemburg

To Leo Jogiches

[Probably Copenhagen 8/29/1910]

This endless bullying and threatening in letters is so wearisome; as it is I have hardly enough strength to drag myself around the city. The situation here is as follows: the section[1] has been formed and has received instructions—so far, everything in order; but no instructions can prevent people, in their human weakness, from committing blunders. I was horrified to hear of the idiocies which [Karl] Radek committed in the Military Commission; no one could have anticipated that. Then I spoke with the French, Germans, etc., and wrote a declaration which Radek introduced to the section today. Unfortunately, one can do no more. On the other hand, it appears that Julek [Marchlewski] in a different commission, spoke foolishly (against the Czechs) and, above all, did not deal with Horvic's campaign[2] regarding the "division of the trade union movement." So, today I also wrote a declaration for Julek; he will have it put in the minutes. I spend most of my time here ascertaining what new blunders our people have made, and repairing them. Because of these "Frakers"[3] I remain stuck in this idiotic commission on the death penalty, which makes it impossible to work on a different commission concerned with something more important.[4] I have written a resolution on the death penalty, which [Clara] Zetkin proposed today as a German, at which point the Frakers courageously withdrew their own resolution in order not to embarrass themselves. For the Russian section, I must draw up a declaration to the German Executive in the form of a forceful protest against Trotsky's article in *Vorwärts*.[5]

To begin an action against the Frakers here, in this whirlpool, would be like a little dog yelping under the table in the midst of great uproar. Nothing will bring me to this "action." When I start something, I want to see results. At the next regular meeting of the International Bureau, I will quietly but firmly take up the matter. [Ignaz] Daszyński[6] is here, he has suddenly gotten completely gray. K[arl] K[autsky] has left quite unceremoniously because he has suffered a "complete nervous breakdown." Some people have already suggested to me that it's my fault. I will try to return on Saturday. By the way, it's better not to scold Radek. It makes no sense and he is very submissive. Even less should one allow Julek to notice anything.

Notes

[1]The Copenhagen Congress of 1910 showed the effect of the conservative reaction to social democracy, insofar as a weakening of the International's stand on militarism and internationalism took place. The SDKPL formed a "section" there.

[2]Maksymilian Horwitz-Walecki (1877-1937): A prominent member of the PPS, who later joined the KPD and the Comintern, it was Horvic who represented the PPS at Copenhagen.

[3]The Frakers, or Fracja, refers to the right wing of the PPS.

[4]Rosa Luxemburg wrote a well-known essay entitled "Against Capital Punishment."

[5]The reference here is to Trotsky's "Russian Social Democracy." Rosa did indeed draw up a protest with the collaboration of Lenin.

[6]Ignaz Daszyński was a well-known member of the PPS and one of Rosa's most prominent antagonists in the Polish movement.

To Luise Kautsky

[Undated. Postmarked Friedenau 9/9/10]

Dearest Lulu,

Whatever you think is right will be all right with me. You know that my feelings for you are always the same.[1] Still, it grieves me that you should feel so miserable. You really have no reason: you mustn't, you shouldn't see everything in such a black light. Take everything calmly, do preserve your cheerfulness! What is most difficult for me is that, this time, I cannot comfort you and cheer you up. Farewell and be happy.

Your
Rosa

Notes

[1]This letter marks the final split with Kautsky. The differences had been building for years, but they burst into the open with the mass strike debate to which Kautsky opposed his "strategy of attrition." Though Rosa broke with Karl Kautsky, she maintained her intimate friendship with Luise.

To Leo Jogiches

[Magdeburg or Berlin. Friday evening,
probably 9/23/1910]

I received the letter. I feel like a beaten dog, and it seems to me that I have suffered a spectacular defeat.[1] I can't describe it all now.

Please read the report in *Vorwärts*, and then come to Friedenau on Saturday, that is tomorrow, but no later than five o'clock since I want to go to bed early. I want to explain only this much for now: my copetitioners have forced me to withdraw the motion, since they became scared that they would remain in the minority! . . . I would like to know what impression this whole affair has made. The rest in conversation.

But one thing I must say from the start: I am in a state of physical collapse. For the next 3-4 days, any type of work is out of the question. I am not able to think, or to sleep or to eat. How I am to prepare the

Luise Kautsky. (Courtesy International Institute of Social History, Amsterdam)

Karl Kautsky. (Courtesy International Institute of Social History, Amsterdam)

important speech to the metal workers on the first is a mystery to me. This Party Convention has cost me two months' strength and health.

So I will wait until 5 (please no later, since it will get late anyway before I get to bed).

Notes

[1]At the Magdeburg Congress Rosa Luxemburg's radical mass strike resolution was overwhelmingly defeated. A sop was thrown to the left wing when the party executive passed a resolution that abstractly called for the continuance of the struggle for the suffrage.

To Konrad Haenisch

11/8/1910

Dear Comrade Haenisch,

Both of your letters gave me a great deal of pleasure, but particularly your Freiligrath paper.[1] I meant to express my pleasure to you much sooner, but I was very busy.

Why, what you tell me about the most recent "resolutions" is simply deplorable. They are, however, only the fruits of the "strategy of attrition."[2] Let's hope that the present discussion and its sequel in Magdeburg[3] will shake up our friends and arouse their vigilance against the powers that be. I, for one, consider it now my duty to the Party to proceed openly at any cost. That K[arl] K[autsky] has gotten himself ever deeper into this fix is a very embarrassing thing for radicalism. But from this too, some benefit might emerge in that our people will learn to think for themselves more, parrot less, and rely less on authorities.

Regarding the "republic,"[4] a curious bit of tough luck happened to K[arl] K[autsky]. That passage about the republic which he refused to accept has now appeared as a separate article in the Breslau paper, the Dortmund paper, and in about a dozen other papers. Now K[arl] K[autsky] accuses me of having personally waived its publication!

Clara Z[etkin] is coming here today. I sent her your letter to inform her.

By the way, do you know my brochure on the mass strike (1906)?[5] It treats precisely those issues which K[arl] K[autsky] is now raising. As it turns out, even our best people have actually not digested the lessons of the Russian Revolution at all. I would consider it very useful were this brochure to be circulated more widely at present.

Now, perhaps, the ground has been better prepared for its acceptance. How about printing the brochure—which is after all short, in your theoretical supplement in some installments? I really don't think that the people in Hamburg could have any objection.[6] . . .

Affectionate greetings.

Your
Rosa Luxemburg

Notes

[1]Ferdinand Freiligrath (1810-1876): A poet and, for a time, a close friend of both Marx and Engels. As a poet, Freiligrath began as a romantic and gradually turned to more political themes. As editor of Marx's *Neue Rheinische Zeitung*, Freiligrath was also a member of the Communist League. In the 1850s, after the failure of the 1848 revolutions, he grew less and less concerned with political affairs.

[2]Kautsky's tactical position regarding the growth of reaction in German society, termed "the strategy of attrition," involved a lessening of demands for reform in the name of the defense of existing gains.

[3]Magdeburg was to be the site of the next party congress.

[4]The polarization in this period led Rosa Luxemburg to take the position that the SPD had to fight openly for a republican constitution. Though it was always assumed that the SPD was republican—and though all its factions in some sense agreed on the need for democracy—the party never felt it safe to declare itself on the issue.

[5]The reference is to *Mass Strike, Party, and Trade Unions*, perhaps Rosa Luxemburg's most important work.

[6]Haenisch was based in Hamburg.

To Leo Jogiches

[Berlin. Early March 1911]

. . . [Clara] Zetkin writes me that she has received nothing.[1] It could be that L[enin] has not even contacted her since he knows of our relationship. Possibly he has gone to Kautsky on the assumption that we have influence with him. I am for sending Adolf [Warski] to K[arl] K[autsky] to explain the situation, but we must simplify the explanation greatly since even *my* head spins when I read the letters relating to this business; after a while I can no longer repeat what I just read. Luise [Kautsky] is here again; if necessary I could talk to her, but she usually twists the sense of such assignments, and so a beautiful mix-up might result. It's better to stick with Adolf.

For my part, I must say that this business—snatching part of the money from them—doesn't please me one bit. I know very well that the Party needs the money, that it will be for the public benefit, and that in such matters, all sentiments must take second place. But I also maintain that we mustn't step on each other's toes and that noblesse oblige. To me the whole business stinks, with your permission, of robbery and extortion. In the end, I assume, the Bolsheviks will feel that they are infested with leeches and that they will prefer an open fight with the Mensheviks to Party unity with us on their back. Should this affair grow into a scandal, our position within the Russian Party would be deeply shaken, and no doubt Dan & Co.[2] will seize any opportunity to compromise us and our alliance with the Bolsheviks. Therefore, careful, careful, gentlemen. . . .

Notes

[1]The reference is to a fund that had been set up for the Russian Social Democratic Labor Party. Despite the fact that a formal unity existed, the Bolsheviks and the Mensheviks quarrelled over the uses to which this fund was to be put and over its management.

[2]Fyodor I. Dan (1871-1947): A Menshevik, Dan later became a chauvinist during the war and an opponent of the Bolsheviks.

To Luise Kautsky

[Undated. Summer 1911]

Dearest Lulu,

I had to go to Kolberg for two days when your letter arrived, hence the delay. I am sitting tight here, and I have no plans for traveling (except for purposes of agitation). Also I feel quite well and happy. Despite the heat, I am working diligently, though, for the most part, not for the *L[eipziger] V[olkszeitung]*. Still, I am enclosing a little dart which once again earned me a great deal of love from the Party Executive Committee;[1] you needn't subscribe. By the way, *Vorwärts* immediately took a similar stand on the article without, of course, mentioning what prompted it to do so.

I don't hear much either from the tumult of the battle taking place in [the Russian Party]. Leo [Jogiches] is there, but he is so busy that he barely has time to catch his breath. His address is: Monsieur J. Goldenberg, for Leo, 39 Port Royal, Paris.

The vigorous behavior of the trustees[2] has had a good effect upon Lenin & Co.: they have yielded and have given up on attempting to destroy the newly created institutions. On the other hand, the

Mensheviks fell into a veritable delirium. After having declared such a thing impossible for 18 months, now all on their own, they are hastily calling a plenary session of the Central Committee or a party conference. Naturally, this will only serve to help deepen the split and insult the Bolsheviks, the Poles, and the unification commission in the most unbelievable manner.

Our friend Trotsky is revealing himself more and more as a rotten customer. Even before the Technical Commission obtained its financial independence from Lenin in order possibly to give its money to *Pravda*,[3] Trotsky in *Pravda* opened fire on the Commission, and on the entire Paris conference, in the most outrageous manner. He denounced the Bolsheviks and the Poles in so many words as "party-splitters," but did not utter a syllable against Martov's[4] pamphlet against Lenin. This pamphlet surpasses anything that has ever existed in baseness, and is obviously aimed at splitting the party. In a word, it's a pretty mess. If only the conference were taking place soon! In spite of everything, the unity of the Party could still be saved if both sides were compelled to call the conference jointly.

As to the painting, I am anxiously awaiting Hans' [Kautsky's] opinion.[5] I only fear that you have already biased him in my favor. Right now I don't get to painting at all. In a few days, Clara will come here again. Yesterday, Hannes [Diefenbach] took off once again, as down in the mouth as is his habit. Write me a line soon.

I kiss you many times,

Your

R.

Notes

[1] The reference is no doubt to Rosa Luxemburg's article entitled "Our Struggle for Power," which appeared in the *Leipziger Volkszeitung* in June 1911.

[2] The trustees of the Russian fund were Karl Kautsky, Franz Mehring, and Clara Zetkin.

[3] *Pravda* (*The Truth*) was the legal daily paper of the Bolsheviks, founded in 1912. It was suppressed quite often over the years and appeared under different titles. It remains the official organ of the Communist Party in Russia.

[4] Martov (Yuli Osipovich Zederbaum) (1873-1923): The leader of the Mensheviks, he was one of Lenin's earliest and closest associates and later his leading opponent within the Russian movement. In 1920, he emigrated to Germany.

[5] One of Rosa Luxemburg's favorite hobbies was painting, and she often showed her work to Kautsky's brother Hans (1864-1937), who was a professional painter and set designer.

To Luise Kautsky

[Undated. Friedenau, mid-August 1911]

Dearest Lulu,

Today I awoke suddenly in a state of panic; I am late in congratulating you on your birthday! I can't tell you how badly I feel about it. But I have a few excuses. Each day for the past 5 days, I have been meaning to begin the letter, but it's as if I were under an evil spell. Since the proclamation of the Party Executive protesting the Morocco affair,[1] I have been receiving telegrams and special-delivery letters daily to address meetings. I decline them all, but that way even more time is taken up since I must write letters of apology. Besides, day before yesterday, my brother and his wife suddenly dropped in. In addition, a courier arrived from Hamburg: [Kaiser] Wilhelm is going to be there and so, of course, I have to go as well. And that, just on the day when I was going to move! This aggravation alone could make me a republican. But I agreed to go. Then too, Ida[2] is turning the house upside down in anticipation of our moving. Is it any wonder that I am upside down too? So, let me embrace you and kiss you at this late date, and don't be angry with me.

How are you otherwise? Since the little card, I have received nothing more from you. Shall we chat a bit about the heat? Probably you are expecting to find here a charred corpse, a wasted skeleton, that would vaguely remind you of the dear features of your late friend from Cranach street. . . . Though I am not a Catholic, I am merry as a lark and in good shape. I get up at 6 o'clock, take cold baths twice daily (in a tub), feel quite refreshed and work so that the fur flies. On the whole, I find that Berlin is a very pleasant city even during the most terrible heat—provided you don't see it, as is the case with me.

Clara Zetkin was here, but only cinematographically—I saw her speeding by. She was fresh and in good humor, although she felt physically sick a few times.

The Russian matter casts a gentle shadow over both her "vacation" and mine. *Nota bene*, the honorable "trustees" have blundered beautifully, or so I, who am "noncommittal," feel in my heart of hearts—with that plan for a conference of all factions! Are the other two of the trustees to come down with the liver-attack which one is having in advance?[3] For, in my opinion, that will be the only practical result of the "conference." Naturally, only a handful of fighting cocks in exile will attend this conference to clamor for the ear and soul of the German trustees. To expect any kind of agreement from these roosters is pure madness. They are already so deeply divided and embittered that a full general discussion would only give them the chance to unburden themselves of their old, oldest, and most recent grievances and only add fuel to the fire. *The only way* to preserve unity is to bring about a general conference with delegates sent from within Russia itself. For the people in Russia all want peace and unity, and they are the only power which can bring those fighting cocks in exile to reason. Thus, only insist upon this type of general party conference and shut your eyes, ears and nose to anything else; that, in my opinion, is the only correct attitude to take.

Unfortunately, the idea of that new conference with the Germans has created a great deal of confusion among the Russians. Trotsky is boasting, in "strictly confidential" letters that now he is the great man who will get everything on the right track. Those Mensheviks who support him have taken courage, and they are boycotting the planned general party conference, while the Bolsheviks, together with the Poles, are getting completely disoriented by the rumors.

Well, all this will pass, I hope, but, in the meantime, even I—innocent lamb that I am—am being bombarded with special-delivery letters and telegrams. I am supposed to explain whether this or that is true, and how this or that is to be understood—while I don't know anything myself. As our poor Paulus [Singer] was in the habit of saying, "I could imagine a prettier world" and in this, as in so many other things, he was right.

As for the rest, the local places are deserted. Hannes is in Flims. Apropos, he sent me his portrait, done by Zündel,[4] for purposes of comparison, which pleases me very much. You'll see it when you come here.

When are you coming, anyway? My moving will probably take place on the 30th since it has to be postponed due to the "Kaiser's" visit. Are you going to attend the women's conference? Can you imagine: I have become a female! I received a credential for the conference and so must leave for Jena on the 8th. But, before that, to heighten the pleasure and shorten the stay, I am to address a voters' meeting in—Düsseldorf. Drop me a line.

I send you many kisses. Greetings to the boys.

Your
R

Notes

[1]The second Morocco crisis. On July 1, 1911, the Kaiser sent the German cruiser *Panther* to Agadir in order to "protect" German interests. A totally unexpected temperamental and patriotic speech by Lloyd George provoked

the SPD to give qualified support to the German position. Rosa saw the German government as provoking war and attacked it as well as the revisionists who, by assuming a nationalist posture, were seeking to recoup the losses that the Party had suffered in the 1907 elections.

2Rosa's maid.

3The reference is to Karl Kautsky.

4The reference is to Clara Zetkin's husband, who was himself an artist and whom Rosa often painted.

To Leo Jogiches

[Probably Berlin 8/29/1911]

A terrible boner: I mercilessly tore apart the Executive's flyer on the Morocco issue and today I learned that . . . K[arl] K[autsky] wrote it![1] A miserable business of the first order, and I didn't have the slightest idea that he wrote it. Today in *Vorwärts* he wrote a whole supplement against me, teeming with rage. A pretty mess for the Russian interests.

Notes

[1]The reference is to Kautsky's "Our Morocco—a Flyer" which Rosa criticized in her "The Morocco Crisis and the Party Executive." For her part, Rosa Luxemburg wrote many articles on the affair, the most important of which is "Regarding Morocco."

To Konrad Haenisch

Südende, Lindenstrasse 2
December, 1911

Dear Comrade Haenisch,

It was, of course, a foolish idea for our dear [Alfred] Henke[1] to suppose that I would allow my "grudge" to prevent me from campaigning for him. The devil take it! I campaign in the election districts of the worst opportunists and, in such a situation, I would not leave my party friends in the lurch because of personal differences. It's ridiculous. But the fact is that I simply can't afford to do it. Since December 1, and up to Janurary 12, all of my evenings—except for the holiday week—have been booked solid for months; so, nothing doing. Today, I am also writing Henke to this effect.

And now, a few words more about the "grudge." Of course I was furious at you in Jena precisely because, while you undertook to defend me, with your totally inappropriate strategy you stabbed me right in the back.[2] You meant to defend my "morality" and to that end surrendered my *political* position; it was the worst possible way to proceed. My "morality" needs no defense. You must have noticed that since I have been in the German Party, since 1898, I have been unceasingly villified *personally*—and most viciously—especially in the south, without *ever* responding with a single word or sentence. Silent contempt is my reaction, prompted—aside from personal pride—by a purely political consideration: all these personal insults are simply maneuvers to divert attention from the political issue. It was clear before Jena that the Executive, which was in a fix, had no other choice than to shift the conflict on to the "moral" personal terrain. It was just as clear that whoever saw the importance of the *principle* would have had to counteract this maneuver, and not let himself be drawn onto this personal terrain. But that is just what happened to you; by concentrating the entire conflict on *my person*, you sacrificed my position on the issue.

Of course, you don't have to share my opinion on every issue and it is your damned right to advocate your divergent opinion openly. But that is no reason for you to dress it up as a "defense" of my person. For this type of "defense" does more damage than an open attack. Doubtless you were not the least bit aware of the impression which your article would make: a lachrymose and magnanimous plea for extenuating circumstances in the case of a poor woman sentenced to death—it's enough to make one's blood boil especially when one is on such an important and advantageous political battle station as I was in Jena. You will just have to stop overreacting to every threatening rumor from a "knowledgeable source"—and let's say it bluntly, from *that slanderer [Rudolf] Hilferding* [3]—and, above all, never transform political questions into personal, sentimental ones. When the revisionists do this to oppose us, they very well know why. But when our people follow them onto the slippery ice, that is just too stupid for words.

So much in order to clear up the matter. I forgot my "grudge" long ago and truly I have other problems which prevent me from dragging around old trifles. So, enough of this.

Thanks very much for your articles. I knew a few of them from press reprints, and I'm very pleased about them. I already obtained the illustrated flyers in Saxony, and I consider the idea and the execution

to be very fine. And now, all my best for the holidays, and
best regards from

Your Rosa Luxemburg

Notes

[1]Alfred Henke (1868-1946): A Party functionary, Henke held many posts in
the SPD. He was also an editor of the *Bremer Bürger-Zeitung* and a
Reichstag deputy. In opposition to the war, he joined the USPD and then in
1922 rejoined the SPD.

[2]The reference is to the defense that Haenisch offered for Rosa Luxemburg
in regard to the Morocco crisis at the Jena Congress. The issue emerged in the
following way. In the midst of the crisis, the party functionary Molkenbuhr
wrote a private memo for the International Socialist Bureau, of which Rosa
Luxemburg was a member. In it, Molkenbuhr argued that if the SPD were to
take up the issue, the electoral possibilities of the SPD would be hampered at
the next election. Rosa Luxemburg published this private memo with a
scathing attack on it and the reformist policy of the SPD. She was attacked
quite viciously for her "indiscretion." For his part, Haenisch sought to
defend her by pointing to the loyalty that she had always shown to the
movement. A scandal had broken, with Rosa Luxemburg in the middle.
Indeed, a motion was put forward to censure her, which was later withdrawn.
Not only did the issue of secrecy in regard to the bureaucracy, as against the
right of the masses to know what was happening, arise, but Rosa Luxemburg
emerged as the outspoken critic of militarism and imperialism.

[3]This line does not appear in Benedikt Kautsky's *Briefe an Freunde*, but has
been restored by Haupt. Rudolf Hilferding (1877-1941): A leading social
democrat, he also became one of the most prominent members of the USPD.
A finance minister in the Stresemann cabinet of 1923, he was the author of the
seminal *Das Finanzkapital* in 1911. When Hitler took power, Hilferding fled
to France, where the Petain government turned him over to the Gestapo in
1940. He died the following year in a German prison camp.

To Franz Mehring

Südende, April 19, 1912

Dear Comrade,

The end of your kind note has upset me so intensely that I have a
strong desire to write you immediately. You say that perhaps you will
no longer stay at the *Neue Zeit*. Today I read in the *Neue Zeit* Bebel's
attack on you and this same day I learned that Kautsky had given
telegraphic orders to drop your reply from the issue. I feel that the way
Kautsky is dealing with his coeditor-in-chief is outrageous, and
Bebel's explanation sounds like senile drivel. Every honest man in the

Party who is not intellectually the Executive's servant will take your side.

But how can all this permit you to leave a post that is so important? I beg you, always keep in mind the general situation of our Party. Surely you too sense that we are approaching the time when the Party masses will need a leadership that is aggressive, pitiless, and visionary—while our higher leadership cadres, the party paper, parliamentary group, as well as our theoretical organ, if they were deprived of you, will grow shabbier and shabbier, more cowardly, more besotted with parliamentary cretinism.

So, facing this pretty future, we must occupy and maintain the positions that, in spite of the official "leadership," allow us to use our right of criticism. Surely you know this better than I! And yet, in spite of all this, we have been shown by the last general meeting of the Berlin people, and even more by the attitude, throughout the country, of all the general meetings of militants, that the masses are behind us and want a different leadership.

It follows that we have a precise obligation to hold fast and not do the official Party bosses the favor of decamping; we have to expect continuous fights and frictions, especially when we touch on the Holy of Holies, parliamentary cretinism, as brutally as you have done. In spite of it all, the best watchword seems to me not to retreat one inch. The *Neue Zeit* must not be left entirely since it is the semiofficial Party organ, nor must it be delivered to the senile and the doddering. Laugh at all these miseries and go on writing in the journal the same way that you have been, which has always pleased our hearts.

To Alfred Henke

Südende, November 15, 1912

Dear Comrade Henke,

Your letter of the 8th, in which you ask me to polemicize against Kautsky in the *Bremer Bürger-Zeitung* amazed me a good deal. You allude to the answer I gave you a year ago when you asked whether I was still angry at you: I said you were really childish. That was about a tactless and tactically mistaken article which you had published, allegedly in my defense—hence, a personal injury which you inflicted upon me. For *personal* slights, I have very little sensitivity and a very short memory. *Now*, something quite different is involved.

For months, your paper has been insulting not me personally, but rather the Polish Social Democrats in an unheard-of manner—a party to which I belong, for which I work, and in whose founding and management I have taken part as best I could. You have insulted this party and its leadership—without the least knowledge of the situation—simply because of a certain individual[1] and the insinuations of this individual. Though you pride yourself on being a pillar of "radicalism" in Germany, in your paper you have insulted leading Polish comrades whose radicalism is different from your own in that it has been proven for decades in prisons, hard labor and continual hunger. For a man such as you it would be appropriate to respectfully take off your hat when they pass.

For the sake of one individual, you have rigidly committed your paper in advance, without ever objectively checking or investigating the situation. An editor who took his paper seriously would never be this blatant. In the same personal matter you also publicly engaged the Bremen membership in a way that a serious politician would never force upon his organization. You have most seriously damaged the reputation of the Bremen paper and the Bremen organization— and all that to save one individual who evidently has become the essence of radicalism for you. I do not call this a serious radical politics, but rather the *machinations of a clique,* which is utterly alien to radicalism. Finally, by reinstating this individual on the editorial staff—a provocation, since it was done without investigating the matter—you have shown that you do not take seriously either your paper or the Bremen organization and that you consider your own "Investigatory Commission" a farce.

And one more thing! As a radical, you often speak of the "masses" and the "self-regulation of the masses." At the same time you automatically push through this Radek business in your paper, even though you know very well that the mass of the comrades in Bremen feel embarrassed by this affair. As long as these conditions prevail in the *Bremer Bürger-Zeitung,* my cooperation with the paper must remain out of the question.

With Party greetings,
Rosa Luxemburg

Notes

[1]The reference is to a now long-forgotten scandal in which Karl Radek played the leading role. From a conflict over a small paper in Württemburg, the *Freie Volkszeitung,* of which Radek was the editor, a debate escalated to the point where a conflict over tactics with Rosa Luxemburg and Leo Jogiches led to Radek's expulsion from the SDKPL—beginning a rift that

Rosa Luxemburg addressing her accusors in court. (Courtesy Dietz Verlag)

would seriously damage the party. At this point, a motion was put forward in the SPD that would have prevented any member who had been expelled from one socialist party from being a member of any other; this rule was to be retroactively applied to Radek. The motion was passed at the Jena Congress of 1913, and Radek was expelled from the SPD. Lenin came to his aid and attacked Rosa Luxemburg for her position on the whole affair.

To Leo Jogiches

[Probably Berlin 2/14/1913]
Today [Franz] Mehring came to see me at the school to ask for my advice about the note which he recently sent to *V*[*orwärts*]. The note is childish (it explains that he wishes to register a complaint with the Control Commission). But I did not advise against it in order not to discourage him and, besides, a little storm now wouldn't do me any harm. . . .

Korn[1] has already read my book.[2] Judging from hints he dropped, he agrees with me and is "enthralled." I suggested the idea of his writing a review for the "Hamburger Echo" or some other paper. He liked the idea. If I know [Clara] Zetkin, she will only finish her review in a few weeks. I am on the best footing with the old man. In line with your suggestion, I am preparing an article for the *L*[*eipziger V*[*olkszeitung*] which will be directed against both *Vorwärts* and the Frakja (on the occasion of the internal politics) as everyone agrees. The entire action by *Vorwärts* has been set in motion by Hilferding. He's fit to be tied. Korn said to me today: "You see, if you had only cited Hilferding once, then the whole thing never would have happened." In response to an inquiry of Mehring's, Korn characterized Hilferding's book[3] as the work of an educated bank clerk.

Notes

[1] Karl Korn (1865-1942): SPD functionary and long-time editor of *Arbeiter-Jugend* (*Worker-Youth*).
[2] *The Accumulation of Capital.*
[3] *Finance Capital.*

To Gertrud Zlottko

[Postcard with postmark Zurich 7/17/1913]
Dear Gertrud!
I had a hideous night in Frankfurt, and arrived half-dead from

the strain. I stood at Bebel's coffin a long time. He looked wonderful, even more beautiful than while he was alive. The burial is today. I don't know when I will be back, probably on Tuesday. I'll send a telegram. I am staying here with Frau Zetkin. She sends her best regards. Affectionate greetings from me to you and Mimi.

R.L.

To Walter Stöcker[1]

Berlin-Südende
March 11, 1914

Dear Comrade Stöcker,

I cannot recommend to you any of the bourgeois works of political economy because they would only make you lose time and bore you. Better continue reading *Das Kapital*. Before beginning the second volume of *Das Kapital*, I would advise you to consult my book on the accumulation process. Unfortunately, I don't know any other work which might serve as an introduction to the second volume of *Das Kapital*; this volume is very difficult insofar as it sets out problems instead of working them through. Nevertheless, try it. If the book appears disconcerting, then perhaps you can try mine. What appears most dangerous to me is that in the second volume of *Das Kapital*, one is able to master every factual detail, and even with a certain facility, but most of the time one does not see the elucidation of the fundamental questions in terms of which the research is carried out, and where the real problems of the volume are actually to be found.

It amuses me greatly—if it were not at the same time a bit saddening—that there are comrades who can believe that I would flee Germany due to fear of imprisonment. My dear young friend, I assure you that I would not flee even were the gallows threatening, for the simple reason that I consider it thoroughly necessary to accustom our party to the fact that sacrifice is part of the socialist's craft and that this should be obvious. You are right: "Long live the struggle!"

Best regards,
Rosa Luxemburg

Notes

[1]Walter Stöcker (1891-1939): A onetime member of the SPD who, as a member of the USPD, participated in the Cologne workers' and soldiers' council movement in 1918. Afterwards Stöcker joined the KPD and served as a Reichstag deputy from 1920-32. Arrested in the aftermath of the Reichstag fire, he died in the Buchenwald concentration camp of typhus.

To Hans Diefenbach

11/1/14[1]

My dear Hannesle,[2]

Today's the day! For weeks I've been writing you the most elaborate detailed letters "in spirit," though I haven't gotten around to putting them on paper. This has weighed upon my heart like a stone. But I have so little quiet and privacy, even though everything has come to a standstill. But now it should get better. Once again, I have decided to begin "a new life": go to bed early, throw all visitors out the door—and work! But hard! And the first step of the "new life" is this letter to you. Your last two comprehensive letters, via Hans [Kautsky] made me terribly happy. At least I can imagine how you are living and what you are doing. . . .

First, since you wished it, a little account of myself. Well, by now, my initially despairing mood has changed. Not as if I were judging the situation in a rosier light, or as if I had reason for cheer—not at all. But the intensity of the first blow which you receive is blunted once the blows become your daily bread. There is no doubt that the Party and the International are in shambles, thoroughly in shambles. But the very dimensions of this disaster have turned it into a world-historical drama, in the face of which the objective historical judgment is restored and displaces any personal breast-beating. Of course, the sometimes almost unbearable pain is always there with each new villainy and baseness committed by former "friends," and the unheard-of degradations practiced by the press. Yet, in the face of all this, in my heart I am ever more convinced that—if for all that it can't be helped—I can still find all sorts of consolation for my modest personal needs—a good book, a walk in the beautiful autumn weather, like in those days when I walked over the stubble with you, Hannesle, and lastly—music! Ah, music! How I miss it, and how I long for it! Up until now, I couldn't obtain any. At first, for weeks on end, there was nothing. Then, on every occasion, there were political demonstrations in the opera and the concert hall. Now, at last, one can take a chance; but Hannesle isn't there to get the tickets. And also, when one is so without any company, music is no consolation.

Finally, I still count on Hans [Kautsky]. He came to me a week ago to deliver your letter. He looks fresh, red-cheeked, younger. Rome was excellent for him. Even aside from all that, he made a very pleasant impression and I promised to drop in on him immediately— didn't get around to it, though. Maybe I'll pass by tomorrow. He promised to play for me two hours daily, if only I would come.

Probably he has already told you of his children: Gretl, the happy fiancee of a touchingly shy Slovak, Fritz—a dashing lieutenant, Robert—a perfect painter; only Hansl remains a *fils perdu*. He makes fun of Papschi[3] in his letters to Robert, and poor Papschi has to come upon just these letters and read them. Luise is, as H. explains, so under the weather that I had better not go there; even a telephone conversation is too much for her. Next week they (H. and L.) are driving to the south again; I envy them. Karli has made a successful career in Frankfurt/Main; Bendl, since he had typhus, is as fat as a little pig; Felix is the same as always. All in all, the K[autsky] clan flourishes as they find their way through life's vicissitudes.

Last week, Donna Clara [Zetkin] stayed with me for six days; she is in terrible physical shape. Kostia is still at home and works at the editorial office. From Maxim, again not a word for a month. Yes: I received a dear sign of life from Medi again. She was sick, you know; now she's home again and working. Brandel's father finally arrived here again last week together with Clara. The poor guy has changed considerably; half his face is immobile. He showed me a very interesting letter from Brandel, which shows the young fellow in the best light. He's not far from you. Write him: Vizefeldwebel B. G. XVIII Armeekorps, 25th Division, aktives Regiment NR. 116, 6th Kompagnie. He will certainly be pleased to hear from you.

Kurt Rosenfeld[4] writes me very often; he is in the east, most recently in Wilkowyscky, where he—as a quartermaster—fixed sales taxes on the prices of kosher and nonkosher meat, performed house searches, and carried out similar juridical functions. Then he got into a hot battle, went through terrors, and is now, I believe, back on German soil. He remains mentally very alert and mobile, and naturally is loyal to the flag.

You want to know what I'm doing and particularly what I'm writing. Well, above all, I now want to finish my study on political economy, which is very advisable, if only on purely personal economic grounds. This is a work which will take several months. The Party School is closed, as you know, during the war year and so I would have enough time if it weren't for visits, conferences, and meetings from morning until night. But now, this—as I said—is to stop. Also, of course, I want to write a study about the war, which—as you can imagine—will soon become an urgent necessity.[5]

For the present, to be sure, a "civil truce" reigns. But silently, we live like dogs and cats with the Südekums,[6] etc., and on the whole the mood is getting livelier and livelier. The problem intrigues me greatly, both on purely theoretical grounds and as a writer. "If only we had time, my woman, only time!" as Dehmel[7]—the enlisted "volunteer"—once sang. The declarations of all the German poets, artists and scholars will, by the way, one day form a *document humain* of the first order.[8]

It seems that soon I will have to move my private "civil truce" to the Tower. I cannot pretend that, under the circumstances, I am particularly pleased about this. Six months ago, I was looking forward to it like a celebration; today, this honor falls on my chest like the Iron Cross falls on yours. Well, I comfort myself that, at the end of the war, I will once again be able to breathe air. Then we will both enter the capital at the same time: you as the victor with an oak garland over your brow, I as your maid of honor clad in white. The Bundesrat, as a matter of fact, in yesterday's declaration on price control, figures on the war continuing beyond the harvest of 1915; so do the English and Russian press. A pretty kettle of fish! Everyone asks: How will the harvest reserves hold up? I ask: How will the nerves of the officers and the soldiers hold up? God keep you peaceful in the hospitable cottage of your peasant woman, where you so touchingly try to substitute yourself for the absent husband. I see from your last letter, by the way, that after all you have discovered a few sympathetic souls under the masks, and I am very happy about that. Continue writing as often as possible, it is always a cause for celebration in my house when a letter from you arrives. Even Mimi sniffs it lovingly (she calls that "reading").

Gertrud [Zlottko] has been gone since the fifteenth; however, I've been able to fend for myself. Don't worry about me, Hannesle, I'll get by all right. But if you, as a newly rich *Conquistadore*, would wish to throw away a 100-mark bill monthly. . . . Tell me, couldn't you sacrifice this for a young man who wants to go to college, who is highly talented, and who has no money? If in this way he could at least put the war year to use, maybe later he can create his own career. Gertrud, by the way, wrote you and complains of your silence. Now, best regards from me and Mimi. Write soon whether you received the letter.

Your R.

Notes

[1]The Austrian Archduke Francis Ferdinand was assassinated on June 28, 1914, precipitating the crisis that ultimately resulted in World War I. Mobilization took place by the various nations of Europe in what was a chain reaction, despite the negotiations that were being carried on to avert the war. These negotiations also took place within the Executive Bureau of the Second

International. But a wave of nationalist hysteria seemed to grip the nations of Europe. When, on August 4, the matter of war appropriations came before the German Reichstag, the SPD supported the government's request for funds. Concretely, this marked the demise of the Second International and called into question the revolutionary ideology, the oppositional stance, and the internationalism of the SPD. The new policy of the socialists was to propagate a "civil truce," which meant nothing other than a "suspension" of "class war" for the duration of the European conflict. It was August 4 that became associated with the SPD's "great betrayal."

[2]A diminutive of Hans; another diminutive is "Hänschen"; Rosa will employ it in many of the letters that follow.

[3]The reference is to their father, Hans Kautsky.

[4]Kurt Rosenfeld (1877-1943): One of Rosa's lawyers and friends. In 1918, he entered the Prussian Ministry of Justice as a USPD member, and was a Reichstag deputy for the USPD in 1920. In 1922, he rejoined the SPD.

[5]The first intimation of the epochal *Junius Brochure: The Crisis of Social Democracy*. This was Luxemburg's magnificent antiwar tract, which argued that the struggle against the war should be turned into a revolutionary struggle against the bourgeoisie.

[6]Albert Südekum (1871-1944): A revisionist social democrat who became the Prussian minister of finance in 1918.

[7]Richard Dehmel (1863-1920): A German avant-garde poet, "Nur Zeit" is one of his labor poems that pressed the demand for the eight-hour day. He served as an officer in the war.

[8]Writers and scholars in both camps had written and signed manifestos to justify the causes of their respective countries.

To Camille Huysmans[1]

11/10/1914

My dear friend,

I am happy at having the chance to send you a few words and delighted to know that the solution which you found for the Executive Committee is most felicitous. I beg you to hold your ground there and to remain at your post despite all attempts to wrest away your mandate or persuade you to renounce it. . . . Our situation here is very difficult. I am convinced that the mass of workers will be on our side as soon as the possibility arises for presenting the issue to them. But, in the meantime, the *arrivistes*[2] profit from the state of martial law in order to terrorize us and demoralize the masses. Still, this state of mind is changing more and more. . . .

The bankruptcy of the International is as complete as it is terrible! At least let us oppose the efforts to substitute a farce and a delusion for it. The reconstruction in my opinion, can only begin to take place after the past betrayals have been severely and frankly criticized; that is to say, after the war. If only I shall be able to enjoy freedom the very moment the war is ended! I can say nothing much about that, since the prison can engulf me at any moment. That decision is made by . . . the gods.

Clara [Zetkin] was in Switzerland, attending the congress.[3] She has spoken to the Italians too. She did a good job and has discovered a number of cute tricks used by our "Party Fathers" abroad.

I cordially clasp your hand, my dear friend; greetings to you and your family. If you have a chance of getting a letter across the frontier, write me at the address of Herrn Hugo Eberlein,[4] Berlin—Mariendorf, Ringstrasse 82 (nothing more). The little volume which I mailed you on the 2nd of August was returned to me by the post office.

R.L.

Dear Comrade!

I am in complete agreement with the above. Now, they say that "charity begins at home." Unfortunately, today, we are still in fetters. Apparently, either Terwagne told some complete nonsense about our meeting, or the *Telegraf* has been grossly lying.

From my heart, I greet you and yours, and all our friends. We feel in solidarity with you in the struggle over your position in the International.

Your
K. Liebknecht

Notes

[1]See letter of summer, 1905, note 2, p. 99.

[2]This must refer to the right-wingers who had "arrived"—taking cabinet seats in Paris and occupying the positions of power in the *Vorwärts* offices in Berlin.

[3]The reference is to the Zimmerwald Conference formed by left-wing socialists who wished to remain internationalist. It was the germ of what would become the Third International.

[4]Hugo Eberlein attended the founding congress of the Third International under the alias Albert. There he voted for the creation of the new International, although Rosa Luxemburg's instructions were that he abstain.

Camille Huysmans. (Courtesy International Institute of Social History, Amsterdam)

To Mathilde Jacob[1]

[Undated, from the Women's
Prison in Berlin]

Dearest Fräulein Jacob!

I am sending you a brisk, happy winter's greeting for the coming Sunday. Please write Clara [Zetkin] that, in the meantime, I have received news from her son, so that she needn't worry.

I would like to hear how you liked *Pitt and Fox*.[2] On Sunday you will receive the Boileau[3] which I just finished and which I had promised you for quite some time. Boileau is rather boring but, due to "classical education," one still has to have read him. Sometimes he is also quite humorous; thus, the beginning of his VIth Satire is very nice, and the ending of the VIIth is also excellent.—Have you found the Anatole France[4] yet? Another question: Do you have Meyer's *Encyclopedia* at home? For if so, I would ask you to regularly copy out some things for me. My own is, due to the cold in Südende, of no use to me. Work is odious when you cannot immediately look up what you need. I affectionately embrace you and Mimi.

Your
R

Notes

[1]Mathilde Jacob was Rosa Luxemburg's secretary and friend who smuggled manuscripts and letters out of prison. In these letters that passed through the censor, the mode of address is more formal.

[2]Book by Friedrich Huch (1873-1913).

[3]Nicholas Boileau (1636-1711): French neoclassical poet and critic.

[4]Anatole France (1844-1924): A humanist and champion of Dreyfus, he was one of the most popular writers of his generation.

To Marta Rosenbaum[1]

3/12/1915

Dear Comrade Rosenbaum,

At last I have a chance to write you a few lines which, however, you had better not mention in your next letter to me. Many heartfelt thanks for your greeting on the 5th and for the flowers, which are still on my little table. Really, they have kept wonderfully well. I also cared for them like the apple of my eye; every single snowdrop and every narcissus was inspected every day. Actually, all of it was "contraband," but they were delivered to me anyway. In fact, on the 5th, unexpectedly—and, as if by prearrangement—I received such a quantity of letters and also flowers that they broke down the rigid "dam of rules" all by themselves.

About my suddenly being cut off like in the middle of a telephone conversation, at first I was rather dismayed, although I still had to laugh. Some plans of mine have been destroyed in this way, but not all, I hope. At last, after two weeks, I have received my books and the permission to work. You can imagine that they didn't have to tell me twice.

My health will eventually have to adjust to the local, somewhat peculiar diet. The main thing is that it doesn't bother me in my work. Imagine, I get up every day at exactly 5:40! To be sure, by 9 o'clock I must be in "bed"—if you can call this instrument by that name. I push it up every morning and down every night; by day, it is as closely pressed against the wall as a board.

As I can see from the papers, which are my only connection with world history, things are progressing vigorously. You are probably enthusiastic about (Hugo) Haase[2] since you do have a great weakness for him. But, apart from the fact that all his complaints and criticism clash loudly with his voting record, he would never have found the right tone had not Karl Liebknecht's mighty tunes in the Landtag shown that there is something to be said for the way we do things while reminding the people of the tones that used to move them.

On the whole, I am in a very good and confident mood. History is really working into our hands. Enclosed a greeting for Kurt [Rosenfeld]. So long, thanks for everything, and write me a line now and then. After all, I am only allowed to write "one letter per month."

Affectionately, your
R. L.

P.S.: Please be careful when talking about me and this letter on the telephone.

Notes

[1]Marta Rosenbaum (1867-1940): One of Rosa Luxemburg's dearest friends and a member of the SPD. Kurt Rosenfeld was her cousin.

[2]Hugo Haase (1863-1919): A longtime member of the SPD, he became its leader after Bebel's death. Though he personally opposed the war, he voted for war appropriations in accordance with party discipline. In 1915, he resigned the leadership and entered the USPD. In 1919, he was assassinated.

To Mathilde Jacob

Friday, April 9, 1915
Berlin, Barnimstrasse,
Women's Prison

Dearest Fräulein Jacob,

I hope you will receive these lines in time for a Sunday greeting. Many heartfelt thanks for your letters, which I read many times and which bring me great cheer. The second one came today (from Jena, where I don't know your hotel) with the nice enclosures.

The picture of Mimi made me terribly happy. I always have to laugh when I look at it: I have observed these scenes of wildness so often, when someone would make "advances," that I almost heard her growl as I looked at the little picture; it came out perfectly. At once, I felt the most lively sympathy for the young doctor who showed so much interest in my Mimi.

A very special thank you for the flowers; you can't know what a kindness you did me. For I am able to return to my botanizing once again; it is my passion and the best relaxation after working. I don't know whether I have ever shown you my botany notebooks in which, from May 1913 on, I entered about 250 plants—all magnificently preserved. I have them all here, just like my various atlases, and now I can begin a new notebook especially for Barnimstrasse. It so happens that I did not have any of the flowers which you sent, and now I have entered them into the notebook; the little yellow flowers in the first letter particularly pleased me, as did the pulsatilla (which is not to be found around Berlin). Also, the two ivy leaves of Frau von Stein[1] have been immortalized—sure enough, I did not yet have ivy (*Ledera helix* in Latin); its pedigree makes me doubly pleased. Except for the liverwort, all the flowers were pressed very nicely, which is important in botanizing.

I'm happy for you that you are seeing so much; for me it would be a hardship if I had to visit museums and the like. It never fails: I immediately get a migraine and am completely worn out. For me the only relaxation is lounging or lying in the grass, in the sun, observing the tiniest beetles or gazing at the clouds. Remember this in case our future trip together should ever come to pass. I won't keep you from visiting anything which interests you, but you will have to excuse me. Certainly, you combine both likings which, after all, is the best.

I saw a picture of Lady Hamilton in the French 18th Century exhibition. I don't remember the painter's name, I just have the recollection of a strong and glaring artifice—a robust, aggressive beauty which left me cold. My taste is for somewhat more refined types of women. I still vividly see, in the same exhibition, the picture of Madame de Lavallière painted by Madame le Brun[2] in a silver-grey tone which stands in such perfect harmony with the translucent face, the blue eyes, and the light-colored dress. I was barely able to tear myself away from the painting, in which the whole sophistication of prerevolutionary France, a truly aristocratic culture with a light touch of decay, was incarnate.

Wonderful that you are reading Engels' *Peasant Wars*.[3] Have you already finished Zimmerman's?[4] Actually, Engels does not give a history, but only a critical philosophy of the peasant wars. The substantial meat of the facts is given by Zimmerman. When I ride through the sleepy little Württemberg towns between the fragrant dunghills, with hissing, long-necked geese unwillingly making way for the motor car, while the hopeful youths of the village call me names, I am never able to imagine that once, in these same little towns, world history was proceeding at a roaring pace and dramatic characters were bustling about.

For relaxation, I am reading the geological history of Germany. Just imagine that in clay slabs of the Algonkian period—that is to say, from the most ancient time in the history of the earth, before there was even the least trace of organic life, uncounted millions of years ago— that impressions of the droplets from short downpours of rain were found in such clay slabs in Sweden. I can't tell you how magically this distant greeting from the most ancient time affects me. I read nothing with such excitement as geology.

By the way, with regard to Frau von Stein, with all due reverence for her ivy leaves: God forgive me, but she was a cow. For, when Goethe showed her the door, she behaved like a shrewish washerwoman, and I stand by my belief that the character of a woman shows itself not where love begins, but rather where it ends. Of all Goethe's Dulcineas,[5] the only one I like is the refined, reserved Marianne von Willemer, the "Suleika" of the *Westöstliche Divan*.[6]

I am overjoyed that you are recovering; you needed that! I am very well. Affectionate regards,

Your
R. L.

Notes

[1]Charlotte von Stein (1742-1827): She was one of Goethe's great loves. Their relationship spanned the years 1776-1788, and the references to her in Goethe's works are innumerable.

[2]The painter to whom Rosa is referring is probably Marie-Anne Vigee-Lebrun (1755-1842).

[3]Engels' well-known *The Peasant Wars in Germany.*

[4]Wilhelm Zimmerman (1807-1878): A participant in the revolution of 1848, he was a democrat and wrote *The History of Peasant War in Germany,* which was published in 1843.

[5]Dulcinea is Don Quixote's ideal love in Cervantes' *Don Quixote.*

[6]Marianne von Willemar (1784-1860): Goethe's last love. Her responses to Goethe's own poems were included by him in his *Westöstliche Divan.*

To Mathilde Jacob

                                                               November 5, 1915

Dearest Fräulein Jacob,

I just want to write you a few lines to tell you that thanks to your generosity, for the time being I am well stocked with food and on Tuesday I would just like you to bring a few sardines. It was so thoughtful of you to send me poems; I haven't read any for so long (except for Goethe, with whom I never part). I hardly know Hölderlin[1] at all (Oh! The shame!). He is a little too stately. If, for example, you compare his "To Hope" with Mörike's[2] piece on the same theme, how much more sincere and poetic is Mörike! By the way, Hugo Wolf[3] set this last piece to heavenly music. On Tuesday, along with Hölderlin, I will give you *Federigo Confaloniere* by Ricarda Huch,[4] which you probably don't know. I have read almost everything she has written, but I consider *Confaloniere* to be the best.

You wanted to transplant the big Meyer *Encyclopedia* from Südende to here! You dear soul! I had a good laugh over this. What am I supposed to do with the 22 quarto volumes here? No! I'll get along as is. Forget about it.

                                                                          Your

                                                                          R

Notes

[1]Friedrich Hölderlin (1770-1843): Some critics place Hölderlin's poetry beyond that of even Goethe. Another legendary figure in literature, Hölderlin went to school with the philosophers Hegel and Schelling at the university in Tübingen. After writing some extraordinary works, he was sent to an asylum in 1806 and spent the remainder of his life in seclusion in a tower in Tübingen. His most famous works include *Hyperion* and *Empedocles.*

[2]Eduard Mörike (1804-1875): One of the major figures of German

romanticism. His works include *An Idyl from the Bodensee* and *Mozart on a Trip to Prague*; but he is best known for his poems.

[3]Hugo Wolf (1860-1903): A composer as well as a music critic, who put many of Goethe's and Mörike's poems to music. His work occupies a central position between the music of Brahms and Schönberg.

[4]Ricarda Huch (1864-1947): One of Germany's most popular writers around the turn of the century. Her works show strains of both romanticism and naturalism.

To Mathilde Jacob

November 10, 1915

Dearest Fräulein Jacob,

You are incorrigible! Another cornucopia in the form of a shopping bag, even though I haven't yet finished the gifts from the week before last. I may as well open a little grocery store shortly with the sugar (for I use 1½ lumps a day, and you bombard me with kilos). Many thanks for the gorgeous asters and for Ricarda [Huch]. Of course, I diligently read the poems at once, but I must confess: female eroticism in public has always been embarrassing to me. As our [Ignaz] Auer once said, "One doesn't say things like that, one does them."[1] Anyway, I like her prose better. But still, your present pleased me. . . . I affectionately embrace you and Mimi.

Your

R

Notes

[1]An allusion to the famous remark that Auer made in regard to Bernstein's position in the "revisionist" debate, where he tried to bring the party's revolutionary theory into line with its reformist practice. (See also the letter of 5/1/1899, note 1, p. 78.)

To the Editors of the Neue Zeit

Berlin, December 25, 1915

Comrades,

Franz Mehring will be 70 years old in February. I should like to ask whether you would wish me to write a short article of approximately 1½ printed pages to commemorate the event, and what would be your deadline. I cannot direct this inquiry to you openly since the article would have to be in your hands before my release (2/18), and since I want to publish it without it being censored here. (Of course, it would only appear after my return to freedom.)

For this reason, I request that you send me your reply by the same route.

With socialist greetings,
Rosa Luxemburg

To a Comrade Westphal

Südende, Lindenstrasse
2/25/1916

Dear Comrade Westphal,

I don't know how to thank you and all the comrades from Mariendorf for the proof of your friendship and goodness which you have shown me on the occasion of my release! I could not have imagined such a reception. After all, a prison is a natural extension of our calling as fighters for the freedom of the proletariat and, from Russia, I have become accustomed to considering the entry and exit from these walls as the purest circumstance.

Now I know that it was not basically in regard to my own person that all this revolved, but rather it was the attitude of our communal struggle which was expressed in this instance. From this standpoint, the heartwarming reception by so many of our male and female comrades gave me great pleasure, because in this attitude we unite completely and fully. I came out of prison with the happiest and most impatient desire to work and I hope that I will not disappoint you in your expectations. Our concern must go forward; in spite of it all I am full of hope and in the best of spirits. Most affectionate regards to you and all the comrades of Mariendorf.

Your
Rosa Luxemburg

To Marta Rosenbaum

[Postmark 5/11/16]

My dear Marta!

Many thanks for your postcard greetings and for the letter.

Previously, I did not have your address and so, if only for that reason, I could not write. Besides, I barely get to thinking, because of all the running about and the meetings. You can imagine that, since the 1st of May, there has been much to do! Of course, above all, you would like to know how Karl [Liebknecht] is doing. Unfortunately, there's nothing much to say. The investigation is still underway, the indictment is still not formulated. The prospects are not unfavorable, but, as you know, what is decisive in such cases is the political *raison d'état*; so we'll have to wait and see. It has already been settled that the entire bourgeois Reichstag will refuse to give him immunity. So much the better: that will mark the political suicide of parliamentarism. The demonstration on the 1st of May was very successful and surpassed all our expectations, especially since we planned it all alone with few forces and in the shortest possible space of time. The Lebedour people were asked to work with us and—they refused![1]

Once again, I have received rather bad news from Clara [Zetkin]: Following a "trip" into the city (after all, she lives outside the city), she felt so poorly that the doctor forbade her—in the strictest terms— to leave the house. You probably know of the tempest in the local Berlin teapot from its echo in *V[orwärts]*. The crisis goes on, no end is in sight, and meetings proliferate from morning until late into the night. Unfortunately, because of all this tumult, I do not get to work quietly, and I don't have a free minute!

Your azalea is in bloom—and is indescribably beautiful. Right now, it's at its zenith. The whole world abounds in the beauty and glamor of spring, but I hardly even have the time to take notice of it in passing. I hope that, at least, you are recovering thoroughly and getting rid of that unbearable pain in your arm.

Take care of yourself properly and don't get upset over reports from our local "theater of war!"

Your
R. L.

Notes

[1] The reference is to the USPD.

To Sonja Liebknecht

[Postcard]
Leipzig 7/7/16

My dear little Sonja!
As is often the case in Leipzig, today is oppressively muggy—I

can't stand the air here. This morning I sat for 2 hours in the park near
the pond reading *The Man of Property*.[1] It's brilliant. A little old
woman sat down next to me, threw a glance at the title page, and
smiled: "That must be a fine book. I also like reading books."

Before I sat down to read, naturally, I scanned the trees and
shrubs of the park—all of them were known to me, as I established
with satisfaction. On the other hand, my contacts with people are ever
less satisfying. I believe that soon I really will withdraw to
anchoritism like St. Anthony, but—without "temptations." Be
cheerful and calm.

Affectionate regards,
Rosa

Notes

[1] The novel by John Galsworthy (1867-1933), one of the most popular
English novelists around the turn of the century and author of *The Forsyte
Saga*.

To Marta Rosenbaum

[Undated, from prison]

Dearest Martchen!

I was so happy about yesterday's visit. It was so nice and pleasant,
and I certainly hope that today and Sunday will be the same. For me,
it was a great mental refreshment which I will feast upon for many
weeks. You warmed me so comfortably through your closeness, you
dear soul. After a while, you will come again, won't you? I am already
looking forward to the next time. That is, if I am still doing time here.

In general, you can really feel reassured about me. I am now
meticulously following doctor's orders, and I firmly hope to come
away from here healthy and strong so that all of you will be proud of
me in struggle and work. There will be many struggles, and much
work to do. But I am absolutely not discouraged. Dearest, history
itself always knows best what to do when conditions appear most
desperate. I am not giving voice here to a comfortable fatalism. On the
contrary: Human will must be spurred on to the utmost, and our job
is to struggle consciously with all our might. But what I mean is:
now, where everything seems so absolutely hopeless, the *success* of
this conscious influence on the masses depends on the elemental,
deeply hidden coiled springs of history. And I know from historical
experience, as well as from personal experience in Russia, that

precisely when on the surface everything seems hopeless and miserable, a complete change is getting ready, which to be sure will be all the more violent. Above all, never forget: we are tied to historical laws of development and these *never* break down, even when they do not exactly follow the plans we have laid. Well, in any case, keep your head up and never say die. I strongly embrace you in the warmest love.

Your
R

To Marta Rosenbaum

[Undated]

My dearest Martchen!

Go to Posen to my physician, Dr. Lehmann, Posen, Viktoria-strasse 26/27. Write down everything that he will say and pass it on to me in exactly the same way (without bruiting it about). Kisses,

Your
R.

To Sonja Liebknecht[1]

[Postcard]
Wronke 8/24/1916

Dear Sonitschka,

That I can't be with you now! The sentence has affected me deeply. But please, keep your chin up. Things will turn out differently from the way they now appear. For the present, however, you must leave—go somewhere: to the country, to where it is green, to where it is beautiful and where you can be cared for. It makes no sense, and there is no purpose, in sitting here any longer and being brought lower. Weeks can pass until the appeal has been heard. I beg you, leave as soon as possible. . . . It will certainly also be a relief for Karl to know that you have gone away for a rest.

A thousand thanks for your dear lines of the 10th and for your nice gifts. Surely we will be together next spring, roaming the fields and the botanical gardens. I am already looking forward to it!

But, for now, get away from here, Sonitschka! Couldn't you get to Lake Konstanz so that you might experience the south a bit?

Before you go, I absolutely must see you. Make an application to the commander's office. Write me another few lines soon. In spite of everything, be calm and cheerful! I embrace you.

R

Notes

[1]The letter was written on the day that Karl Liebknecht was sentenced to four years at hard labor.

To Sonja Liebknecht

Wronke 11/21/16

My beloved little Sonitschka,

I learned from Mathilde [Jacob] that your brother was killed in action. I am completely shaken by this new blow which has been dealt to you. What you have had to bear of late! And I can't even be with you to comfort you and cheer you up.

. . . Also, I am anxious about how your mother will bear this new grief. These are bad times, and we all have a long list of casualties to live with. Now truly every month . . . can count for a year.

I hope that I will be able to see you very soon. I long for it with all my heart. How did you receive the news of your brother, through your mother or directly from the War Department? And what do you hear from your older brother? I would so much have liked to send you something through Mathilde, but unfortunately here I have nothing other than a little colored kerchief—don't make fun of it; it is only meant to tell you that I love you very much. Write a few lines soon, so that I can see what state you are in. A thousand greetings to Karl. I affectionately embrace you.

Your
Rosa

To Emanuel and Mathilde Wurm

Wronke 12/28/16

Dearest Tilde,

I want to answer your Christmas letter immediately, as long as I am in the state of rage which it has evoked in me. Yes, your letter made me seethe with rage because, despite its brevity, it shows me in every

Emanuel and Mathilde Wurm. (Courtesy International Institute of Social History, Amsterdam)

line how very much you are again under the influence of your milieu.
This whining tone, this "alas" and "alack" about the "disappointments" which you have experienced—disappointments which you
blame on others, instead of just looking into the mirror to see the
whole of humanity's wretchedness in its most striking likeness! And
when you say "we" that now means your boggy, froggish friends,
whereas earlier, when you and I were together, it meant *my* company.
Just you wait, I will treat "you" in the plural.

In your melancholy view, I have been complaining that you
people are not marching up to the cannon's mouth. "Not marching"
is a good one! You people do not march; you do not even walk; you
creep. It is not simply a difference of degree, but rather of kind. On the
whole, *you* people are a different zoological species than I, and your
grousing, peevish, cowardly and half-hearted nature has never been
as alien, as hateful to me, as it is now. You think that audacity would
surely please you, but because of it one can be thrown into the cooler
and one is then "of little use!" Ach!—you miserable little
mercenaries. *You* would be ready enough to put a little bit of
"heroism" up for sale—but only "for cash," even if only for three
mouldy copper pennies. After all, one must immediately see its "use"
on the sales counter.

For you people, the simple words of honest and upright men
have not been spoken: "Here I stand, I can't do otherwise; God help
me!"[1] Luckily, world history, up until this point, has not been made
by people like yourselves. Otherwise, we wouldn't have had a
Reformation, and we probably would still be living in the *ancien
régime*.

As for me, although I have never been soft, lately I have grown
hard as polished steel, and I will no longer make the smallest
concession either in political or personal intercourse. When I think of
your heroes, a creepy feeling comes over me: the adorable Haase;
Dittmann[2] with the lovely beard and those lovely Reichstag speeches;
the uncertain pastor Kautsky whom your Emmo naturally follows
through thick and thin; the magnificent Arthur [Stadthagen]—Ah,
there's no end to it!

I swear to you: I would rather do time for years on end—and I do
not mean to say here, where after all compared to those previous places, I am in heaven, but rather in the joint on Alexanderplatz where,
morning and night without light, I was squeezed between the C (but
without the W) and the iron cot in an 11 cbm cell and where I recited
my Mörike—than (excuse the expression) "struggle" along with your
heroes, or, generally speaking, have anything to do with them! Even

Count Westarp[3] would be better—and not because in the Reichstag he spoke of my "almond-shaped velvet eyes," but because he is a *man*!

Let me tell you, as soon as I can stick my nose outside again, I will chase and hunt your company of frogs with trumpet calls, cracks of the whip and bloodhounds—I was going to say like Penthesilea, but by God, not one of you is an Achilles![4]

Do you have enough now for a New Year's greeting? Then see that you remain a *Mensch*! Being a *Mensch* is the main thing! And that means to be firm, lucid and cheerful. Yes, cheerful despite everything and anything—since whining is the business of the weak. Being a *Mensch* means happily throwing one's life "on fate's great scale" if necessary, but, at the same time, enjoying every bright day and every beautiful cloud. Oh, I can't write you a prescription for being a *Mensch*. I only know how one *is* a *Mensch*, and you used to know it too when we went walking for a few hours in the Südende fields with the sunset's red light falling on the wheat.

The world is so beautiful even with all its horrors, and it would be even more beautiful if there were no weaklings or cowards. Come, you still get a kiss, because you are a sincere little dear. Happy New Year!

R

Notes

[1]These were Martin Luther's famous words, which he uttered before the Emperor Charles V and which ushered in the Reformation.

[2]Wilhelm Dittmann (1874-1954): A German social democrat, leader of the USPD, people's commissar in 1918. After 1920, he rejoined the SPD.

[3]Count Westarp was the leader of the conservative forces in the Reichstag and later leader of the German nationalists. In this and the following letter, Rosa Luxemburg expresses sentiments that account for the occasional rapprochements between the far Left and the far Right.

[4]In Heinrich von Kleist's drama *Penthesilea*, the Amazon queen kills Achilles, whom she loves.

To Hans Diefenbach

Wronke in Posen Fortress
1/7/17

Hänschen, today is Sunday, which has always been a noxious day for me. For the first time since my stay here began, I feel "as poor and abandoned as that God from Nazareth." Because of this, just today a feeling arose: I must write to Hänschen. You aren't angry with me that I've been silent for so long, are you? For all that, I was thrilled each time I received your letters; I laughed myself silly over them and thought of you a great deal. Hänschen, when will we once again have our beautiful nights in Südende? Nights when you will read Goethe aloud, between countless cups of tea, and I, with Mimi on the sofa, will give myself up to happy laziness; or, when we will argue about everything under the sun, until at midnight, with a despairing glance at your watch, you will snatch up your hat and run to the railway station at a mad gallop, still whistling *Figaro* back to me from around the corner.

I fear that after the war, quiet and comfort will cease to exist entirely. And by God I feel so little inclination for the impending brawl! Eternally, to have the same sweet personages around; the same Adolf Hoffmann[1] with his Berlin "natural wit" and his Inexpressibles (I beg your pardon!), those pants which look like two collapsing Doric columns; and eternally to have to look at that same broadbrimmed brown plush hat of Father Pancake.[2] I have a horror that these things will surround me to my life's end. "Thrones burst, kingdoms crumble," the world has been turned upside down—but in the end I still cannot break out of the "vicious circle"; eternally the same few dozen people—*et plus ça change, plus ça reste tout à fait la même chose.* So resign yourself to any eventuality! I still don't know what will become of me for, as you know, I too am a land of boundless possibilities.

For you, however, I have at last found a proper calling. That is to say—*entendons-nous*—a side line! Your principal calling remains, now as before, to bring brightness and light into my earthly existence; or, as you with such chivalry put it in your last letter, to be my court jester. Besides that, you are to create a genre for us that does not yet exist in German literature: the literary and historical essay.

For this form is not, as a Franz Bley[3] would imagine, the perfect refuge for spiritual impotence in all other domains. Rather, the essay is just as strict and legitimate an art form as is the *Lied* in music. Why is it that the essay, so brilliantly represented in England and France, is completely lacking in Germany? I think the reason is that the Germans possess too much pedantic thoroughness and too little intellectual grace; when they know something, immediately a heavy dissertation with a bagful of citations results instead of a light sketch. Since alas, Hänschen definitely possesses more grace than knowledge he seems to be ideally suited to brilliantly introduce the essay into Germany. In fact, I am quite serious! After the war, your tippling around on all flower beds like a swallowtail must come to an end, Sir! Get hold of Macaulay[4] in the Tauchnitz ed. (*Historical and Critical Essays*), if you please, and read him carefully.

The drama in Sillenb. dealt me a heavier blow than you can imagine, a blow to my peace and my friendship.[5] You will remind me to be sympathetic. You know that I feel and suffer with every creature; I will rinse off a wasp that slips into my inkwell three times in lukewarm water and then dry it in the sun on the balcony in order to give back to it that little bit of light. But, tell me, why in this case should I not feel sympathy for the *other* side; the one who is being roasted alive and who every God-given day must pass through the seven circles of Dante's hell? And further: my sympathy, like my friendship, has definite bounds; they end a hairbreadth before meanness begins. That is to say, my friends must have their accounts in good order and, at that, not only in their public, but also in their private, most private, lives. But to thunder great words in public about the "freedom of the individual"—and in private life to enslave a human soul through mad passion—I don't understand it and I don't forgive it. Through it all, I miss the two basic elements of a woman's nature: kindness and pride. Dear God, when, if only from a distance, I get a feeling that someone does not like me my very thoughts flee his orbit like a frightened bird. Even a fleeting glance at him seems presumptuous. How can one, oh, how can one prostitute oneself so?

You will remind me of the terrible suffering involved. Well, I'll tell you, Hänschen, if my best friend were to say to me: I have only the choice between committing a base deed and dying of grief, I would tell him with icy calm: Then die. Regarding you, I have a quiet, comforting conviction that you are incapable of meanness even in your thoughts. If your milk-toast temperament and your eternally cold hands irritate me sometimes, still I say: Blessed be this lack of temperament if it reassures me that you will never rampage over others' happiness and peace like a panther. But, in fact, this has little to do with temperament. You know that I possess enough of it to set a prairie ablaze, yet the peace and simple desires of every other human being are a sanctuary to me and I would rather break down before it than violate it. Enough! To no other soul except you will I say a word about this sad affair.

Why, I have not thanked you yet for the Christmas gift. To be sure, it would have pleased me more had I not received it "in nuce" but rather in the finished form of your choice. Still I know that, from your hick town, you could at best have sent me your piano or your orderly, and I have room here for neither one. When will you finally stop this war, so we can once again go to hear *Figaro?* Ach, I am suspicious of you; you leave conquering the French to others and are content with the quieter conquests of French girls; you little good for nothing. That is why the war is not making any headway. But I will not stand for any "annexations," do you hear? And please, above all, let's have a detailed report and a "comprehensive repentant confession." Write here direct to Wronke I.P. Festung, Dr. Lübeck. Write soon. Oh, I forgot, I am well here, don't worry about me. Send me more pictures of you and your nag.

Affectionately,
Your R.

Notes

[1] Adolf Hoffmann (1858-1930): A participant in the founding congress of the Second International, in the Zimmerwald Conference, and in the founding of the USPD. In 1920, he joined the KPD and then returned to the SPD in 1922. An atheist and of modest origin, he was ridiculed by the bourgeoisie in terms not very different from those Rosa Luxemburg uses here. Count Kessler also referred to the "screwdriver pants" of Hugo Preuss, the father of the Weimar Constitution.

[2] The reference is to the social democrat Wilhelm Pfannkuch.

[3] Franz Bley (1871-1942): German avant-garde writer and poet.

[5] Thomas Macaulay (1800-1859): Politician and historian, he wrote essays and a *History of England.*

[5] Refers to Clara Zetkin's marriage troubles. She refused for many years to give a divorce to her (much younger) husband.

To Sonja Liebknecht

Wronke 1/15/17

. . . Oh, today there was a moment in which I felt bitter. The whistle of the locomotive at 3:19 told me that Mathilde was departing, and on my usual "promenade" along the wall I paced back and forth like an animal in a cage, and my heart was convulsed with grief that I could not get away from here as well. Oh! Only to get away from here! But it doesn't matter. Immediately thereafter my heart was given a slap and had to heel; it has already learned to obey—like a well-trained dog. Let's not talk of me.

Sonitschka, do you still remember what we planned for after the end of the war? A trip together to the south. And we will do that! I know that you dream of going with me to Italy, that most exalted land. I, on the contrary, am planning to drag you to Corsica; that's even better than Italy. There, one forgets Europe, at least modern Europe.

Think of a broad, heroic landscape with the strong contours of mountains and valleys. On high, nothing except barren rock formations which are a noble grey; below, luxuriant olive trees, cherry trees, and age-old chestnut trees. And above everything, a prehistoric quiet—no human voices, no bird calls, only a stream rippling somewhere between rocks, or the wind on high whispering between the cliffs—still the same wind that swelled Ulysses' sails. And if you do meet people, they will fit exactly into the landscape.

For example, suddenly, from around the bend of a mountain path, a file of people and animals will appear—the Corsicans always travel behind one another in stretched-out single files, not in crowds like our peasants. Usually, a dog runs in front, then slowly along comes a goat or a little donkey laden down with sacks of chestnuts. Then, there follows a large mule, on which a woman, with a child in her arms, is riding side-saddle, her legs dangling straight down. She sits erect, immobile, slim like a cypress. Alongside, a bearded man is walking in a quiet firm stride. Both are silent.

You would swear: it's the Holy Family. And you encounter such scenes all the time. I was so moved every time that, instinctively, I wanted to sink to my knees as I always must before perfect beauty. There the Bible and antiquity are still alive. We must go there and do it the way I did it: across the whole island on foot, rest at a different place every night, and start out early each morning to greet the sunrise. Does that tempt you? I would be happy to show you this world.

Read a great deal. You must also progress intellectually, and you can do it—you are still fresh and flexible. And now I must close. Be cheerful and calm on this day.

Your
Rosa

To Hans Diefenbach

[No date]

Hänschen! I am so madly looking forward to your visit! Just no surprises. If necessary, send me a telegram when you expect to come.

And another thing: 1) come in uniform; 2) be as natural here as you would be, were we at home. I will not forego the customary kiss on arrival either; because if you are stiff and self-conscious, inevitably I will be even more so, and then neither of us will get anything out of the visit. Well, I await you with impatience!

Affectionately,

Your R.

To Emanuel and Mathilde Wurm

Wronke i. P. Fortress, 2/16/17
(Send your *sealed* letters here
directly, and without marking them
"prisoner-of-war" letters.)

Dearest Tilde,

Received letter, card and biscuits—many thanks. Don't worry, despite the boldness of your parry, even to the point where you declare war, I will remain as fond of you as always. I had to smile: you want to "fight" me. Young lady, I sit tall in the saddle. No one has yet laid me low, and I would be curious to know the one who can do it. But I had to smile for yet another reason: because you do not even want to "fight" me, and also you are more dependent upon me politically than you would wish to believe. I will always remain your compass, because your straightforward nature tells you that I have the most infallible judgment—because with me all the annoying side issues are forgotten: anxiousness, routine, parliamentary cretinism, which cloud the judgment of others. Your whole argument against my watchword—"Here I stand, I can't do otherwise!"—amounts to the following: Good, so be it, but the masses are too cowardly and weak for such heroism. *Ergo*, one must fit tactics to their weakness and to the axiom: "Walk softly, and you'll walk safely."

What a narrow historical view, my little lamb! There is nothing more mutable than human psychology. The psyche of the masses like the eternal sea always carries all the latent possibilities: the deathly calm and the roaring storm, the lowest cowardice and the wildest heroism. The mass is always that which it *must* be according to the circumstances of the time, and the mass is always at the point of becoming something entirely different than what it appears to be. A fine captain he would be who would chart his course only from the momentary appearance of the water's surface and who would not know how to predict a coming storm from the signs in the sky or from the depths! My little girl, the "disappointment over the masses" is always the most shameful testimony for a political leader. A leader in the grand style does not adapt his tactics to the momentary mood of the masses, but rather to the iron laws of development; he holds fast to his tactics in spite of all "disappointments" and, for the rest, calmly allows history to bring its work to maturity. With that, let us "close the debate." I will gladly remain your friend. Whether, as you wish, I am to remain your teacher, that depends on *you*.

You remind me of an evening six years ago, when we went to Schlachtensee together to wait for the comet. Strange—I can't recall it at all. But you awaken another memory in me. At the time, on an October evening, I was sitting with Hans Kautsky (the painter) at the Havel river, opposite the Peacock Island, and we were also awaiting the comet. There was a deep twilight, yet a dark purple streak was still gleaming on the horizon, which was reflected in the Havel, and which transformed the water's surface into a huge rose petal. A white squall passed over it, and created dark scales on the water, which was sprinkled with a swarm of black dots. These were wild ducks, which had stopped in their flight for a rest on the Havel, and their muted cries—in which so much longing and breadth resounded—were transmitted over to us.

There was a wonderful ambience and we sat quietly, as if bewitched. I looked at the Havel, and Hans accidently looked at me. Suddenly he rose in terror, and grabbed my hand: "What's the matter with you?" he shouted. You see, a meteor had descended behind his back and had bathed me in a phosphorescent green light; I must have appeared as pale as a corpse. And since I had jumped violently seeing this strange spectacle which was invisible to him, Hans probably could not help thinking that I was dying. (Later he made a beautiful, large painting of that evening at the Havel.)

That you now have neither time nor interest for anything except the "single issue," namely the quandary of the Party, is calamitous. For such one-sidedness also clouds one's political judgment; and above all, one must live as a full person at all times.

But look, Lady, since you so rarely get to open a book, at least read only *good* books and not kitsch like the "Spinoza-novel" which you sent to me. What do you want with this particular suffering of the Jews? The poor victims on the rubber plantations in Putumayo, the Negroes in Africa with whose bodies the Europeans play a game of catch, are just as near to me. Do you remember the words written on the work of the Great General Staff about Trotha's campaign in the

Kalahari desert? "And the death-rattles, the mad cries of those dying of thirst, faded away into the sublime silence of eternity."

Oh, this "sublime silence of eternity" in which so many screams have faded away unheard. It rings within me so strongly that I have no special corner of my heart reserved for the ghetto: I am at home wherever in the world there are clouds, birds and human tears. . . .

Your

R

To Sonja Liebknecht

Wronke 2/18/17

. . . For a long time, nothing has shaken me like Marta's short report of your visit to Karl, how you found him behind bars and how this affected you. Why have you kept this from me? I have a claim to take part in anything that hurts you, and I will not have my proprietary rights abridged!

By the way, this vividly reminded me of my first reunion with my brother and sisters in the Warsaw citadel 10 years ago. There, one is brought out into an actual double cage of wire netting: that is to say, a little cage stands within a larger one, and you must converse through the moiré-like glimmer of the double mesh. On top of it all, since the meeting took place right after a 6-day hunger strike, I was so weak that the captain of the fortress nearly had to carry me into the visiting room, and in the cage I had to hold onto the wire with both hands, which probably reinforced the impression of a wild animal in a zoo.

The cage stood in a fairly dark corner of the room, and my brother pressed his face very close to the wire: "Where are you?" he asked over and over, wiping from his pince-nez the tears which kept him from seeing me. How gladly and happily I would now sit there in the Luckau cage in order to spare Karl!

Extend my heartiest thanks to [Franz] Pfemfert[1] for the Galsworthy. Yesterday I finished it and am very pleased with it. To be sure, I liked this novel much less than *The Man of Property* not in spite of—but rather because—in it the social message is more predominant. In a novel, I do not look to the message, but rather to the artistic value. And in this respect, what bothers me, in *Fraternity*, is that Galsworthy is too sophisticated. That will no doubt make you wonder. But he's the same type as Bernard Shaw and also Oscar

Wilde, a type which today seems quite common among English intellectuals: a very clever, refined, but *blasé* man who looks at the whole world with a smiling skepticism. The fine, ironic remarks which Galsworthy makes about his own *personae dramatis* often make me laugh out loud. But, as truly well-brought-up and distinguished people never, or only rarely, deride their surroundings, even should they consider everything laughable, so a true artist never uses irony on his own characters.

Don't get me wrong, Sonitschka: this does not exclude satire of the grand style. For example, *Emanuel Quint* by Gerhart Haupt-mann[2] is the most lethal satire on modern society that has been written in a hundred years. But Hauptmann himself does not smirk; at the end, he is standing with quivering lips and wide open eyes in which tears are glistening. Galsworthy, by contrast, with his witty asides affects me like a dinner companion who, at a soirée, will whisper some malice into my ear about each new guest who enters the parlor.

Today is Sunday once again, the deadliest day for those who are imprisoned and lonely. I am depressed, but ardently wish that you are not, and that Karl is not either. Write soon as to when and where you will finally be going for a rest. I affectionately embrace you and regards to the children.

Your Rosa

Couldn't Pfemfert possibly send me something else that's good? Perhaps something by Thomas Mann? I still have read nothing by him. One more request: outdoors, the sun is beginning to blind me. Could you perhaps send me one meter of thin black veiling with scattered black dots in an ordinary envelope? Many thanks in advance.

Notes

[1]Franz Pfemfert (1879-1954): He was a major force in the avant-garde movement with his journal, *Die Aktion*.

[2]*The Fool in Christ: Emanuel Quint*. (See next letter, note 5).

To Hans Diefenbach

Wronke i. P. 3/5/17

Dearest Hänschen,

Your assumptions regarding my impulsiveness, youthfulness

and similar flattering things are based on error. First of all, I did write you—a beautiful 8-page letter. I just haven't sent it off yet (for proof, I enclose the drawing which decorated the letter, perhaps you will like it). Secondly, I have been living in constant anticipation, spurred on by longing, that any day now you appear before me in person. It seems that Herr von Kessel [1] has found out how he can hurt me the most, and now he means to put me to the test as to whether I can "hold out." Don't make it harder for me by being angry. Keep on writing me. Don't get tired—be loving and patient with me as always, even if I'm not worth it.

To tell you the truth, I am now going through a somewhat difficult time. It has happened again, exactly like last year at Barnimstrasse: for 7 months I hold myself erect; during the eighth and ninth my nerves suddenly fail me. Each day that I have to spend here becomes a minor mountain to be wearily climbed, and every little thing irritates me grievously.

In 5 days, fully 8 months of the second year of my solitude will have come to an end. Then, surely, like last year, a revival will occur of its own, especially since spring is coming. By the way, everything would be a lot less difficult to put up with if only I wouldn't forget the basic resolution which I made for my life: to be *good*. That's the main thing! To be good—plain and simple; that resolves and binds everything. It's better than all the intelligence in the world. But who is going to remind me of this if even Mimi isn't here? At home, with her long silent look, she often knew how to lead me on to the right path, so that (just to spite you!) I simply had to smother her with kisses and say: "You're right, being good is the main thing." So, if you should ever notice, either from my speech or silence, that I am sulking or being cranky, just remind me of Mimi's motto and—set me the example: you be good, even if I don't deserve it.

Now, before anything else, many thanks—the list has grown long—for the booklets, for the saccharin (to be returned with interest, since I received a large provision, and you need it for yourself), for the picture, for the thermometer, for the sweets, for the last two books and especially, for the portraits of the Roman emperors, which serve as a vivid education in republicanism. But, above all, thank you for the letters, which are a great comfort to me. Your adventure in Wronke amused me greatly; a pity that I couldn't join it, or even catch a glimpse of what was happening. I tremendously enjoyed the letter in which you most artfully try to seduce me into reading Hebbel [2] and look forward to my ignorance. How glad I am that you are still the same irrepressible Hänschen, who cannot imagine that I should know of and understand something which I have not received from your hands, the dear hands of the mentor.

Oh Hanneslein, I've known Hebbel much longer than I've known you. I borrowed him from Mehring during the period of our most glowing friendship. This was when the area between Steglitz and Friedenau (where I was still living) presented a tropical landscape in which the *Elephas primigenus* and giraffes picked the green leaves off the phoenix palms. At that time, when Hänschen hadn't even been thought of in Berlin, I read *Agnes Bernauer, Maria Magdalena, Judith, Herodes and Marianne.* I did not get any further, for the tropical climate abruptly had to make way for the great glacial period and my fat Gertrud had to travel to Steglitz, with a basket full of presents and borrowed books, in exchange for . . . a similar cargo which arrived in Friedenau because of our annual "disengagement."

Anyway, I know Hebbel and I have a great, if cool, respect for him. I place him, however, far below Grillparzer[3] and Kleist.[4] He has a great deal of intelligence and a beautiful style, yet his characters have too little blood and life; they are, all too often, simply the carriers of artificial and overrefined problems. If you wish to make me a present of him, however, perhaps I might exchange him for Grillparzer? This is a writer whom I seriously love. Do you know him and do you value him highly enough? If you want to read something excellent, then read *Judith.* There you have the purest Shakespeare in his conciseness, pertinence and popular humor, along with a soft, poetic touch which even Shakespeare does not have. Isn't it ridiculous that Grillparzer should have been a dry civil servant and a bore? (See his autobiography, which is almost as insipid as Bebel's.)

But what about your reading? Are you well supplied? Lately, in fact, I have made a number of good acquaintances whom I dearly wish to introduce to you. Especially—in case you don't know him already—*Emanuel Quint* by Gerhart Hauptmann[5] (a novel). Do you know the Christ pictures by Hans Thoma?[6] Well, in this book, you will experience the vision of a slender Christ passing through ripe cornfields in a shimmer of reddish light, while around his dark figure, to the left and right, soft lavender waves flow over the silver sheaves.

Among countless others, one problem struck me which I have never seen presented above, a problem which I have deeply known in my own experience: the tragedy of an individual who preaches to the masses and who feels, at the very moment the words fall from his mouth, that each becomes crude and caricatured in the heads of the listeners. The preacher is nailed onto this distortion and, from the disciples who surround him, he can only hear the crude clamor: "Show us the miracle. So you have taught us. Where is your miracle?" The way Hauptmann depicts this is sheer genius. Hänschen, one should never make final judgments about men; they can still surprise one—sometimes in the worst sense but also, thank God, in the best. I considered Hauptmann a complete fool, and then the fellow pulls off this type of book, so full of depth and grandeur that I would have loved immediately to write him a feverish letter. I know, *you* would have encouraged me, just as you wanted me to write to Ricarda Huch. But I am too shy and reticent for such ostentatious confessions. It is enough for me that I confess to you.

I still have a thousand things to say. When are you finally coming?

Affectionately,
Your R.

Notes

[1]Herr von Kessel was Rosa Luxemburg's prosecutor.

[2]Friedrich Hebbel (1813-1863): One of the finest German playwrights of the period.

[3]Franz Grillparzer (1791-1872): Austrian playwright of the Biedermeier period.

[4]Heinrich von Kleist (1777-1811): A major playwright in world literature, he is best known for his play *Prince Friedrich of Hamburg* and for his short stories *Michael Kohlhaas* and *The Marquise of O.*

[5]Gerhart Hauptmann (1862-1946): An early naturalist, Hauptmann's *The Weavers* made his fame. Rosa's sympathetic consideration of *Emanuel Quint* is not shared by Hauptmann himself. In the book, one of the uncomprehending disciples is a shrill, hot-tempered Polish agitator of Jewish descent—clearly, Rosa Luxemburg herself. It's fascinating that she does not recognize—or perhaps chooses not to mention—her own caricatured portrait. By that time, Hauptmann was no longer a socialist.

[6]Hans Thoma (1839-1924): The neoclassical canvas by Thoma is as idealistic and pretty as Rosa describes. It is a perfect example of pre-World War I popular taste that was shared by radicals.

To Hans Diefenbach

Wronke i. P. Fortress
3/8/17

Hänschen,

Of those thousand things that I had to say, here are another handful. Now, once again, I'm in a quieter frame of mind, and therefore, I want to write you. Because I didn't want to sadden you, I did not send you that torn-up letter; in black and white, a passing depression looks much more tragic than it is in reality. I am now writing you principally for the following reason. Frl. Mathilde Jacob, who is here, will be travelling to Posen and hopes to see you. I instigated that idea, because I thought that it would be all right with you. She will report to you about me in detail and will transmit to you my most burning greetings—but something else too! And this something is my manuscript of the *Anti-Critique*,[1] the reply to Eckstein, Bauer[2] and Co., in defense of my book on accumulation! You, poor devil, have been chosen to be the second reader of this opus. (The first was Mehring, of course, who has read the manuscript several times. After the first reading, he called it "simply a work of genius," "a truly magnificent, ravishing achievement" the like of which had not appeared since Marx's death. In a later report—in the meantime we had become temporarily "embroiled"—his praise was more measured! . . .) As a matter of fact, this is a work which I am pretty proud of, and which will certainly outlive me. It is much more mature than the *Accumulation* itself: its form is extremely simple, without any accessories, without coquetry or optical illusions, straightforward and reduced to the barest essentials; I would even say "naked," like a block of marble. This is, in fact, where today my taste lies. In theoretical work as in art, I value only the simple, the tranquil and the bold. This is why, for example, the famous first volume of Marx's *Kapital*, with its profuse rococo ornamentation in the Hegelian style, now seems an abomination to me (for which, from the Party standpoint, I must get 5 years' hard labor and 10 years' loss of civil rights. . . .) Of course, in order to intelligently appreciate it, the reader of my *Anti-Critique* must thoroughly master political economy in general and Marxian economics in particular. And how many such mortals are there today? Not a half dozen. From this standpoint, my works really are luxury items and could be printed on handmade paper. The *Anti-Critique*, however, is at least free of the algebraic formulas which provoke such panic in a "simple reader." In general, I believe that you will understand my stuff, for Mehring praises precisely its "crystal clarity and the transparency of the presentation." Well, you shall read it and give me your judgment as "a simple man of the people." Your opinion on the artistic aspects of the presentation is of the greatest importance to me. But I also want to see how much of it you will grasp. All right, now to work! "Up, boy" or if you aren't able, read it while lying down. But get to it, and write me your impressions. Nor will getting another taste of political economy do you any harm.

Ah, Hänschen! If only winter were over! This weather crushes me; at this point, I just can't withstand any cruelty from people or nature. Every year, by this time, I would be making my travel arrangements so that by the 7th or 10th of April I would be at Lake Geneva. It's now three years since I saw it last. Oh, that beautiful dreamy-blue Lake Geneva. Do you recall the amazement which is experienced when, after the desolate Bern-Lausanne stretch and the last terribly long tunnel, you suddenly float above a great blue sheet of sea! Every time my heart would soar up like a butterfly. And then, that glorious stretch from Lausanne to Clarens, with those tiny stations every twenty minutes. Deep down, near the water, those little houses grouped around a small white church and then the tranquil, sing-song call of the conductor, the station bell tinkles—three times, and again three times, and again; the train slowly starts, but the bell still keeps ringing so bright and gay. And the blue mirror, the water surface keeps changing in relation to the train tracks. Sometimes it appears to be at an upward angle, sometimes it trails downwards, and you see the steamers creeping like June bugs falling into the water and a train of white foam. And that white embankment beyond—the steep white mountainside, its foot hidden in blue haze most of the time so that only unreal, snow-covered tops float high up in the sky. And above everything, the splendid, powerful Dent du Midi. Dear God, when will I ever again experience April there! Every time, the air and the quiet and the serenity flow into my soul like balsam.

In my Chailly sur Clarens, the vineyards are still overgrown with last year's weeds, the clearing-away begins only gradually. I am still allowed to saunter around the vineyards and pick the red dead-nettles and the hypnotizingly fragrant sapphire-blue hyacinths which grow there in countless bunches. At 11 o'clock, the peasant is brought his lunch in a basket; the father, in shirt sleeves, puts down the spade and sits down on the ground while his wife, and the children who came along, squat around him. The basket is opened and the family silently eats the meal. The father wipes the sweat from his brow with his sleeve because the April sun is mighty strong here in the vineyard. And I am lying silently nearby, letting the sun glow through me, watching the vine grower's family through squinted eyes, chewing on a blade of grass, without a single thought in my head, but with one simple feeling all over my body: Dear God! How beautiful the world is, and life! And above, on the Col de Jamen, a little train creeps upward from Glion like a dark caterpillar. On high, there is a tiny veil of smoke fluttering in the air like the distant wave of a departing friend! . . .

Hänschen, adieu,

R.

Notes

[1]The *Anti-Critique* was Rosa Luxemburg's response to the critics of *The Accumulation of Capital.* This work also restates the essential thesis of her larger opus in a much more accessible form.

[2]Otto Bauer (1882-1938): A leader of the Austrian Social Democratic Party, who was also influential in the Second International and one of the major critics of Rosa Luxemburg's *The Accumulation of Capital.* It is generally to his arguments that she responds in the *Anti-Critique.*

To Hans Diefenbach

Wronke i. P. 3/27/1917
Evening

Dear H.,

What's going on?! On the 13th you write that "tomorrow" you will send me a comprehensive letter, and then I hear nothing for two weeks. I was already making the blackest conjectures about your illness, sudden departure, etc., etc. What's more: After the bitter disappointment caused by the refusal, letters are my only consolation. Well, mend your ways: Don't work so long on one letter or, at least, send me more postcards in between.

By the way, what do you mean saying that you are "working hard?" After all, you are still a patient!! Or, what type of "work" do you mean?

You can well imagine how the events in Russia threw me into an inner turmoil. So many an old friend, who for years languished in jail in Moscow, Petersburg, Orel or Riga, now walks free.[1] How this lightens my incarceration here! A funny *change de places*, isn't it? But I'm content and begrudge no one his freedom, even though precisely because of this my own chances for freedom have grown slimmer. . . .

As far as my consulting Dr. L. is concerned, the cure essentially reduces itself to the advice which the good old Ufenau parson gave to the deathly ill Hutten:

Now try to rest
Don't listen to the outside world

> In this quiet bay the tempest of the age dies down
> Forget, Hutten, that you are Hutten.

And Hutten's reply:

> Your advice, my dear friend, is wonderful indeed.
> I am supposed not to live . . . so that I may live.[2]

Well, I never grieve long over the unattainable. Instead, I concentrate with all my soul on the present and the beauty it offers. By the way, the worst period is already past and I breathe more freely—the ominous 8th month ended yesterday. We had a bright, sunny day, if somewhat cool, and in the sunshine the tangle of the barren shrubs in my little garden shimmered in all the colors of the rainbow. In addition, the larks, high in the sky, were already warbling and, in spite of the snow and the cold, still one could sense that spring was near. This brought to mind that last year, around this time, I was free, between two jail terms, and at Easter I sat listening to *The St. Matthew's Passion* with Karl and his wife in the Garnison Church.[3]

Still, who needs Bach and *The St. Matthew's Passion*! When I simply stroll on the streets of my Südende on a warm spring day—I think that everyone there knows me by my dreamy wanderings—both hands in the pockets of my jacket, walking without any purpose except that of gazing around me and absorbing life. . . . From the houses, one can hear the clang of spring cleaning—of mattresses being beaten, a hen cackling loudly somewhere, little school boys wrestling on their way home amid bright cries and laughter. A train passes, whistling a short greeting into the air; a heavy beer wagon rattles down the street and the hooves of its horses knock rhythmically and forcefully on the railway bridge. In between, the sparrows chirp noisily. Thus, in the brightest sunlight, a symphony emerges, an *Ode to Joy*, which neither a Bach nor a Beethoven could reproduce. And my heart exults over everything, over each sober detail.

I stand near other gawkers at the little Südende Station in front of which there are always little groups of people hanging around. Do you remember? Left, the flower store; right, the cigar store. How magnificent the tangle of colors in the flower shop window! From inside, the pretty salesgirl smiles at me while looking over the flowers which she is selling to a lady. She knows me well, since I never pass by without buying a little nosegay, even if it should cost me my last 10 pfennigs. Lottery tickets are displayed in the window of the cigar store; aren't they adorable? I smile, happy about the horse racing tickets. Inside the store, with its door wide open, someone is speaking (for 5 pfennigs) loudly into the telephone: "Yeah. What? Yeah. I'll be there around 5 o'clock. OK, fine. All right. Goodbye. Around 5 o'clock. Goodbye. Adieu." . . . How likable this greasy voice and this stupid talk! How delightful that this gentleman will arrive somewhere at 5 o'clock. I would almost like to call out to him: Please give my regards—to whom I don't know. Whomever you like. . . .

Two old women are standing here with shopping bags on their arms, gossiping with their usual expressions of having confided sour secrets. I find them lovable. . . . On the corner, the gaunt, one-eyed news vendor trips along. Rubbing his hands, he cries, automaton-like, his eternal "Voschsche Paapar with Pitchurs". . . . When the weather is bad—after all, I must pass by here every day on my way to the Party School—this fellow's enunciation drives me to despair and, every time, I lose hope that I can ever make something worthwhile out of my life. But now, since he is bathed in the April sunlight from top to bottom, I find his "Pitchurs" touching. I smile at him as I would at an old friend and, by buying a paper, try to apologize for the grim looks which I hurled at him in winter. . . . On the other corner is a little tavern-restaurant with yellow blinds which are always lowered. Those dirty opaque windows and the tables outside in the front garden on the gravel, with the eternal red-blue checkered tablecloths, which usually make me so melancholy that I just must rush past in order not to burst into tears, seem decidedly pretty today. Look how the shadows of the maple tree branches nearby play upon the tables. Notice how quietly they sway to and fro—can there be anything lovelier?

And here at the baker's, the door creaks loudly as it continually opens and closes. Spruce house maids and small children go in and, loaded with white paper bags, come out again. Doesn't the continual creaking somehow mix with the appetizing pastry fragrance from the baker and the sparrows chirping in the street? Isn't there a flavor of competence and quiet assurance? Doesn't it all seem to say: "I am life and life is beautiful?" . . .

Now, from the bakery, where I stand gazing, the grandmother of the shoemaker who lives on my street emerges, old as the hills. "Fräulein, I thought you were going to visit us for coffee," she says with a toothless mouth. (In Südende, everyone calls me "Fräulein." I don't know why.) I can barely understand her, but cheerfully promise to come sometime, for sure. Smiling, she nods and her whole wizened old face beams: "But, be sure!" she calls back to me. Dear God, how nice and good people really are; there again, a lady whom I don't even know, bids me hello and, smiling, looks back at me. Probably, I look a bit peculiar with my happy, beaming face and my hands in my pockets. But what do I care? Is there any higher happiness than such aimless hanging around in the spring sun, hands in your pockets and a little nosegay for 10 pfennigs, in your buttonhole?

Hänschen, I think that Posen is farther east than Wronke; the April sun reaches you first. So, send it to me posthaste. Once again, let it show me the wonders of life that can be found spread all over the place; let it make me good, clear-sighted and tranquil once again.

R.

Notes

[1]She is obviously referring to the February Revolution that overthrew the Czar.

[2]Conrad Ferdinand Meyer (1825-1898): One of Rosa's favorite writers. The lines are from Meyer's *Hutten's Last Days.*

[3]Compare this with Lenin's famous reaction to Beethoven's *Apassionata*: "Beautiful, but one must not listen to such beauty for too long, or else one might forget the revolution."

To Hans Diefenbach

Wronke i. P. 3/30/17

D. H.

With a great effort, I had just regained my composure, when a despair gripped me which was far blacker than the night. And today, once again, it is grey instead of sunny—a cold east wind. . . . I feel like a frozen bumble bee. Did you ever find such a bumble bee in your garden in the first frost of an autumn morning? It lies on its back, quite numb as if it were dead, with its little legs tucked in and its fur covered with hoar frost. Only when the sun warms it through, do the legs slowly begin to stir and stretch. Then the little body rolls over and finally, clumsily, rises into the air with a buzz. I always made it my duty to kneel down by such frozen bumble bees and, with the warm breath from my mouth, bring them back to life. If only the sun would awake me, poor soul that I am, from my cold death! In the meantime, like Luther, I'm fighting the devils inside me—with an inkwell.[1] That's why, as a sacrifice, you must withstand a barrage of letters. Until you have loaded your large gun, I will so bombard you with my low-caliber one that you will be in fear and trembling. By the way, if at the front you have been loading your cannon with the same speed with which you have been writing your letters, then I'm not at all surprised by our present retreat at the Somme and Ancre. It will surely be on *your* conscience should we have to conclude peace without annexing beautiful Flanders.

I thank you very much for Ricarda Huch's little book on Keller. Last week, when I felt most wretched, I read it with pleasure. Ricarda is really an extremely bright and intelligent person. Yet, her style, which is so very etiolated, reserved, and controlled, seems to me somewhat contrived; her deliberate classicism suggests something pseudoclassical to me. Someone who is really rich and free in his mind can be natural at any time and allow himself to be carried away by his passion without becoming untrue to himself.

I also reread Gottfried Keller; the *Zurich Novellas* and *Martin Salander*. Please don't go up the wall, but I maintain that Keller cannot write either novels or novellas. What he always presents are only *stories* about things and people long since dead and gone. I am never involved when something happens. I only see the narrator rummaging up beautiful memories in the manner of old people. Only the first part of *Der grüne Heinrich* really *lives*. Just the same, Keller always does me good because he's such a wonderful guy and, with a fellow whom one loves, it's nice to sit and chat about insignificant things and little remembrances.

I have never experienced a spring more consciously or more intensely than the last one—perhaps because it followed the year in jail, or because by now I know every shrub and every little blade of grass with an exactitude which allows me to follow the development of each. Do you remember how a few years ago, by a blooming yellow bush, we tried to figure out what it was? You made "the suggestion" that we identify it as "laburnum." Naturally, it wasn't. How glad I am that three years ago I suddenly threw myself into botany! And I did it the way I do everything, with all the fervor I possess, with all of my self. The world, the Party and work vanished. Night and day, I was filled with this one passion: roving in spring meadows, collecting armfuls of flowers, then going home, sorting them, identifying them, and mounting them in books. How intensely I lived all that spring! As if in a fever! How I suffered sitting by a new little plant, for a long time not knowing how to categorize it. Sometimes I would nearly faint in those instances, and Gertrud would angrily threaten to "take the plants away." But I now feel myself at home in the green kingdom. I've conquered it, in storm and in passion—and what one seizes with so much ardor grows deep roots within one.

Last spring I still had a partner on those hikes: Karl Liebknecht. Perhaps you know how he had been living for so many years. Parliamentary sessions, commissions, conferences; hurry-scurry, continually on the go, from train to tram and from tram to automobile, all his pockets stuffed with note pads and all his arms full of newly bought newspapers which he would never have time to read. His body and his soul were covered with the grime of the street, and yet there was always that genial young smile on his face. Last spring, I had convinced him to take a little rest, to remind himself that a world exists outside the Reichstag and the Landtag. Many were the times that he sauntered through the fields and botanical gardens with Sonja and me. How he enjoyed himself—like a child—looking at a birch tree with new catkins!

Once we hiked across the fields to Marienfelde. You know the way—do you remember? We took the trip in autumn and had to walk over stubble. But, last April with Karl, it was morning and the fields still carried the fresh green of the winter crop. A mild wind pursued the grey clouds to and fro in the sky. And the fields now were beaming in the bright sunlight, now they were darkening like emeralds in the shadows—a splendid play, and we silently marched along. Suddenly, Karl stopped and began making strange leaps into the air, while keeping a solemn look on his face. I watched him amazed, even a bit frightened, and asked: "What's wrong with you?" "I'm so blissfully happy," he answered simply, at which point we naturally broke into fits of laughter.

Affectionately,

R.

You unjustly wanted to have me classified as "the most beautiful and precious stone" in Hindenburg's[2] pearl necklace. But, according to the official statement, I am *not* a prisoner of war. Proof: I must pay the postage for my letters.

Notes

[1]Martin Luther is said to have thrown an inkwell at the devil.

[2]Paul von Hindenburg (1847-1934): To whom the victory over the Russians was attributed; later commander-in-chief on the Western front. The symbol of German nationalism, he became president of the Weimar Republic in 1925 and named Hitler chancellor in 1933.

Karl and Sonja (or Sophie) Liebknecht on a hike, shortly after their marriage.

To Marta Rosenbaum

Wronke, April, 1917

Dearest Martchen!

Many thanks for your affectionate card. For me too, your visit was refreshing; my body and my spirit are still feasting on it. All that love and goodness radiating from you, after all, must warm anyone. Also, this time everything went much better and more "humanely," than I feared it would, and I hope that the next time you are here it will be even better yet. As for the rest, I continue to live in the same way: during my walks in the ugly prison courtyard, I dream of something beautiful so intensely that I don't even notice the surroundings; I spend the remaining hours in my cell, reading all the time and working in a calm mood. For about a week, naturally, all my thoughts have been in Petersburg, and every morning and evening I grab the latest newspaper with impatient hands. But, unfortunately, the information is scant and confused. A lasting success there is, surely not to be counted upon; yet the very beginning of a seizure of power is a punch in the face of the local Social Democrats and the entire slumbering International. Sure, Kautsky knows nothing better than to prove statistically that Russian social conditions are not yet ripe for the dictatorship of the proletariat. A worthy "theorist" of the Independent Socialist Party! He has forgotten that "statistically" France in 1789 and even in 1793 was even less ripe for the rule of the bourgeoisie. . . . Luckily, history has long since stopped following Kautsky's theoretical prescriptions. So, let's hope for the best. . . .

Your

R.

To Marta Rosenbaum

Wronke April, 1917

Dear Marta!

I fear that this time it won't be the real thing. Friday (and probably today, too) I was so dazed, and my head spun so, that I just couldn't chat with you quietly and openly. Why? Because of the double supervision—and there is nothing to be done. You are, as I can guess, in the same frame of mind. But it is still a comfort at least to see you and feel your closeness. Too bad that it all goes at such a pace. Next time, you must come on Thursday and stay until Monday or Tuesday. I don't know yet whether tomorrow's kiss of departure will take place. But, if it doesn't, we must get by anyhow! By now I am composed. How thankful I am that you came!

Don't worry about me. In terms of health, my stomach is still not better, but there are signs of slow progress with my nerves. Probably my stomach will quiet down too. If only spring were here! Sun, warmth, and fresh foliage are the most important things for my general condition. After all, you know me!

Well, the wonderful things in Russia affect me like an elixir of life. Isn't what comes from there a message of salvation for all of us? I fear that you all underestimate what is happening there, that you do not realize that it is our own cause which is victorious there. It *must*, it *will* serve as a deliverance for the entire world, it must radiate to all of Europe. I am absolutely convinced that a new epoch is beginning, and that the war cannot last much longer. For that reason, I would like to hear that you are in a better frame of mind, that you are all in high spirits and a happy mood—despite all the misery and horror. Do you see, history knows how to manage where things seem most unmanageable. Be happy and cheerful for me. I embrace you a thousand times, and many regards to Kurt [Rosenfeld].

Your
R.

To Hans Diefenbach

Wronke i. P. 4/16/17

Nr. 2

Hänschen,

Receiving your No. 1 yesterday made the Sunday much more beautiful. Here today, it's raining in torrents. Still, early in the morning, I wandered about in the little garden for two hours—as usual without an umbrella, wearing only an old hat, and wrapped in Grandmother Kautsky's cape. It was so lovely to meditate and dream as I walked while the rain poured through my hat and hair, over my face and down my neck. The birds were also awake. A titmouse, with whom I am especially friendly, often goes for walks with me and he does it this way: I always walk on two sides of the garden, along the walls; the titmouse jumps along in step next to me, from shrub to shrub, once forward and then back. Isn't that adorable? There is no type of weather which we fear, and the two of us have even taken our daily walk in a snowstorm. Today the little bird looked as disheveled, wet, and totally scruffy as I most surely did—and we both felt splendid.

Now, in the afternoon, it is so stormy though that we won't venture outside. The titmouse is sitting on my window grating and is twisting his little head to the right and to the left in order to peer at me through the pane while I sit here at my desk and work, enjoying the ticking of the clock which makes it rather pleasant in the room.

This weather—from what I understand—is calamitous for food production. It is impossible now for the fields to be prepared for the summer crops. Everything is late, and the winter crops have surely suffered the most from the late frost. By this time last year, the winter wheat in Südende was 20-25 cm. high, and the summer field had been prepared by March. Besides, there are also the floods. The poor "from the depths" will, as always, be the ones to suffer. . . . Now, your old man has good reason to grumble: even the heavens seem to be in the pay of the English.[1]

Your Berlin-Stuttgart odyssey sounds frightening. Probably what you missed the most was that, this time, you could not lay the blame on my sinful head for all the mischief of the inanimate—like on our famous Christmas trips to Stuttgart. The idea of traveling peacefully for a few days to Nuremberg and the other provincial towns of the Palatinate, is very enticing. I have only the vaguest idea of Nuremberg and all those other cities to which I only went in order to attend a meeting or a Party Convention. Of the last meeting before the war, I remember only a huge bouquet of glaring red carnations on my lectern, which bothered me while I was speaking, and then, just as I was going to open my mouth, a call resounded which I could not make out at first: "First-Aid!" The hall was in fact overcrowded to the point where three people had to be carried out unconscious. This always has a very depressing effect upon me, and at first I had to pull myself together before I could get warmed up again. Once during the Party Convention, however, someone or other abducted me from the evening session and drove me slowly around the city for a few hours in a comfortable landau. It was the end of September, and the city held a bluish autumn haze, above which emerged a castle, overgrown with green foliage, and the pointed roofs and churches, fantastically colorful as out of the Middle Ages. And over everything there hung the dark-red glimmer of the parting day while, down in the alleys and corners, shadows grew denser in the twilight. A most wonderful remembrance of that hour has remained with me, particularly of the contrast between the heavenly quiet and beauty outside accentuated, so to speak, by the steady clatter of our horses' hooves—and the ragged confusion and tormenting tastelessness seen at the convention. I don't know who sat next to me in the carriage, I know only that, during the entire ride, I didn't say a word and that, upon getting out in front of my hotel, for a moment I glimpsed a disappointed face. I absolutely want to return to Nuremberg, but without meetings or conventions. Instead, I want to bring along a volume of Mörike or Goethe, from which you have so often read to me with your deep bass voice.

What a pity that now, here, you cannot read Shakespeare to me, the way we went through the entire *Wallenstein*.[2] I have had my William brought to me here. (Do you still remember Goethe's:

> To belong to one beloved
> To admire one hero
> Makes heart and mind into one.
> Lida, bliss so proximate
> William, star so high
> To you I owe what I am.

Lida is naturally Frau von Stein.) My renewed interest in him was awakened—believe it or not—by the theater critic of the *Leipziger Volkszeitung*. His reviews are brilliant and very stimulating. Here, for example, is how he describes a female character in *As You Like It*:

> Rosalind is a woman after the poet's own heart. She is a lady as well as a child of nature. She knows what is right and proper, and is able to thumb her nose at all propriety. She is not learned, but knows how to say the most intelligent things. She is full of spirit and full of modesty. She can be all of this because she has sure instincts; trusting in her healthy instincts, she is able to waltz, skip, and stride through the world as if no danger could ever seriously threaten her. This is by no means the only case where Shakespeare draws this type of assured young woman: in his work, one encounters several of this sort. We do not know whether he ever met a woman like Rosalind, Beatrice, or Portia, or whether he had models to work from, or whether he created pictures from his longings. But this we definitely know: from these characters, there speaks his own belief in women. His conviction is that women can be so magnificent because of their special nature. At least for a time in his life, he extolled women as few poets ever did. In women, he saw a force of

nature working which culture could never harm. They take in everything culture offers, adopt it, but do not allow themselves to be led astray from the path which nature prescribes for them.

Isn't this a fine analysis? If you knew what an insipid, dried up, queer fish Dr. Morgenstern is in private! But his psychological penetration is what I would wish for the future creator of the German essay. . . . Apropos: so you are a descendant of Justinus Kerner![3] By God, that's a distinguished ancestor! Yet I know nothing about him. I have had only a general remembrance of brassy rhythms, strong pathos, and a revolutionary gesture. At any rate, the name itself works wonders. Isn't it true that there are certain names made for eternity which ring with an Olympian chord, even though we know nothing specific? Who today knows even one verse of Sappho's?[4] Who (except for myself) reads Machiavelli?[5] Who has heard an opera by Cimarosa?[6] But, for everyone, such a name gives a flash of eternity before which one reverentially removes one's hat. However, *noblesse oblige*. Hänschen, you must make something out of yourself—we owe it to Justinus Kerner.

R.

You say nothing of Clara [Zetkin]. Hope you see her often.

Notes

[1]The following winter did come to be known as the "hungry winter."
[2]*Wallenstein*, written in 1798, is one of Schiller's most important plays.
[3]Justinus Kerner (1786-1862): A minor Munich poet and essayist.
[4]Sappho was a Greek poet, famous for her beautiful love songs.
[5]Nicolo Machiavelli (1469-1527): One of the crucial figures in the development of political thought, who brought the study of politics down from the theological into the secular realm. Machiavelli is best known for his *Prince* and *Discourses*. Machiavelli also wrote some plays, such as *The Mandrake* and *Clizia*.
[6]Domenico Cimarosa (1749-1801): Italian composer whose works include *Il Matrimonia Segreto*. A precursor of Mozart.

To Hans Diefenbach

Wronke i. P. 4/28/1917

Nr. 3
Hänschen,
        Unfortunately, it is impossible for Frau Marta to make a visit to

Lissa at this time. Her vacation is too short. Already you must pay the price for your new home being so far out of the way. You see, I immediately looked up your city in Dierke's old school atlas (in the same old Dierke which traveled with you to the Stuttgart Karls-Gymnasium; I received this copy from Kostia). I found that Lissa lies midway between Posnan and Breslau; that is to say, in the opposite direction from Berlin. In turn, you will certainly see Hans and Luise [Kautsky] in about two weeks. Luise has received permission to visit during the period between the 10th and 15th of May.

I seriously resent your not visiting Clara [Zetkin]. You simply *had* to find the time. Do you understand my psychological situation in this instance? The more I inwardly reproach myself for not standing by her enough at present, the more it was both a necessity and a consolation for me that you were acting better than I. You, so to speak, were to make good the measure of warmth and delicacy of feeling which I could not give. And now you fail me completely! So help me God, I don't remember whether I blurted out that you had been in Stuttgart at Easter. But I ask you to write her directly, with complete openness and honesty, and make up for the negligence with an affectionate letter. Just don't be cowardly and dissemble, Hänschen, it's not worthy of you.

I've finished Ricarda Huch's *Wallenstein*. At first it greatly refreshed and excited me, but in the end the picture comes to nothing. With all the details and miniatures, the whole never emerges. From this piece, you can clearly learn how not to write an essay and how you must improve upon the genre. I still maintain: It is the German's thoroughness which prevents them from creating a picture of a life or of the times, sketched in light strokes, which at the same time could be a full and precious experience. Even Ricarda—though she is a woman—lacks the mental grace which should have told her that exhausting every detail is tiring and offensive to a refined and sensitive reader. Just a few traits, artistically selected, excite the reader's fantasy so that, on his own, he can turn the work into a finished and rounded picture—exactly as in the private intercourse of clever people light intimations are appreciated much more than heavy distinctness.

Very soon, I would like to send you a comedy, *The Philanderer*, by Bernard Shaw. Initially, I was impatient with the screaming paradoxes and absurdities of all the characters involved. But then, a few serious passages appear which one reads with mixed feelings: On the one hand there is relief, for finally one is learning the author's real meaning and intention, but, on the other hand, a certain reserve occurs in regard to his tasteless moralizing maxims. At the end, one discovers that these "serious passages" were the most farcical of all and that Shaw is simply making fun of the whole world, the reader, and also of himself, as if he were following the motto: Nothing in life is worth taking tragically. The closing scene, in which a masked ball breaks in upon two attorneys in the midst of a bone-dry juristic deliberation, and where the two are led out waltzing, actually works in a Shakespearean manner; it wafts into one's face the giggly hobgoblin of *A Midsummer Night's Dream*. Reading this last scene—sitting in my room alone, around midnight—I broke into those cascades of laughter by which you know me. This was just after another little fit of despair had come over me, and so this terrific book did me a world of good.

Since I am talking about literature, listen, can you tell me where I got the following few lines:

> He walks so proud, he stands so tall,
> His smile and eyes the noblest of all,
> His words, a spring of magic bliss,
> The clasp of his hand—

More, I don't know. I could swear that it's Gretchen at the spinning wheel.[1] At the same time, I could swear that Gretchen at the spinning wheel is singing something entirely different, namely The King in Thule. I only have your little Harnack edition of Goethe with me, but not *Faust*, and I can't check. These few rhymes have been going around in my head since Easter to the point where I'm beginning to believe that I have my own spinning wheel inside my head. Do you know how tormenting it is when you are unable to remember from where you have taken a scrap of a poem or a melody?

Directly above my place is the schoolroom of our "panopticon." Just as I'm writing this, class is in session. First I hear the boisterous clattering of several feet, then quiet, then an old teacher's voice lecturing, and now the monotone of a girl's voice reciting—exactly the way small children read out loud, without any pauses, in a high, somewhat diffident, half-questioning tone. I can't distinguish a word, but just this muffled murmuring has such a soothingly homey effect. From this invisible little scene above me, from which only a distant noise breaks through to me, I get the clear feeling again that life is very beautiful.

R.

Notes

[1] Rosa is right; the quote does come from "Gretchen at the Spinning

Hans Diefenbach. (Courtesy International Institute of Social History, Amsterdam)

Wheel" in *Faust*. It is interesting that she should forget the last line—"And ah! His kiss!—" though the German rhyme suggests it. See letter of 6/23/17, p. 212.

To Sonja Liebknecht

Wronke 5/2/17

. . . One morning last April, you may remember, I urgently called the two of you on the telephone at 10 o'clock to go hear the nightingale who was giving a full concert in the botanical gardens. Once there, we sat quietly on the rocks, by a little trickling pool of water hidden in the dense shrubbery. After the nightingale had finished, however, we suddenly heard a monotonous plaintive call which sounded something like: Gligligligliglick! I said that it sounded like some type of marsh or aquatic bird and Karl agreed, but we were absolutely unable to find out what it was.

Just imagine that a few days ago, early in the morning I suddenly heard the same sound here, nearby. My heart pounded with impatience finally to learn what it could be. I had no peace until I found out today: it is not an aquatic bird, but rather a wryneck, a kind of grey woodpecker. It is only a little bigger than a sparrow, and it takes its name from the fact that, when in danger, it attempts to frighten its ememies through comical gestures and contortions of its head. It lives only on ants, which it collects on its sticky tongue like the anteater. That's why the Spaniards call it *Hormiguero*—the ant-bird.

By the way, Mörike wrote a very pretty comical poem about the bird; Hugo Wolf set it to music. For me, it's as if I had received a present, since I learned the nature of this bird with the wailing voice. Perhaps you could also write Karl about it, it would please him.

What am I reading? For the most part, natural science: geography of plants and animals. Only yesterday I read why the warblers are disappearing from Germany. Increasingly systematic forestry, gardening and agriculture are, step by step, destroying all natural nesting and breeding places: hollow trees, fallow land, thickets of shrubs, withered leaves on the garden grounds. It pained me so when I read that. Not because of the song they sing for people, but rather it was the picture of the silent, irresistible extinction of these defenseless little creatures which hurt me to the point where I had to cry. It reminded me of a Russian book which I read while still in Zurich, a book by Professor Sieber about the ravage of the redskins in North America. In exactly the same way, step by step, they have been pushed from their land by civilized men and abandoned to perish silently and cruelly.

I suppose I must be out of sorts to feel everything so intensely. You know, sometimes, it seems to me that I am not really a human being at all, but rather a bird or beast in human form. Inwardly, I feel so much more at home in a plot of garden like the one here, and still more in the meadows when the grass is humming with bees, than at one of our party congresses. Surely I can tell you this, since you will not immediately suspect me of betraying socialism! You know that, in spite of it all, I really hope to die at my post, in a street fight or in prison.

But, my innermost self belongs more to my titmice than to the "comrades." And not because I find a restful refuge in nature like so many morally bankrupt politicians. On the contrary, in nature too, with every step, I find so much that is cruel that I suffer very much. For example, imagine that I cannot get the following little experience out of my mind. Last spring, I was coming home from a walk in the fields, along my silent, empty street, when I noticed a little dark spot on the pavement. I bent down and saw a silent tragedy: a big dung beetle lay on its back, helplessly defending itself with its legs, while a large group of tiny ants swarmed around on top of it and ate it alive! It made my flesh crawl! I took out my handkerchief and began to chase away the brutal little beasts. But, they were so insolent and stubborn that I had to fight a long struggle against them. When I finally freed the poor victim, and placed it far away on the grass, I saw that two of its legs had already been eaten away. . . . I walked away with the agonizing feeling that in the long run I had done it a very dubious favor.

Now, in the evenings, the twilights are long. How I used to love this hour! In Südende there were many blackbirds, here I neither see nor hear any. I fed a pair all through the winter, and now they have vanished. In Südende, around this time of evening, I used to saunter around the streets; it's so lovely when, still in the last violet light of day, suddenly the rosy gaslights on the street lamps flicker on and still look so strange in the twilight as if they felt a bit ashamed of themselves. Through the streets, the vague figure of some tardy woman scurries by, a porter or a servant girl running to the baker's or grocer's in order to buy something. The shoemaker's children, with whom I have made friends, would still play in the dark street until, from the corner, they would be vigorously called to come home. At this hour, some blackbird would remain who couldn't settle down and who suddenly, like a naughty child, would screech in his sleep and then noisily fly from one tree to another. And I would stand there, in the middle of the street, counting the first stars, not wanting to go home and get out of the mild air and the twilight, in which the day and the night would so softly nestle against one another.

Sonjuscha, I will write you again soon. Be calm and cheerful. Everything will be all right—for Karl too. So long, until the next letter.

I embrace you.

Your Rosa

To Hans Diefenbach

Wronke 5/12/17

No. 4

Dear H,

Received No. 5, many thanks. I await your stylistic corrections (some mistakes are those of the typist). Your remark that some passages in the *Anti-Critique* are mutilated to the point of incomprehensibility causes me to revise the manuscript once again. Usually I am never able to reread what I have written; the more strongly I am involved in something while writing it, the more decidedly it is finished for me afterwards. I fully understand, Hänschen, that it appears that I write my economic tracts for a half dozen people. Yet, in fact, I write them for only one person: myself.

The period in which I wrote the *Accumulation* belongs to the happiest of my life. I lived in a veritable trance. Day and night I neither saw nor heard anything as that one problem developed so beautifully before my eyes. I don't know which gave me more pleasure: the process of thinking, when I mulled over a complicated question slowly walking back and forth across the room, closely observed by Mimi, who lay on the red plush tablecloth, her little paws crossed, her intelligent head following me—or the literary creation with pen in hand. Do you know that I wrote the whole 900 pages in 4 months at one sitting? An unheard-of thing! Without checking the rough copy even once, I had it printed. At Barnimstrasse, it was the same with the *Anti-Critique*. Yet then, after the strong involvement, I lose all interest in the work to the point where I hardly trouble myself about finding a publisher. To be sure, due to "circumstances" over the last year and a half, that was a bit difficult anyway.

You decidedly overestimate Eckstein. His "criticism" was nothing but revenge for his long, fruitless attempts at friendship which I brusquely rejected. This very transfer of the "all too human" into the alpine regions of pure theory filled me with disgust for him. However, he was also capable of being quite nice and witty. Once, at the Kautskys' as I was desperately trying to get my jacket down from the clothes rack in the hall, damning my lilliputian form, he chivalrously held the jacket out for me and smilingly hummed, from Wolf's song, "Small things can also enchant us. . . ." (I suppose you know that Hugo Wolf was associated with the Eckstein family in Vienna and was the household god there.)

Your idea that I write a book about Tolstoy does not excite me at all. For whom? What for, Hänschen? After all, everyone can read Tolstoy's books. As for those who cannot get the strong breath of life from Tolstoy's books, my commentary will not get it across either. Can one "explain" what Mozart's music is? Can one "explain" the magic of life to someone who cannot perceive it from the smallest everyday things or, better, who does not carry it in himself? For example, I consider the whole immense bulk of Goethe literature (that is to say, the literature about Goethe) a waste of paper and I feel that too many books have been written; for all the literature, people forget to look out at the beautiful world.

Anyway, since the 1st, we have had a series of sunny days. The first morning rays greet me when I awake, for my windows here face east. In the Südende, where, as you know, my apartment stands like a lantern which is open to the sun on all sides, the morning hours are beautiful. After breakfast, I would take the heavy crystal prism with its countless corners and edges, which sits on my desk as a paperweight, and place it in the sun. The rays would immediately burst into a hundred small rainbow spurts scattering over the ceiling and walls. Mimi would watch it all in a state of fascination, especially when I would move the prism and let the many multicolored spots jump and dance to and fro. At first she would leap up to try and catch them. But soon she would realize that these forms were "nothing," just optical illusions, and would then follow their dance wide-eyed and motionless. We achieved exquisite effects with the prism as, for example, when such a little rainbow lit upon a white hyacinth on the flower table, the marble head over the desk, or upon the big bronze clock in front of the mirror. The clean, tidy room, full of sunshine, with its bright wallpaper, breathed such quiet and comfort. Through the open balcony door nothing intruded but the chirping of the sparrows, the hum of the electric tram which would pass once in a while, and the ringing metallic hammering of workers repairing rails somewhere. Then I would take my hat and go into the fields to look at what had grown during the night and collect some fresh, succulent grass for Mimi.

Here I also go into the little garden right after breakfast. I have a wonderful job, watering my "plantation" under the window. I had a cute little watering can brought to me, and I have to walk to the water tub with it a dozen times until the flowerbed is finally moist enough. The water spray sparkles in the morning sun and the drops quiver for a long time on the red and blue hyacinths, which are already half-open.

After all that, why am I sad? I almost believe that I overestimate the power of the sun in the sky. No matter how strongly it shines, sometimes it is unable to warm me when my heart fails to lend it warmth.

R.

To Hans Diefenbach

Wronke, 5/14/17

No. 5
D. H.,

This time, only a few short lines. They might arrive at the same time that Louise [Kautsky] and the Igels will be visiting. Please: do not discuss the *Anti-Critique* with them. Up until now, I have not mentioned the work to them, and it would cause me some embarrassment should they learn of it from a third person. On the other hand, naturally, I will present a copy to Luise as soon as the work is in print, and perhaps she will be able to read it.

Hänschen, be good to Luise. Give her the warmth and happiness which, unfortunately, I was not able to give her. Alas, it wasn't my fault—it just didn't work out. I could barely manage the words necessary to speak to her. My heart, which for days has been shivering and trembling like a puppy, grew still more timorous and shy. I feel so very bad for Luise. Most certainly she will think that she has been getting on my nerves. But that is completely untrue. Convince her of this.

I can't tell you how wretched I felt this evening. For comfort, I turned over the pages of *Westösliche Divan* a bit. I love it so much, not only because of the imperishable passion which radiates from it, but also because of Suleika—Marianne who is, for me, Goethe's only lovable female character. Her own songs, I feel, are really equal to Goethe's in terms of their intimacy and simplicity. How pretty, for example, is the way she dispatches her winged messenger: "Tell him, but tell him modestly: His love is my life. Only his closeness can give joyous security of both."[1] Unfortunately, only some of the songs have been included in the Harnack edition.

As regards serious reading, I'm going over *The Lessing Legend*[2] for the nth time. Do you know it? It gives me such manifold stimulation and refreshment.

Affectionate regards,
R.

Notes

[1] An interesting and perhaps revealing misquote. Suleika only expects a "joyful sense of both" whereas Rosa also hopes for "security."

[2] *The Lessing Legend* is Franz Mehring's classic of Marxist literary criticism.

To Sonja Liebknecht

Wronke 5/23/17

. . . Your last letter of the 14th had just arrived when I sent mine off. I am very happy to be in touch with you again, and I would like to send you my warmest Pentecost greetings. "Pentecost, that sweet holiday, had come," so begins Goethe's *Reinecke, the Fox*. Let's hope you will spend it somewhat cheerfully. Last year, of course, on Pentecost we took that wonderful trip with Mathilde to Lichtenrade where I picked stalks of grain for Karl and that wonderful branch of birch catkins. In the evening, carrying roses in our hands, we then went like the "three nobelwomen of Ravenna" to take a walk in the Südende field.

Here the lilacs are already in bloom. Today they opened up; it's so warm that I had to put on my lightest muslin dress. In spite of the sun and warmth, however, my little birds are by now almost completely silent. Obviously, their time is taken up with the business of hatching. The females sit in the nest and the males have their beaks full procuring food for themselves and their spouses. Also, they probably nest more outside in the fields or on tall trees. At least it's quiet now in my little garden. Only now and then does the nightingale sing briefly, or the greenfinch make its rapping steps, or late at night the catfinch blares once again; I don't see my titmice anymore.

Still, yesterday, all of a sudden, I received a short greeting from afar. It came from a blue titmouse, and it completely unnerved me. For the blue titmouse, unlike the great titmouse, is a migratory bird, it normally doesn't return to us before the end of March. At first, it had always stayed near my window, had come with others to the window, and diligently sung its funny "Tsi-tsi-ba." But it stretched the sound to such lengths that it sounded like a naughty child's bantering. I had to laugh every time, and I would answer it in the same way. Then, at the beginning of May, it disappeared with the others in order to breed somewhere outside. I neither saw nor heard it for weeks. Yesterday, suddenly, from out there, from beyond the wall which separates our yard from another prison area, I heard the familiar greeting. But it was so completely changed, only very short and hasty, three times one after the other, "Tsi-tsi ba, tsi-tsi ba." Then silence fell. My heart pounded convulsively; so much was said in this hurried call from far away, a whole bird history: the blue titmouse's remembrance of the beautiful times of courtship in the early spring where one sang and beckoned all the time; now, however, all day long he must fly and collect gnats for himself and the family. Hence, just a short reminiscence: "I don't have time!—Oh yes, it was nice!—Spring will soon come to an end—Tsi-tsi ba—tsi-tsi ba—tsi-tsi ba——"

Believe me, Sonjuscha: such a little bird call, in which there is so much expression, can affect me deeply. My mother, who next to Schiller, held the Bible to be the highest source of wisdom, stubbornly believed that King Solomon understood the language of birds. At the time, I grinned at this motherly naiveté with all the superiority of my fourteen years and a modern scientific education. Now, I myself am like King Solomon: I also understand the language of birds and animals. Naturally, not as if they were using human words, but rather I understand the most varied nuances and feelings which they put into their sounds. Only to the crude ear of an indifferent person is a bird song always one and the same. If we love animals and have an understanding for them, we find great differences of expression, an entire language, even in the general silence now, after the racket of early spring. And I know that if I am still here in autumn, which in all probability will be the case, then all my friends will return and seek food at my window. I am already looking forward to the one great titmouse with whom I am especially friendly.

Sonjuscha, you are bitter over my long imprisonment and ask: "How is it that people can judge other people? What's the use of it all?" I beg your pardon, but I had to laugh out loud while reading. In [Fyodor] Dostoyevsky's *The Brothers Karamazov*, there is a Madame Khokhlakova who at a party used to ask those very same questions, and look around helplessly from one guest to another. But, before even one person would try to answer her question, she would already have jumped to some other subject. My little bird, the entire cultural history of humanity, which according to conservative estimates comprises some 20,000 years, is based on "people judging other people," and this has deep roots in the material conditions of existence. Only a further agonizing development can change this. In fact, right now, we are witnesses to one of these agonizing chapters. And you ask what's the use of all this? "What for" is not, in fact, a concept for the whole of life and its forms. To what purpose are there blue titmice? I really don't know, but I am happy that they exist and I feel a sweet comfort when suddenly, from beyond the walls, there resounds a quick Tsi-tsi ba from afar.

By the way, you overestimate my "mellow wisdom." My inner equilibrium and my bliss, unfortunately, can be disturbed by the lightest shadows which fall over me, and then I suffer unspeakably; it's only that I possess the peculiarity of then falling silent. Literally, Sonjuscha, then I am unable to get out a word. For example, in the last few days I was really so cheerful and blissful; I was enjoying the sunshine, when suddenly on Monday an icy storm seized me and all of a sudden, my radiant cheerfulness was changed into the deepest misery. And if my very soul's happiness suddenly stood before me incarnate, I wouldn't be able to get out a sound; at best, I might reveal my despair with a mute gaze.

To be sure, it is rare enough that I get the temptation to speak. I don't even hear my own voice for weeks on end. By the way, that's the reason why I reached the heroic decision not to allow my Mimi to be brought here. The little creature is used to cheerfulness and life. She likes it when I sing, laugh, or chase her through all the rooms. Surely, she would become melancholy here. So, I am leaving her with Mathilde. Mathilde will come to visit me one of these days and I hope to pull myself together again. Perhaps Pentecost will be that "sweet holiday" for me as well. Sonitschka, I want you to be cheerful and calm. Everything will turn out all right, believe me. Send my most affectionate regards to Karl. I embrace you many times.

Your Rosa

To Sonja Liebknecht

Wronke 6/1/1917

. . . I know orchids well. In that wonderful greenhouse in Frankfurt a.M., where one whole section is full of them, I studied them diligently for several days. This was after my trial in which I received a year's sentence. I feel that they have something quite overrefined and decadent in their light grace and fantastic, unnatural forms. They affect me like the elegant, powdered marquises of the rococo age. I admire them with an inner resistance and a certain disquiet since, in general, my nature is offended by anything decadent or perverse. I get much more pleasure, for example, from a simple dandelion, which has so much sun in its color and which, like myself, opens itself completely and thankfully to the sunlight, only to close up shyly at the slightest shadow.

What evenings and what nights we are having now! Yesterday an indescribable magic lay over everything. Long after sunset, the sky, an incandescent opal light, was smeared with streaks of indeterminate color, just like a huge palette on which a painter has wiped off his brush with a broad gesture after a hard day's work. The air was a bit sultry, and a light tension weighed upon the heart. The bushes stood completely still; the nightingale was not to be heard; but the indefatigable bird with its little black head still hopped around in the branches and called forth in a shrill voice. All of nature seemed to be waiting for something to happen. I stood by the window and waited too—God knows for what. After "lock-up" at six, you know, between heaven and earth there is nothing for me to await. . . .

R.

To Mathilde Jacob

June 1, 1917

My dearest Mathilde,

You aren't angry at me, are you?! . . . You do understand that I am thankful for every minute that we can be together, but. . . . By now, you must have come to know my "buts," and make allowances, no? Yesterday your Maréchal roses filled the whole room with a sweet aroma. I lay on the sofa and dreamt until 10 o'clock, then I went to sleep without lighting the lamp. Now, there are the most beautiful days of the year, when the twilight has no end and when, in the evenings, the birds can find no peace. As late as nine-thirty (that is to say, 8:30 according to bird time), restless spirits could still be heard chirping. The lilac panicles glimmered lightly in the twilight and the air was so still that everything seemed to be listening with the most tense expectation. I could barely tear myself away from the open window, and I would have loved to stand there all night in order to drink in the delicious freshness.

Good morning my dearest Mathilde. Have a good trip and keep loving me in spite of it all.

Your R.

To Mathilde Jacob

June 8, 1917

. . . Oh, Mathilde! How I long for you! To tell the truth, I feel utterly miserable. I sometimes think that I shall go mad. But don't make too much of it. Perhaps I shall overcome it once again as I have so many times before. I embrace you and Mimi many times in the most painful longing.

Your R.

To Mathilde Jacob

June 13, 1917

My dearest Mathilde,

. . . It pains me so much that I should have upset you with my letter. I regretted it as soon as I sent it off. I'm already feeling better, the migraines are letting up. We'll speak of the doctor when you get here. Do apply for the 22nd, which is again a Friday; that day, after all, suits you best. Write me immediately whether you have made your application. By then, I hope to be far enough along so that I will actually be able to enjoy you. . . . I embrace you and Mimi a thousand times.

Your R.

To Hans Diefenbach

Wronke 6/23/17

Hänschen,

Hello! I'm back again. Today I feel so lonely that I must refresh myself a bit by chatting with you.—This afternoon on my sofa I was taking the siesta which the doctor prescribed for me. I was reading the newspaper, and at two-thirty I decided to get up but then, immediately, I fell asleep unawares and had a wonderful dream which was very vivid but of indeterminate content. I know only that someone dear to me was there that I touched his lips with my finger and asked: "Whose mouth is this?" He answered: "Mine."—"Oh, no!" I cried laughing. "Why, that mouth belongs to me!" I awoke still laughing over this nonsense and looked at my watch: It was still two-thirty. My long dream had, in fact, only lasted a second. But it left me with the feeling of having had a precious experience, and then, comforted, I went back into the garden.

There, I was to have another beautiful experience: a robin sat down on the wall behind me and sang a little song to me. In general, the birds are now completely involved with family concerns; only now and then can one be heard for a short moment, as with today's robin, which has visited me only a few times early in May. I'm not sure whether you know this little bird and its song. Like so much else, I really got to know it only here, and I love it incomparably more than the renowned nightingale. The ringing recital of the nightingale reminds me too much of a prima donna, of audiences, of noisy triumphs, and of enthusiastic hymns of praise. The robin has a tiny, delicate little voice and it gives forth a singularly intimate melody which sounds like an up-beat or a bit of reveille. In the jail scene from *Fidelio*,[1] do you know the distant trumpet call of deliverance which seems to pierce the darkness of night? The robin's song sounds something like this, only it has a soft, tremulous tone of infinite sweetness, like a misty remembrance lost in a dream.

My heart trembles in delight and pain when I hear this song and at once I see my life and the world in a new light, as if the clouds were to disperse and a new bright sunbeam were to fall on the earth.

Because of this soft little song, today I felt at peace with myself. Immediately I regretted all the wrongs I ever had done anyone and all the harsh thoughts and feelings I ever had. Once again, I resolved to be good, simply good—at any price. It's much better than "being right" and keeping accounts of every little insult. And then I decided to write you, today, right away, even though, since yesterday, a writing pad with seven resolutions has been sitting upon my table. The first reads: "Do not write letters." You see, that's how I keep to my own "ironclad" resolutions! That's how weak I am! If, as you write in your last letter, the stronger sex like women the most when they show their weakness, then you will now be delighted with me: Here I am! Oh, so weak! More so than I could wish.

By the way, there your babe's mouth speaks truer than you could imagine, for I just recently experienced this in the funniest manner. Surely, at the Copenhagen Congress, you saw Camille Huysmans, the tall youth with the dark curly hair and the typical Flemish face? Now, of course, he is the big mover at the Stockholm Conference.[2] For ten years, the two of us both belonged to the International Bureau and for ten years we hated each other—as far as such a feeling is possible for my "dove's heart" (the term was coined by Heinrich Schulz MdR!!![3] . . .) Why? It's difficult to say. I believe that he cannot stand politically active women. For my part, I suppose his impertinent face got on my nerves. Well, it so happened that, during the last session in Brussels, which took place towards the end of July 1914 in the face of the approaching war, we found ourselves together for a few hours. We were at an elegant restaurant and I was sitting by a bunch of gladiolas which were on the table. I lost myself looking at them and did not take part in the political talk. Then the discussion turned to my departure, at which point my helplessness in "mundane things" became an issue. My eternal need for a guardian who would take care of my ticket, stick me on the right train and retrieve my lost handbags—in short, they brought up all those shameful weaknesses which have given you so many happy moments.

Huysmans silently watched me all the while, and within an hour, the ten-year hatred was transformed into a glowing friendship. It was laughable. At last he had seen me in my weakness and he was in his element. Right away he decided to take my fate in hand. Together with Anseele,[4] that delightful little Walloon, he dragged me to his house for supper, brought in a little kitten, and played and sang Mozart and Schubert for me. He owns a fine piano and possesses a nice tenor. It was a new revelation for him that musical culture should be my life's blood. He played Schubert's *Limits of Mankind*[5] very nicely and he sang the closing verse, "And with us play the clouds and the winds" a few times in his funny Flemish accent—with the deep throaty L, something like "cloouds"—with deep emotion.

Afterwards, naturally, he took me to the train, carrying my suitcase himself. He even sat in the compartment with me and then suddenly decided: "Mais il est impossible de vous laisser voyager seule!"[6]—as if I really were a baby. I was barely able to talk him out of accompanying me, at least to the German border; he jumped off just as the train was getting under way, still calling "Au revoir à Paris!" For in two weeks we were to hold a congress in Paris. That was on the 31st of July. But, as my train pulled into Berlin, the mobilization was in full progress, and two days later poor Huysmans' beloved Belgium was occupied. I had to repeat to myself: "And with us play the clouds and the winds. . . ."

In two weeks, a full year of my imprisonment will be over, or—if you disregard a short interval—two full years. Oh, how much good an hour of harmless chatter would do me now! During visiting hours, of course, we hastily discuss business matters and, most of the time, I am on tenterhooks. Apart from this, I neither see nor hear a human soul.

Now it's 9 p.m., but naturally it's light as day. It's so quiet all around, only the ticking of the clock, and from the distance, the muffled barking of a dog. Isn't it strange how it reminds you of home when in the country you hear dogs barking at night? Instantly I imagine a comfortable peasant's farm house, a man in shirt sleeves standing on the doorstep chatting with a neighbor's wife, his pipe in his mouth. From inside, the bright voices of children and the clatter of dishes. Outside, there is the smell of ripe wheat and the first diffident croaking of frogs. . . .

Adieu, Hänschen

Notes

[1]*Fidelio* was the only opera written by Beethoven.
[2]The reference is to the socialist Stockholm Peace Conference.
[3]MdR is the abbreviation for Member of the Reichstag.
[4]Edouard Anseele (1856-1938): One of the founders and leading members of the Belgian Workers' Party and a member of the executive committee of the Second International.
[5]Based on Goethe's poem.
[6]"But it would be absolutely impossible to allow you to travel alone."

To Hans Diefenbach

Wronke 6/29/17

Nr. 8
Good day, Hänschen!
    Well, all right, for your sake the first of my seven maxims will be

broken. The other six, however, are very reasonable and will certainly meet with your approval. It is touching that Gerlach[1] would exchange me only for a field marshal. By the way, his letter makes a good impression. It seems that he has inwardly matured through the war, and I will be pleased to see him again in our "Swabian" circle. When will that be. . . ?

Every night while sitting at my barred window, where I can breathe in the fresh air and dream, with my legs stretched out on another chair, somewhere in the neighborhood the muffled sounds begin of someone diligently beating carpets, or something like that. I have no idea who is doing it or where. But I have already gained an intimate, though indeterminate, relation to whoever it is through the regular recurrence of those sounds. They awake in me some vague idea of competent housework, of a little place in which everything is sparkling clean. Perhaps it is one of our female officials, who finds time only late at night, after the daily work, to take care of her tiny household—a lonely old maid or widow, like the majority of prison officials, who uses the little leisure time she has to forever put her few rooms into meticulous order. Of course, no one ever enters these rooms, and she only rarely makes use of them herself. I just don't know; yet, every time, these rapping sounds bring me the feeling of ordered, circumscribed quiet and, at the same time, a slight feeling of being enclosed within the narrowness and hopelessness of a penurious existence—china cabinets, yellow photographs, artificial flowers, a hard sofa. . . .

Do you also know this strange effect of sounds whose origin is unknown to us? I have experienced this in every prison. For example, in Zwickau, every night at exactly two o'clock, ducks who were living somewhere nearby in a pond, woke me with a loud "quack-quack-quack-quack!" The first of the four syllables was called in a high pitch with the strongest emphasis and conviction. From that point, it scaled down to a deep bass murmur. Awakened by the noise, for a few seconds I was always forced to reorient myself in the blackest darkness on a stone-hard mattress and remember where I was. That feeling of being in the jail cell, always somewhat oppressive, the special accentuation of the "quack-quack," the fact that I had no idea where the ducks were and that I only heard them at night, gave their call something mysterious and meaningful. It always sounded to me like some type of philosophical saying which, through its regular recurrence every night had something irrevocable about it, something that had been valid since the beginning of the world like some kind of coptic maxim.

And on the nights of Indian air
And in the deep of Egyptian graves
Have I heard the sacred word. . .

That I could not decipher the meaning of this duck wisdom, that I only had a vague idea of it, called forth a strange disquiet in my heart every time, and I used to lie awake, anxious, for a long time.

It was completely different in Barnimstrasse. At 9 o'clock it was lights out, and I would always willy-nilly lie down in my bed though, naturally, I was unable to fall asleep. Shortly after 9, in the stillness of night, from some nearby tenement the crying of a two- or three-year-old boy would regularly begin. Then, after a few pauses, the little fellow would gradually sob his way into a true, plaintive crying which, however, had nothing vehement about it and which expressed no clear pain or desire. Instead, it only manifested a general discontent with existence, and an inability to come to terms with the difficulties of life and its problems, especially since Mommy was not by his side. The helpless crying lasted a good three-quarters of an hour. At exactly ten, however, I would hear the door opening firmly; light, quick steps resounded loudly in the little room, and a full-sounding young woman's voice, from which one could still sense the freshness of the street air, would say: "Why aren't you asleep? Why aren't you asleep?" At that point, three hearty smacks would follow from which one could clearly feel the appetizing roundness and bed warmth of that particular part of the little body. And—oh, wonder!—the three smacks would suddenly solve all the difficulties and complex problems of life with ease. The whimpering would stop, the little boy would immediately fall asleep, and a quiet relief would rule again in the tenement.

This scene recurred so regularly every night that it became a part of my own existence. By 9 o'clock, I would be waiting with tensed nerves for the awakening and whimpering of my little unknown neighbor. I knew his whole vocal register in advance and could follow that crying, in which the feelings of helplessness in the face of life were fully communicated to me. Then I would wait for the young woman's return home, for the sonorous question, and especially for the liberating smacks. Believe me, Hänschen, that old-fashioned method of solving the problems of existence, by way of the little fellow's behind, also worked wonders in my own soul. My nerves would immediately relax with his and, every time, I would fall asleep at almost the same time as the little one. I never learned from which window decorated with geraniums, from which garret, those human threads stretched to me. In the harsh light of day, all the houses which I was able to see appeared equally grey, sober and sternly reserved. They all had the expression: "We know nothing." Only in the darkness of night, through the soft breath of the summer air, were spun the mysterious relations between people who neither knew nor saw one another.

Ah, what a beautiful memory I have of Alexanderplatz! Hänschen, do you know what Alexanderplatz is? That one-and-a-half-month stop-over there left me with grey hair and rents in my nerves which I shall never repair. And yet, I recall a small scene which breaks forth like a flower in my memory. The nights there began—it was late autumn, October, and there was no lighting at all in my cell—as early as 5 or 6 o'clock. There was nothing left for me to do in the 400-cubic-foot cell except stretch myself out on the cot, squeezed in between indescribable pieces of furniture. Into a hell's music of the incessantly thundering elevated trains, which shook the cell and struck red reflections of light on the rattling windowpanes, I would recite my Mörike under my breath. From 10 o'clock on, the diabolical concert of the trains would quiet down somewhat, and after, from the street, the following little episode could be heard. First a subdued masculine voice, which had something summoning and admonishing about it, and then, in response, the singing of an 8-year-old girl. Evidently she was singing a nursery song while skipping and jumping around; her silvery laughter resounded as pure as a bell. Probably the voice belonged to some tired and grouchy doorman calling his little daughter home to bed. The little rascal didn't want to obey. She played tag with her father, that bearded, gruff bass voice, and fluttered around the street like a butterfly, teasing the feigned strictness with a lively nursery rhyme. You could practically see the short shirt flap up and down and the little legs fly into a dancing stance. In this jumping rhythm of the nursery song, in the bubbling laughter, there was so much carefree and victorious lust for life that the whole dark, mouldy building of the police presidium seemed enveloped in a coat of silvery mist; it was as if, all of a sudden, my malodorous cell smelled of falling dark-red roses. Thus, wherever we are we can gather up a little happiness from the street, and we are reminded again that life is beautiful and rich.

Hänschen, you have no idea how blue the sky was today! Or was it just as blue in Lissa? Usually, before the "lockup," I go out into the evening for a half-hour to water my little flower bed (self-planted pansies, forget-me-nots, and phlox!) with my own little can, and stroll around a bit in the garden. This hour before nightfall has its own peculiar magic. The sun was still hot, but one was happy to allow its slanted rays to burn one's neck and cheeks like a kiss. A low breath of air moved the bushes like a whispered promise that the coolness of evening would soon arrive and relieve the heat of the day. In the sky, which was a sparkling, glimmering blue, some dazzling-white cloud formations stood towering; a very pale half-moon swam between them like a phantom, like a dream. The swallows had already begun their nightly communal flight. Their sharp pointed wings cut the blue silk of space into pieces. They shot to and fro, somersaulting with shrill cries in the dizzying heights. I stood with my dripping water can in my hand. My head was held high, and I had an uncontrollable desire to plunge into the moist, shimmering blue above, to bathe in it, to splash in it, to give myself up to the foam and then disappear. Mörike came to mind—you know:

> Oh river, my river in the morning light!
> Receive this once, receive
> This yearning body
> And kiss its breast and cheek!
> The sky, azure and of childlike purity,
> In which the waves are singing,
> The sky is thy soul,
> Oh let me permeate it!
> With my mind and my senses I immerse myself
> Into thy deepest azure
> And cannot wing to its ends! . . .
> Is anything as deep, as deep as this azure?
> Only, only Love,
> Love is never satiated, she never sates
> With her everchanging light. . . .

For God's sake, Hänschen, don't follow my bad example. Don't you also become so talkative. It won't happen again, I swear!!!

R.

Notes

[1]Gerlach was an SPD member and suitor, as well as friend, of Rosa Luxemburg.

To Sonja Liebknecht

Wronke July 20, 1917

Sonitschka, darling!

Since my life—or rather, nonlife—here has been drawn out

longer than I originally expected, here is another last greeting from Wronke. How could you think that I wouldn't write you any more letters! Nothing has changed my feelings for you, and nothing could change them. I did not write because, since your departure from Ebenhausen, I knew that you were in a state of turmoil because of a thousand different things and also, in part, because I was momentarily not in the mood.

You probably know that I'm being transferred to Breslau. Here, this morning, I took leave of my little garden. The weather is grey, stormy and rainy; tattered clouds were rushing across the sky, and still I was able to take full pleasure in my usual early morning walk. I took leave of the small paved path along the wall on which I have walked back and forth for nearly nine months now, and where by now I know exactly every stone and every little weed which grows between the stones. What interests me in the plaster stones is the bright colors: reddish, bluish, green, grey. Particularly during the long winter, in which I waited so very long for a little bit of living green, my color-hungry eyes tried to draw a bit of brightness and excitement from those stones. And now in summer, how many things, even more peculiar and interesting, appear between the stones! For masses of wild bees and wasps dwell there. They bore round holes the size of nuts between the stones, then they build deep corridors inside and, in so doing, they work the soil up from the inside to the surface and stack it into quite sizable little piles. Inside they lay their eggs and work the wax and the wild honey. There is continual slipping in and flying out, and I had to be very careful on my walks in order not to crush these underground apartments.

Then, in several places, the ants make straight paths across the road, on which they continually walk back and forth in such a remarkably straight line that it's as if they knew by heart the mathematical axiom that a straight line is the shortest distance between two points (which, for example, is completely unknown to primitive peoples). The most luxuriant weeds grow exuberantly on the wall; some of the little plants have already bloomed and have scattered fluff, the others are indefatigably budding on. Then there is a whole generation of young trees which, this very spring, before my very eyes, have sprouted up from the soil by the wall or in the middle of the road; a little acacia which obviously this year germinated from a fallen husk of the old tree; several small white poplars; they too have come into the world only last May, but already they are wearing the luxurious ornament of white and green leaves which daintily rock in the wind, exactly like the old ones.

How many times have I walked along their path! And while walking, how many different things has my mind experienced and thought! In the coldest winter, after a fresh snowfall, I often first smoothed a path with my feet, accompanied by my little titmouse which I hoped to see again in the fall, but which will not find me when it returns to the familiar feeding place by the window.

In March, when we got a few days of thaw in the middle of a hard frost, my path changed into a little stream. I remember how, under the mild wind, little waves ruffled on the surface and how the bricks on the wall were vividly and brightly reflected on them. Then, finally, May came and the first violet by the wall, which I sent you.

As I wandered over there today, observing and meditating all the while, a verse from Goethe rang in my ears: "Old Merlin in the luminous grave where as a youth I spoke to him."

Of course, you know the rest. The poem, naturally was in no way connected with my mood or inner concerns. It was only the music of the words and the strange magic of the poem which lulled me into tranquility. I don't know myself why it is that a beautiful poem, especially by Goethe, so deeply affects me at every moment of strong excitement or emotion. The effect is almost physical. It's as if with parched lips I were sipping a delicious drink that cools my spirit and heals me, body and soul.

The poem from *Westöstliche Divan* which you mention in your last letter is unknown to me; please copy it out for me. And there is another thing that I've wanted for quite some time which is missing from the small Goethe volume I have here: *Blumengruss*. It is a short poem of four to six lines; I know it from a Wolf *Lied* which is indescribably beautiful, especially the closing verse which goes something like this:

> In yearning I have picked them
> In searing throes untold,
> And I have pressed them to my heart,
> Well-nigh a thousandfold.

Put to music it sounds so holy, tender and chaste; as if one were kneeling down in silent adoration. But I no longer remember the text, and would like to have it.

Only last night, around nine, I witnessed a glorious spectacle. From my sofa, I noticed the shining reflection of pink color in the windowpane, which surprised me since the sky was completely grey. I ran to the window and stood as if rooted to the spot. On the completely monotonous grey of the sky, a large cloud of an unearthly beautiful pink color was piling up in the east. It was so alone, so isolated in itself, that it looked like a smile, like a greeting from an unknown faraway land. I drew a deep breath as if I were free and instinctively held out both hands toward that enchanted picture. If there are such colors, such forms, then life is beautiful and worth living, isn't it? With a look I attached myself to the shining image, and devoured each of its rosy rays until suddenly I burst out laughing at myself.

Dear God, the sky and the clouds, and the entire beauty of life really will not remain behind in Wronke; I do not have to take leave of them. No! They will leave with me and stay with me wherever I may be and as long as I may live.

Soon I will report to you from Breslau. Visit me there as soon as you can. Affectionate greetings to Karl. I embrace you many times. I'll see you in my ninth prison.

Your faithful
Rosa

To Mathilde Jacob

[Postcard-mark]
July 26, 1917

From: Dr. Luxemburg, Criminal Penitentiary
To: Mathilde Jacob/Hotel Vier Jahreszeiten, Breslau

Dearest Mathilde!

Yesterday I arrived here half-dead from fatigue; after all, I am no longer accustomed to people or turmoil. The first impression of my new lodging was so shattering that it took an effort to hold back the tears. The change from Wronke is too great. But what can be done to lighten my existence here a bit, will surely be done; of that I have no doubt. The worst is the question of food—which, for me is the cardinal point! Today I was informed that there is not one restaurant that will deliver my meals. What will come of that is not clear to me; it would simply mean that I shall starve since, after all, with my serious stomach illness I can't digest prison food! So in case there is really nothing to be found here we must immediately make an urgent appeal for transfer to a different place! Above all, naturally I long to see you and speak to you soon! I embrace you a thousand times.

Your R.L.

Please send newspapers!

To Sonja Liebknecht

Breslau 8/2/1917

My dear Sonitschka,

Your letter, which I received on the 28th, was the first news that reached me here from the outside world, and you can easily imagine how happy it made me. In your loving care for me, you take my transfer in a way which is decidedly too tragic. . . . As you know, I take all the turns of fate with the proper cheerful equanimity. I have already settled down here. Today my boxes of books came from Wronke. Soon, my two cells with the books, little pictures, and unassuming decorations, which I usually lug around with me, will once again look as cosy and comfortable as in Wronke, and I shall get back to work with redoubled vigor.

What I miss here, of course, is the relative freedom to move around which I enjoyed there where I had the run of the citadel all day long. Here, I am simply locked in. Then, think of the wonderful air, the garden and, above all, the birds. You have no idea of how fond I am of this little company. But naturally one can do without all this, and soon I will forget that I ever had it better than I have it here. The entire situation is about the same as in Barnimstrasse; only the pretty green hospital yard is missing, where I was able to make some little botanical or zoological discovery every day. Here, on the paved yard which serves for my walks, there is nothing to "discover." And, while walking, I desperately fix my gaze on the grey pavement to avoid seeing the prisoners at work in the yard, who are always a torture for me to look at in their degrading garb. Amongst them, there are always a few whose age, sex and individual traits have been erased by the stamp of deepest human degradation; yet these very people, through some painful magnetism, again and again draw my gaze.

To be sure, there are also people everywhere whom even the prison attire cannot demean, and who would please a painter's eyes. Thus, I already discovered a young female worker here in the yard whose slim spare form, along with her strong profile, her head wrapped in a kerchief, actually seemed like a character painted by Millet.[1] It's a pleasure to see with what noble movements she carries her loads, and the lean face with the taut skin, chalk-white all over, reminds one of a tragic Pierrot mask. But, from sad experience, I try to stay far out of the way of such promising appearances. For, in Barnimstrasse, I also had discovered a woman prisoner of truly royal stature and bearing. I thought to myself that a corresponding "intérieur" would go with it. Then she came to my station as a trustee, and after two days, it turned out that beneath the beautiful mask there was such stupidity, so base a mind, that, from then on, I always looked away when she crossed my path. At the time, I thought to myself that, after all, Venus de Milo could only have preserved her reputation through the centuries as the most beautiful of women because she has remained silent. Were she to open her mouth, perhaps her whole charm would go to the devil.

Across from me is the men's prison, the usual gloomy red-brick building. But, over across the wall, I see the green treetops of some park: a tall black poplar which rustles loudly during strong gusts of wind, and a few much lighter ash trees draped with bunches of yellow husks. There is a northwest view from the window, so that I sometimes see beautiful evening clouds, and you know that one such reddish cloud can enchant and make up for everything.

At this moment it is 8 p.m. (hence actually 7). The sun has barely gone down behind the gables of the men's prison; it still shines through the skylight in the roof, and the whole sky is lit up in gold. I feel quite well and—I don't know why myself—I have to sing Gounod's[2] *Ave Maria* softly to myself (you probably know it).

Many thanks for the Goethe you copied. "The Men Entitled" is indeed beautiful, although I myself wouldn't have noticed it. After all, sometimes you get the beauty of a thing by suggestion. I would also like to ask you to copy out "Anakreon's Grave" when you get a chance. Do you know it well? Of course, I only came to understand it correctly through Hugo Wolf's music. In the *Lied* it really makes an architectonic impression; you think you are seeing a Greek temple.

Just now—I took a little break in order to watch the sky—the sun has gone down much lower behind the building, and silent myriads of little clouds, which have run together from God knows where, are hovering high above. At their edges there is a silver glow, in the middle a delicate grey, and all their tattered contours are sailing north. There is such a carefree, cool smile in this flight of clouds that I must smile along with them, as I always must participate in the rhythm of surrounding life. With such a sky, how can anyone be "bad" or petty? Just never forget to look around you, and then you will again and again be "good."

It makes me wonder a bit that Karl should want a book specifically on bird calls. For me, the voice of a bird is inseparable from its whole habitat and life; only the whole interests me, not some torn-off detail. Give him a good book on animal geography. That will surely give him plenty of stimulation. I hope that you will come to visit me before long. As soon as you receive permission, send a telegram. I embrace you many times.

Your Rosa

Notes

[1]Jean François Millet (1814-1875): French Barbizon and naturalist painter, best known for his works on peasant labor.

[2]Charles François Gounod (1818-1893): An important composer, best known for his opera *Faust*.

To Mathilde Jacob

August 11, 1917

My dearest Mathilde!

I just can't tell you how your letter, which I received yesterday, upset me. So, my Mimi has been seriously ill for months and only now do I learn of it by chance because I, so to speak, backed you against the wall with my questions! And you, of all people, found it in your heart to hide something which means so much to me! I ask where is the simple respect which prevents you from treating me like an incompetent child, an "object." Why, this is the same story as with the application which you made without my knowledge.[1]

On the grounds of martial law, the military locks me up for years and then my friends, proclaiming their own private martial law over me, treat me like a minor, make decisions in my name, or withhold important news from me. You were the only one left whose words I thought I could trust. Now I don't trust you any longer either. So, now, I am completely alone. Well, o.k!

And then, you simply write me that Mimi is sick! That is to suffice! Not a word about why or what! And this prattle about "old" Mimi! A year ago, when I was arrested, she was still young and beautiful and healthy. Why, at Pentecost you even wanted to bring her to me at Wronke . . . then everything was all right. And now, suddenly, I have to learn of her "age."

Now, if you please, send the most exact information by return mail: 1) since when has Mimi been sick? 2) what symptoms does she have? 3) since when has the illness started to worsen? 4) whether, and what, she is eating? 5) which veterinarian has looked at her?— . . . I will write you as much about my health as you write me about Mimi's—I embrace you, and affectionate regards to your mother.

Your R.

Notes
¹Mathilde Jacob had applied for Rosa's release for health reasons.

To Hans Diefenbach

8/13/17

Hänschen,

I just recently wrote you a postcard with a brief greeting, yet I very much long for a proper letter from you. Here I lead the regularized existence of a convict; that is to say, locked in my cell day and night, I only see the men's prison across from me. To be sure, I am allowed to walk in the courtyard as often as I wish. But it is the usual paved yard in the midst of the prison buildings, upon which working prisoners walk back and forth, and so I keep my visits down to a minimum. I seek only the exercise which the doctor prescribes for health reasons. Also, during these "walks" I look around as little as possible. The descent from Wronke is steep, in every respect. This is not meant as a complaint, however, only as an explanation of why, lately, I have not written you the type of letter which you were accustomed to receiving from Wronke—woven from the scent of roses, the blue of the sky and the veils of the clouds. Still, my cheerfulness will eventually return—after all, I carry an inexhaustible supply within me. Only first I must get my carcass into shape, which, at present is a difficult task to accomplish. For the last week and a half, my stomach has been rebelling violently to the point where I had to stay in bed for a full week. Even now, I live primarily on hot compresses and thin soup. The cause is still unclear to me, probably it is a nervous reaction to the abrupt worsening of general living conditions. Today, I'm already feeling better. I went down into the sun again for an hour, and I believe that the worst is over.

In the yard, there are two pale and consumptive patches of grass, frequently trod upon by the prisoners nearby who are hanging up and taking down laundry. Of course, the grass is never able to flourish. At any rate, I have already determined various species of plants growing there, all in stunted forms. A few diminutive milfoils are blooming, and a dozen Heracium (you surely know them without the botanical name; they look like dandelions, only much smaller) are lifting up their little yellow, sunny heads. Cabbage butterflies, which now flutter about in abundance, like to hang on them. As in every prison yard, there are also a few pigeons. They come from the neighboring area, but feel quite at home here. When grain sacks (from the military) are being unloaded and emptied, they boldly walk up to pick the kernels which probably may be left over here and there. Aside from the pigeons, only a few sparrows silently creep about.

I am now reading Mignet[1] and Cunow[2] on the French Revolution. What an inexhaustible drama, which grips and entrances one again and again! Yet, I still find the English Revolution more powerful, splendid and full of imagination, even though it did run its course in such morose forms of Puritanism. I have already read Guizot three times;[3] still I will take him up many times again in the future.

I am working hard on the Korolenko[4] translation, which I promised to deliver by the end of the month. To be sure, because of my illness, there will be an annoying delay. What do you think of it?

It occurs to me that perhaps you already wrote me under the name Frau Dr. Lübeck, and that nobody here knew that I was she. At any rate, I have received nothing from you and now am longing for a letter. Here I welcome letters as dear guests even more warmly than in Wronke.

Goodbye, until the next letter.

Affectionately,
Your R.

Notes

[1]François Mignet (1796-1884): Rosa is referring to his *History of the French Revolution 1789-1814.*

[2]Heinrich Cunow's *The Parties of the Great French Revolution.*

[3]François Guizot (1787-1874): A French historian and statesman, he wrote a history of the English revolution from a class standpoint. Rosa's predilection for the British revolution is atypical; the Left generally looked to the great French Revolution for its model.

[4]Rosa Luxemburg was translating Korolenko's *History of My Contemporary,* for which she also wrote an introduction.

To Mathilde Jacob

August 18, 1917

Dearest Mathilde,

Just this minute I received your letter of the 15th. It seems you want me to spend additional time on the rack! You go on and on saying that Mimi is ill, without a word about what is wrong with her. The devil take it! I have to know what type of illness she has! Is she still alive? Perhaps she has already been dead a long time, and you are just leading me on! If that were the case, I would not forgive you. I want to know *the truth, immediately, the whole truth!*

Kiss and Greetings
Your R

What happened to Mimi on the first of May?

To Hans Diefenbach

Breslau 8/27/17

Hänschen,

Today it is overcast, abominable and rainy, so I have been sitting shut up in my room all day. Just now, however, my mail was brought to me: a few letters and among them one from you—and so I am happy and cheerful again. I too feel relieved that our correspondence is flowing once again. By the way, I had just written you in Stuttgart. I could, however, retrieve the letter and substitute this one in its place.

Poor Hannesle, I can empathize with the mood in which you find yourself, and it is just your sorrows that I need to hear about. I would also be in favor of you moving to Stuttgart in order to be with your father. So long as one cannot help, you will at least feel relieved to be near him; after all, your presence alone would do the poor fellow good. Later, one always blames oneself bitterly for every hour which one took away from the old people. I wasn't lucky enough even to have done as little as that. After all, I constantly had to look after the urgent business of humanity and make the world a happier place. And so I received the news of my father's death in Berlin, after returning from the International Congress in Paris where I had been wrangling with Jaurès, Millerand, Dazýnski, Bebel, and God knows who else, until the fur flew. In the meantime, the old gentleman wasn't able to wait any longer. Probably he said to himself that there would be no sense anyway in waiting, however long he waited; after all, I never did "have time" for him or myself—and he died. When I came back from Paris, he had already been buried a week. *Now*, of course, I would be much wiser, but one is usually wiser after it's too late. Anyway, if you possibly can, go to your old man and stay with him to the end. This advice means no small sacrifice for me: for it's really as if you were closer to me in Lissa and I would feel completely abandoned if you were to go to Stuttgart. But, after all, I have the time—*now*, I have a lot of time . . . —and then, again, the mail will also bring me your news from there.

Romain Rolland[1] is no stranger to me, Hänschen. He is one of those rare birds—here and abroad—who have not joined the relapse into the psychology of Neanderthal times on account of the war. Of his works, I have read *Jean-Christophe in Paris* in German translation. I'm afraid I'll offend you but still, as always, I'll be completely honest: I found the book very nice and simpatico, but it's more of a pamphlet than a novel. It's not an authentic work of art. I am so inexorably sensitive in these matters that even the most beautiful message cannot substitute for simple God-given genius. But, I would very much like to read more by him, especially in French, which in itself would be a real pleasure. Perhaps I'll find more in other volumes than in this one.

But, how's it going with my Hauptmann's *Fool in Christ?* Haven't you read it yet? Reading it now, in your mood, you would find it a real treasure. If you did read it, then please hurry up with your judgment.

Over the last few days, huge numbers of wasps have been whirring into my cell (naturally I keep the window open day and night). They now have a goal; they are looking for food and, as you know, I am hospitable. I lay out a little bowl of various sweets and they load up. It's a pleasure to see how these little animals vanish through the window every few minutes with a new cargo. They set out for a faraway garden, the green treetops of which I can only see in the distance. After a few minutes, they return straight through the window and to the bowl. Hänschen, what fabulous sense of direction in those little eyes, no larger than pinheads, and what memory! Day after day they come, not forgetting during the night the way to the "middle class restaurant" behind cell bars! In Wronke, on my walks through the garden, every day I noticed how they bored deep holes and corridors into the ground between cobblestones and how they carried the soil up to the surface. On every square meter there were dozens of such holes, completely indistinguishable to the human eye. Yet, every wasp knew precisely how to get straight back to its own hole as it returned from a long excursion!

From the migrations of birds, which I am studying right now, the same riddle of intelligence remains. Did you know, Hänschen, that during the autumn migrations to the south large birds, like cranes, often carry a great many little birds, like larks, swallows, golden-crested wrens, etc., on their backs?! This is no child's fairy tale, but rather a scientifically observable fact. And the little ones twitter briskly and converse with each other on their "omnibus-seat!" . . . Do you know that on such autumn migrations sparrow hawks, falcons, kites and other birds of prey often crowd together with little warblers whom they otherwise feed upon? On such flights, a kind of God's truce, a general cease-fire, rules. When I read something like this, I am so thrilled, so full of joie de vivre, that even Breslau turns into a place where people can live. I don't know why it should affect me in this way. Perhaps, it reminds me that life really is a beautiful fairy tale. In the beginning here, I almost forgot. Now, however, it comes back to me. I will not give in. Write soon.

Affectionately,

Your R.

Enclosed, a touching letter from the front. I don't know who the fellow is at all.

Esteemed Frau Rosa Luxemburg,

Yesterday I took the liberty of mailing you a one-pound package. If the director or the administration permits it, that is to say if you can receive packages with foodstuffs, I would very much like to send a parcel with fruit or some other sort of edibles.

Whenever I think of the past, or the present, your name and your person always come to mind. Even before the slaughter I had read much of yours that was good and beautiful, and at meetings I listened to your words with pleasure. Not only have you remained true to your convictions, but you also had to suffer the most inhuman treatment because of them, especially during the "war."

In closing, I wish you good health, good cheer, and a quick release along with the full human development for us all.

Best regards,

Your Adalbert Ottenbacher

Notes

[1]Romain Rolland (1866-1944): French novelist and pacifist, friend of Herman Hesse, he opposed the First World War. Aside from *Jean-Christophe in Paris*, his best-known work is probably *The Summer*. Rosa Luxemburg's judgment has been vindicated; this brave and generous man is now virtually forgotten.

To Mathilde Jacob

August 24, 1917

My dearest Mathilde,

   . . . I won't write anymore about Mimi; let's forget that sad chapter. But you can see once again that it is more merciful to tell the whole truth immediately, openly and honestly than to keep someone in error for months on end out of a false sense of consideration. How much easier it would have been for me if you had personally broken the sad news to me in Wronke, where I had you with me so often and where I could have asked you about all the particulars so dear to me! And so, here I sit with this naked fact, I know nothing more, and appear to myself to be so cruel and heartless, having been able to live for four months in complete ignorance of her sad end. . . . Well, we'll let it go at that: I won't change you, and most people behave exactly like you in such cases. So, let's drop it.

   Many thanks for the books and things which you sent. But it pains me very much that you are so depressed and morose. Sonja too writes utterly despairing letters. But *you*, of all people, were usually so full of vitality and high spirits. Please don't let all sorts of oppressive influences bring you low. Read something good in every free minute and, above all, go into the fields, into the free outdoors, often. There one always finds comfort and joy of living.

   Surely, it's been an eternity since you last visited the Botanical Gardens. Please get up your strength and pay a visit to Dahlem. Take Sonja with you and then describe exactly how the gardens look, what is in bloom, which birds you hear, etc. Hurry up, since these are the last days for most of the songbirds; at the end of August—beginning of September, they leave for the south again. And a whole bunch of them do nest in the Botanical Gardens. Particularly in the densest part, at the entrance . . . then to the right of the entrance hall. There, one day in April, I presented the nightingale and many other birds to Karl and Sonja. Now, I would like to get a detailed report on everything that is living there. . . . These few hours will refresh you, and prepare you for work, for many days thereafter. And then, you'll be doing it for me.

   Yesterday, I also made an "excursion!" Namely (at my request) to garrison headquarters where I had a few things to discuss. I had so looked forward to the little trip; but, as always, I returned quite exhausted. After all, I am no longer accustomed to human intercourse, so that the racket of the streets numbed me after only a few minutes. Also, the city looked dusty and hot; the trees seemed quite withered. Anyway, it was "something different," and I bought myself a few flowers and a cake along the way.

I am sending you another 80 manuscript pages. I am hurrying very much with Korolenko. Has Hänschen gotten everything you received? Of course, I am writing to him in Stuttgart.

Please do not send the deck chair. Basically, after all, I live only in one cell and I have no room for this piece of furniture. In exchange, I would like to ask you for Gertrud's picture when you get a chance, also for the Turner. . . .[1]

I'll write you again soon. My dearest Mathilde, please don't let your spirit sag and your joy of life fade. Everything will eventually be different! When we can both, again, live in Südende and go picking flowers in the fields! . . . So, be cheerful and happy—in spite of everything, OK? I embrace you, and best regards to yours.

As always, your

R

Notes

[1]Joseph Millard William Turner (1775-1851): English romantic painter known for his landscapes. His use of color and light made him a precursor of the impressionists.

To Franz Mehring

September 8, 1917

. . . It is with one eye laughing, and one weeping that I follow the inexhaustible stream which flows from Kautsky's untiring pen and which, calmly, spins one "theme" after the other with the patience of a spider. Everything is properly laid out in little chapters with subheadings and everything is considered "historically"; that is to say, it begins with the foggy origins of the world and proceeds to the present day. Only in the essentials does he, unfortunately, not know what he thinks he knows. I keep thinking of Fritz Adler[1] who, the last time he visited me, told me that he completely agreed with the *Junius Brochure*; when I said that I thought he was accepting Kautsky's view, he replied: "How is that possible? Even Kautsky does not accept Kautsky's view." But still, [Philipp] Scheidemann's[2] people will soon make him into a martyr and, with that, allow his bald-headed glory to beam afresh. . . .

Notes

[1]Friedrich Adler (1879-1960): Son of Victor Adler, the leader of Austrian social democracy. Friedrich Adler served as secretary of the Austrian party from 1911 to 1916. In that year, as a gesture of protest against the war and the reformism of the party, Adler assassinated the Austrian premier. After a spectacular trial, he was imprisoned and then freed in the revolution of 1918. One of the guiding spirits of what came to be known as the "Second-and-a-Half International," he led the group back into the Second International in 1923.

[2]Philipp Scheidemann (1856-1937): One of the leading right-wing social democrats in Germany; it was Scheidemann who, in a speech, proclaimed the Weimar Republic and became its first chancellor.

To Mathilde Jacob

September 18, 1917

Dear Mathilde,

I have been informed by garrison headquarters that my correspondence is too extensive. Please write me only once a week and more briefly. Also, notify Hans, Clara and Luise that I ask them not to write any more and not to expect any letters from me. Today I received your letter no. 9. For the future, numbering the letters will be superfluous. I have sent you another 100 of my manuscript pages.[1] Please do not mention the restriction *either in letters or otherwise.* Greetings.

Your R

Notes

[1]The reference is to Rosa Luxemburg's Korolenko translation.

To Mathilde Jacob

November 9, 1917

My dearest Mathilde!

... I have such a longing for you: I believe it's high time for us to see one another again. We have never let it go as long as this—4 months!—and I feel so very sad that this was possible. I can't get over the fact that things are different between us now than in former times, and I have no idea of what caused the change. I don't simply mean that it's been so long since we've seen each other, but rather that your letters seem to be elsewhere. I would so much like to know how you feel emotionally and empathize the way I was able in Wronke. Surely, you don't doubt that I would like to write you often; I'm just not allowed. . . .

Hänschen was very enthusiastic about Hauptmann's *"Fool."*. . . Dearest, I would like to write you much more and ask you about many questions, but I must close. When are you coming? I embrace you many times and kiss you affectionately.

Your R.

To Luise Kautsky

Breslau, House of Detention
11/10/17

Dearest Lulu,
I have just received the news that Hannes has been killed. At the moment, I am unable to write more.

Affectionately,
Your Rosa

Letter to Hans Deifenbach's sister Gretl after his death

1917

My dear Mrs. Müller:
Many thanks for your note. If, in an anguish such as this, there can be comfort at all, then your words provide it to me. Our thoughts come together. Even before receiving your letter, I had decided that, as soon as I was at liberty, I would travel to Stuttgart in order to get to know Hans' sister. I feel now as if I needed to go somewhere in the world to find and collect living traces of his existence—and where could I find them as well as through you? Hans told me many times of his deep brotherly friendship for you in the time of his early youth, also of the trip to Venice which you took together. No one can know better what you lost than I; for I think that hardly anyone knew him better.

You are right; Hans surpassed everyone I know in inner nobility, purity and goodness. In my case, this is not the usual urge to speak well of the dead. Only recently, from my last jail, I wrote him—in connection with a particular matter concerning mutual friends— how comforting and calming the thought is that he, Hans, was never capable of committing an ignoble deed, not even unobserved, not even in the most secret compartments of his thoughts. Everything base was alien to his nature, as if he were made from the purest and best stuff of which men can be made. His weaknesses—of course he had them too—were those of a child who always lives with an inner fear of life and who is not equipped to cope with real life, with strife and all its unavoidable brutality. I was always afraid that he would eternally remain a dilettante of life, exposed to all of life's tempests; I sought, as much as I could, by applying gentle pressure, to get him to somehow anchor himself in reality. All is gone now.

At the same time, I have lost my dearest friend, who, like no other, understood and empathized with each of my moods and feelings. In music, in painting, as in literature, which were his lifeblood and mine, we had the same gods and we made the same discoveries.

Just now, in order to relax, I was reading Mörike's wonderful correspondence with his betrothed. From habit, at every beautiful passage, I thought to myself: "I must draw Hans' attention to that!" I cannot get used to the thought that he has now vanished without a trace. . . .

R. L.

I affectionately squeeze your hand.

To Sonja Liebknecht

mid-November, 1917

My dearest Sonitschka,

Soon, I hope to get another chance at sending you this letter, and I seize the pen with longing. How long now have I had to forego the lovely custom of at least chatting with you on paper! But I couldn't help it; the few letters which I was permitted to write I had to save for Hans D[iefenbach] who, after all, was waiting for them. Now it's all over. My last two letters had been written to a dead man; one has already been returned to me. I still cannot comprehend the fact that he's dead. But, let's rather not talk about it. I prefer to settle such matters with myself alone, and when someone, "sparing my feelings," wants to prepare me for the bad news and "comfort" me

through his own lamentation, as N. did, this irritates me
unspeakably. That my closest friends still know me so little! That
they so underestimate me! That they fail to comprehend: the best and
most delicate approach in such circumstances is to tell me quickly the
short and simple words "he is dead"—that offends me. But enough of
that.

What a pity for the months and years which are passing and
in which we could be spending so many beautiful hours together, in
spite of all the horror which is taking place in the world. You know,
Sonitschka, that the longer it takes, and the more the basenesses and
atrocities occurring every day transgress all limits and bounds, the
more calm and resolute do I become. Just as I cannot apply moral
standards to the elements, to a hurricane, a flood, or a solar eclipse,
and instead, consider them only something given, an object of
research and knowledge, these are obviously, objectively, the only
possible paths of history, and we must follow them without getting
diverted from the basic direction. I have a feeling that this whole
moral mire through which we are now wading, this huge madhouse
in which we are living, can overnight, with the wave of a magic wand,
be transformed into its opposite, transformed into something
extraordinarily great and heroic and—if the war should last for
another few years—it *must* be transformed. . . .

When you get a chance, read *The Gods Are Athirst* by Anatole
France. I consider the work to be so great primarily because, with a
genius' insight into all of human nature, it says: Just look! The most
enormous events and the most monumental gestures are made from
these miserable figures and these everyday pettinesses in the decisive
moments of history.

We must take everything that happens in society the same way as
in private life: calmly, generously and with a mild smile. I firmly
believe that, in the end, after the war, or at the close of the war,
everything will turn out all right. But apparently we must first wade
through a period of the worst human suffering.

Apropos, my last words awake a different idea in me, a fact which
I would like to share with you because it seems so poetic and
touching. Recently, I read in a scientific work on the flight of birds—
which until now has been a fairly puzzling phenomenon—that it was
observed how different species which are usually deadly enemies,
making war on one another and eating each other, peacefully make
the great trip south across the sea, flying next to one another.
Gigantic flocks of birds go to Egypt for the winter. They fly high up
like clouds and darken the sky. Among these flocks, right between

birds of prey—hawks, eagles, falcons, owls—there are thousands of little songbirds like larks, golden-crested wrens, and nightingales, who fly without any fear in the midst of the birds of prey which normally pursue them. On the trip, therefore, a tacit truce of God seems to rule; all strive for the common destination and at the Nile fall down half-dead from exhaustion, there to divide back into species and groups of compatriots. Moreover, it has been observed that on this trip "across the great pond" large birds transport many smaller ones on their backs. Thus, flocks of cranes have been seen passing on whose backs tiny migrating birds were merrily twittering! Isn't that charming?

. . . In an otherwise tasteless and pell-mell collection of poems, I recently discovered one by Hugo von Hofmannsthal.[1] In general, I don't like him at all; I feel he is affected, overly refined and obscure—I simply don't understand him at all. But, I liked this poem very much, and it made a strong poetic impression upon me. I enclose it for you. Perhaps it will give you pleasure as well.

I am now deeply interested in geology. You probably think of it as a very dry science, but that is a mistake. I read the material with a feverish interest and passionate satisfaction; it broadens one's intellectual standpoint enormously, and it conveys a more unified, all-encompassing conception of nature than any other science.

I would like to tell you a great deal about it, but for that we would have to talk, while strolling on the Südende field in the morning, or walking each other home a few times on a quiet, moonlit night.

What are you reading? How is it going with *The Lessing Legend*? I want to know everything! Write—if possible—immediately through the same channels or, at least, through official channels without mentioning this letter. I am also silently counting the weeks until I see you here again. That will be soon after New Year's, won't it?

What has Karl written? When will you see him again? Send him a thousand greetings from me. I embrace you and firmly press your hand, my dear, dear, Sonitschka! Write soon and extensively.

Your Rosa

Notes

[1]Hugo Von Hofmannsthal (1874-1919): Major modernist writer and poet, Hofmannsthal's best-known work is perhaps his play, *The Tower*. He was also the librettist of Richard Strauss' *Rosenkavalier* and *Salome*.

To Luise Kautsky

11/15/17

Dearest!

Thank you for those few words, which made me so ashamed, for having broken the terrible news to you so abruptly and indelicately. But I received the news in the same way and I felt in such a case, brevity and bluntness are the most merciful way, the same as in a serious operation. I too am unable to find words.

I only wish that I could be with you and Hans now. I feel as if the atmosphere of love, woven between the three of us around his person, somehow might still keep him alive.

I am still unable to emerge from the profound astonishment: is such a thing possible? It seems like a word that has been silenced in the midst of a sentence, like a chord of which has suddenly been broken off—and which I still hear.

We had a thousand plans for the time following the war. We wanted to "enjoy life," travel, read good books, marvel at the spring, as never before. . . . I can't comprehend it: is such a thing possible? Like a flower which has been ripped off and trampled upon. . . .

Dearest, keep calm. One must remain proud and show nothing. Only, we must pull together a bit closer, so that it will be "warmer." I embrace you and Hans with my sincerest love.

Your

R

To Sonja Liebknecht

Breslau 11/24/17

. . . You are mistaken if you believe that I am opposed to the modern poets sight unseen. About 15 years ago, I read Dehmel with enthusiasm; some prose piece by him—by the deathbed of a beloved woman—I have a vague memory—delighted me. I still know Arno Holz's *Phantasus* by heart.[1] At the time Johannes Schlaf's *Springtime* carried me away.[2] Then, however, I moved away from them and went back to Goethe and Mörike. I don't understand [Hugo von] Hofmannsthal, and I don't know [Stefan] George.[3] It's true: with all of them I am a bit frightened by their complete mastery of form, by their poetic means of expression, and by their lack of a grand, noble Weltanschauung. This dichotomy rings so hollow in my soul that, because of it, the beautiful form becomes a distortion. Usually they render wonderful moods. But moods alone do not make a person.

Sonitschka, there are such magical evenings now, like spring evenings. At 4 o'clock, I go down into the yard. It is already twilight, and then I see this ghastly environment hidden in the mysterious veils of darkness. In contrast, the sky is lit in a light blue, and a clear silver moon floats upon it. Every day at this hour, high above, there are hundreds of crows, in a broad, loose, swarm flying out across the yard to the fields, to their "sleeping tree," where they rest for the night.

They fly with a comfortable flapping of their wings, exchanging strange cries by day—completely different from the sharp *krah* with which they rapaciously pursue their prey. Now, that cry sounds muted and soft, a deep guttural sound which affects me like a little metal ball. And when several of them take turns emitting this throaty *kau-kau*, to me it's as if they were playfully throwing metal balls at one another, which hover in the air in an arc. It is a real babbling about the experience of "the day, the day that was today."[4] . . . They seem so serious and important, as each follows its habits and its prescribed course. I feel something like awe for these large birds whom I follow with my eyes, my head raised, until the last one passes. Then I walk back and forth in the darkness and I see the prisoners, who are still in the yard, hurriedly performing their duties, scurrying about like indistinct shadows, and I'm happy that I, myself, am invisible—so alone, so free with my dreams and the secret greetings between me and the crows flying above. I feel so comfortable in the mild springlike breeze. Then the prisoners, carrying the heavy kettles (evening soup!) pass through the yard and into the house; marching two by two, ten pairs one after the other; I follow last. In the yard, in the buildings, the lights gradually dim. I walk into the house and the doors are double-locked and bolted—the day is over.

I feel so good, despite the pain which Hans' death has caused. For actually, I am living in a dream world in which he isn't dead. For me, he goes on living and I often smile at him when I think of him.

Sonitschka, stay well. I am so looking forward to your arrival. Write again soon—for the time being through official channels, after all that will do—and then when you get a chance.

I embrace you.

Your Rosa

Notes

[1]Arno Holz (1863-1929): A German avant-garde poet.

[2]Johannes Schlaf (1862-1941): A close friend of Holz', Schlaf was also a poet.

[3]Stefan George (1868-1933): One of the major literary figures in Germany after the turn of the century. Strongly influenced by Nietzsche, George's circle considered itself an elite. Though certain members of his circle, such as Ludwig Klages, later became Nazis, George himself repulsed the Nazis' overtures to him. His influence was enormous. His major works include *The Year of the Soul*, *The New Reich*, and *The Tapestry of Life*.

[4]Alludes to a poem by Mörike.

To Sonja Liebknecht

Breslau, mid-December, 1917

. . . It's a year now that Karl's been in Luckau. During the past month, I've thought of this often, and exactly one year ago you were visiting me in Wronke, where you presented me with a beautiful Christmas tree. . . . This year I had ordered one. But they brought me a real shabby one, with branches missing—no comparison with the one of last year. I don't know how I will fasten the eight little candles I bought. This will be my third Christmas in jail. But don't you take it too hard; I am as calm and cheerful as ever.

Well, yesterday I thought: how strange that I continually live in a happy state of intoxication for no particular reason. So, for example, I am lying here on a stone-hard mattress in a dark cell, around me the usual quiet of a cemetery; one imagines oneself in the grave. From the window, the reflection of the lantern—which burns all night in front of the prison—is drawn on the ceiling. From time to time, one hears, quite muffled, the distant rattling of a passing train or, from nearby under the window, a sentinel clearing his throat; he is slowly taking a few steps in his heavy boots in order to move his stiff legs. The sand rustles so hopelessly beneath his steps that the whole desolation and inescapability of existence rises from it into the damp, dark night.

There I lie, quiet, alone, wrapped in those manifold black scarves of darkness, boredom, confinement, and winter—and, at the same time, my heart beats with an incomprehensible, unknown inner happiness, as if I were walking over a blooming field in radiant sunshine. And I smile at life in the darkness as if I were aware of some magical secret which might confute the lies, the baseness and the sadness and transform them into sheer brightness and felicity.

And at the same time, I myself am searching for a reason for this happiness. But I find none, and again I must smile at myself. I believe that this mystery is nothing other than life itself; the deep darkness of night is beautiful and soft as velvet if only one looks at it properly. And in the rustling of the moist sand beneath the slow, heavy tread of a sentry, a beautiful little song of life is also singing—if only one knows how to listen properly. In such moments I think of you, and I would so much like to share this magical key with you so that, always, in every situation, you will be able to perceive the beauty and happiness of life, so that you too will live in a state of ecstasy as if you were crossing a multicolored meadow.

Of course, I wouldn't dream of feeding you on asceticism and imaginary joys. I do not begrudge you any real sensuous happiness. I would only like to add to that my own inexhaustible inner cheerfulness, so that I shouldn't worry about you and so that you walk through life in a mantle studded with stars which will protect you from all that is petty, trivial, and frightening.

You picked a beautiful bunch of black and pink violet berries in Steglitz Park. For the blackberries either elders come to mind—their berries hanging in heavy, thick clusters between large, feathery fronds, surely you know them—or, more likely, privets: thin, dainty, upright panicles of berries with slim, longish, green little leaves. The pinkish-violet berries hidden beneath little leaves could be those of the dwarf medlar; they are really red, but in this late season they are already a bit overripe; they begin to rot, and so they often appear reddish-violet. The leaves resemble those of the myrtle: small, pointed at the ends, dark green, and leathery on top, rough below.

Sonjuscha, do you know Platen's *Lethiferous Fork*?[1] Could you either send or bring it to me? Karl mentioned once that he had read it at home. The poems by [Stefan] George are beautiful. Now I know where the verse originated which you used to recite during our walks in the fields: "And under the rustling of the stalks of grain!" When you get a chance, would you make a copy of [Goethe's] "The New Amadis"? I love that poem so very much—naturally, thanks to Hugo Wolf's *Lied*—but I don't have it here. Have you read further in *The Lessing Legend*? I have again taken up Lange's *History of Materialism*[2] which always excites and refreshes me. I would very much like you to read it.

Ach, Sonitschka! I have experienced an acute pain here. In the yard where I walk, military wagons often arrive, packed full with sacks, or old uniforms and shirts often spotted with blood. . . . They are unloaded here, passed out in the cells, mended, then reloaded, and delivered to the military. The other day, such a wagon came drawn by water buffaloes rather than horses. This was the first time that I saw these animals up close. They are built sturdier and broader than our oxen, with flat heads, their horns bent flat, their skulls rather resembling the skulls of our own sheep; the buffaloes are completely black with large soft eyes. They come from Rumania, they are trophies of war. . . . The soldiers who drive the wagon say that it was a very hard job to catch these wild animals and even more difficult to use them, who were so used to freedom, as beasts of burden. They were beaten frightfully to the point where the words apply to them: "Woe to the defeated." . . . About a hundred of these animals are said to be in Breslau alone. Moreover, used to the luxuriant pastures of Rumania, they receive miserable and scant fodder. They are mercilessly exploited in dragging all kinds of loads, and so they perish rapidly.

Anyway, a few days ago, a wagon loaded with sacks drove into the prison. The cargo was piled up so high that the buffaloes could not make it over the threshold of the gateway. The attending soldier, a brutal character, began to beat away at the animals with the heavy end of his whip so savagely that the overseer indignantly called him to account "Don't you have any pity for the animals?" "No one has any pity for us people either!" he answered with an evil laugh, and fell upon them ever more forcefully. . . . Finally, the animals started up and got over the hump, but one of them was bleeding. . . . Sonitschka, buffalo hide is proverbial for its thickness and toughness, and it was lacerated. Then, during the unloading, the animals stood completely still, exhausted, and one, the one that was bleeding, all the while looked ahead with an expression on its black face and in its soft black eyes like that of a weeping child. It was exactly the expression of a child who has been severely punished and who does not know why, what for, who does not know how to escape the torment and brutality. . . . I stood facing the animal and it looked at me; tears were running from my eyes—they were *his* tears. One cannot quiver any more painfully over one's dearest brother's sorrow than I quivered in my impotence over this silent anguish.

How far, how irretrievably lost, are the free, succulent, green pastures of Rumania! How different it was with the sun shining, the wind blowing; how different were the beautiful sounds of birds, the melodious calls of shepherds. And here: this strange weird city, the fusty stable, the nauseating mouldy hay mixed with putrid straw, the strange, horrible people—and the blows, the blood running from the fresh wound. . . . Oh! My poor buffalo! My poor beloved brother! We both stand here so powerless and spiritless and are united only in pain, in powerlessness and in longing. . . .

Meanwhile, the prisoners bustled busily about the wagon, unloading the heavy sacks and carrying them into the building. The soldier, however stuck both hands into his pockets, strolled across the yard with great strides, smiled and softly whistled a popular song. And the whole glorious war passed in front of my eyes. . . . Write quickly. I embrace you, Sonitschka.

Your Rosa

Sonitschka, dearest, in spite of it all, be calm and cheerful. That's life, and that's how one must take it: courageously, intrepidly and smilingly—in spite of it all.

Notes

[1]August Graf von Platen-Hallermünde (1796-1835): A poet of the Biedermeier period. Platen's works include *Sonnets from Venice* and *The Romantic Oedipus*.

[2]Friedrich Albert Lange (1828-1875): A left Kantian, Rosa is referring to his *History of Materialism*, which was published in second edition in 1876 and widely read by socialists.

To Emanuel and Mathilde Wurm

[Postcard. Postmarked
Breslau 12/17/17.]
Dearest Tilde!

I received your card bearing the sad news [of Stadthagen's death]. Now I am waiting patiently until you are in a position to make use of the permit to visit me. It grieves me that your husband is so depressed. I was also deeply shaken by Arthur's [Stadthagen's] death. Still, the prevailing pessimism is totally out of place.

Don't let it get the better of you, and hold your head high. One never sees things and life properly through black lenses. So be of good cheer, and look bravely into the future. In the meantime, my affectionate regards.

Your
R. L.

To Emanuel and Mathilde Wurm

Breslau; January 1918
Tildchen!

I just wanted to elaborate a bit on Proudhon[1] because,

unfortunately, it was so uncomfortable yesterday that the words froze in my throat. Besides, I can't very well give full lectures, which might appear suspicious to the outsider.

Well, you can find the dates on Proudhon's life and works in Mühlberger.[2] If necessary, you might also consult Diehl.[3] (His three-volume work on P[roudhon] will surely be available in either the Reichstag library or the Royal Library.)

Three aspects could be used in your lecture: 1) his theory of "direct exchange," which is the central point of his theoretical and practical system; expressed more simply, the abolition of money while retaining commodity production. That is to say, Proudhon believed that it was the use of money which shielded the "injustice" of the exchange between worker and capitalist (labor power for wages): one needs only to introduce the notion that commodities will be exchanged directly according to the labor time which they contain for exploitation to become impossible. Naturally, a completely utopian idea.

According to Proudhon's conception, the exploitation of the proletariat does not rest on capitalistic private ownership of the means of production, but rather on a *swindle* in the payment of wages; a swindle which is made possible through the use of money. Hence, his introduction of simple notes certifying the hours of work which every commodity contains; an equitable exchange must then lead to general economic equality.

He completely forgot that the proletariat does not sell commodities to the capitalists, but rather sells his only single commodity—labor power. Consequently, exploitation will continue when, and especially when, labor power is paid according to its value and according to its costs of subsistence. The most disastrous and most reactionary aspect of this utopia is that it draws the worker's attention to economic quackery, and turns him away from the political struggle, from the struggle for the conquest of state power. This is to be understood as one of the many reactions to the disappointment over the purely political struggle for power in the Great French Revolution.

By the way, don't forget that Proudhon did not invent the idea. Owen[4] already discovered it in the 20s and 30s in England (see Engels' Introduction to *The Poverty of Philosophy*). Proudhon is just the most brilliant in working out the idea.

2) Practical role of these ideas in the February Revolution: the experiment with the "Bank of Direct Exchange" and naturally its quick bankrupty. Proudhon's ideas, together with those of Louis Blanc's[5] "Organization of Work," formed the predominant currents of the Revolution of 1848. Fighting against both types of utopian-

economic experiments, the Blanqui group[6] was the only truly revolutionary proletarian association working directly towards the social revolution and the conquest of political power in the February Revolution.

By the way the experiment with the "Bank for Just Exchange" had also already been tried in England, I think around 1836 in Manchester. Naturally, it also went bankrupt within a few months.

3) In spite of the complete untenability of his ideas and the 1858 bankruptcy Proudhon had a great and long-lasting influence on the French and on the whole Latin labor movement into the 1860s and 70s. In the First International,[7] Marx had to fight primarily against Proudhonism, whose principal representative was Tolain[8] (later a renegade and a senator). You would probably have to check that in Jaeckh (*History of the International*).[9] The influence of Proudhonism is naturally more important than Proudhon the person. Only the new basis for the labor movement in France following the collapse of the Commune—the entry of Marxism in the 1880s—shoved the Proudhonist ideas in France into the background.

For all that, don't forget that Proudhon's most important and principal effect does not lie in the subtleties of his mistaken theories of commodity exchange and money, but in his directing the attention of the labor movement to purely economic remedies, rather than to the political struggle for the conquest of state power. And for all that—once more—don't forget the historical perspective: Proudhon, as well as Louis Blanc and all the economic groupings are an understandable reaction to the disappointment with the Great French Revolution and the reign of the Jacobins. It was Marxism which first established the correct relationship between economics and politics (with the splendid result which we are witnessing today. . . .)[10]

Notes

[1]Pierre Joseph Proudhon (1809-1865): A leading theorist of anarchism and utopian socialist, Proudhon is best known for his *Philosophy of Poverty*, to which Marx responded with *The Poverty of Philosophy*.

[2]Arthur Mühlberger (1847-1907): A physician who became a publicist for anarchist ideas deriving from Proudhon.

[3]Karl Diehl (1864-?): Author of one of the standard works on Proudhon, *P. J. Proudhon: Seine Lehre und Sein Leben*, published in 1896.

[4]Robert Owen (1771-1858): One of the outstanding examples of what Marx and Engels would call "utopian socialism." An English industrialist, Owen founded the New Lanark colony in Scotland.

[5]Louis Blanc (1811-1882): A French socialist, Blanc participated in the revolution of 1848, and later opposed the creation of the Paris Commune. His slogan: "Right to work."

[6]Auguste Louis Blanqui (1805-1881): A French revolutionary who spent many years in jail. Blanqui sought to foster the revolution through conspiratorial politics. He took part in the revolutions of 1830 and 1848.

[7]The First International was founded in 1864 and lasted until 1876. Marx was a member of the provisional committee of the International and wrote the "Inaugural Address of the International Working Men's Association." The squabbling never stopped between Marxists and anarchists—headed by Bakunin—and, after the defeat of the Paris Commune, the First International virtually ceased to exist, though it carried on another few years.

[8]Henri Louis Tolain (1828-1897): A right-wing Proudhonist, he was a leading member of the First International who went over to the "Versailles" enemy during the Commune. He was later expelled from the International.

[9]Gustav Jaeckh (1866-1907): An editor of the *Leipziger Volkszeitung*. He was the author of a well-known *History of the First International*.

[10]The sarcastic ending refers to Rosa Luxemburg's belief that it was the Party's subservience to the trade union movement that prevented it from undertaking a more revolutionary course of action.

To Sonja Liebknecht

Breslau 1/14/1918

My dearest Sonitschka,

How long has it been since I've written you! I believe it's been months. And even today, I don't even know whether you are already in Berlin. But, I'll hope that these lines will still reach you in time for your birthday. I asked Mathilde [Jacob] to send you a bunch of orchids from me. But now the poor dear is in the hospital and will hardly be able to carry out my instructions.

Still, you know that I am with you in my thoughts and with all my heart and that on your birthday I would like to surround you completely with flowers: with lavender orchids, with white irises, with strong fragrant hyacinths, with anything available. Perhaps, instead, next year on this day I will be granted the happiness of bringing you flowers in person and taking a glorious walk with you in the botanical gardens and in the fields. How wonderful that would be!

Today it's 32 degrees. At the same time, however, there is such a gentle, refreshing breath of spring in the air, and above, between plump, milk-white clouds, a deep blue sky is glimmering and, in addition, the sparrows are chirping so happily you would think it was late March. I am so looking forward to spring, the one thing of which you never get tired, so long as you live, and which, to the contrary, you learn to better appreciate and cherish every year.

Do you know, Sonitschka, that the beginning of spring in the organic world—that is to say, the awakening of life—really starts in early January? It doesn't wait for the calendar. You see, at the time when, according to the calendar, winter begins, we are—astronomically speaking—closest to the sun. This has such a mysterious effect on every living thing that, even on our northern hemisphere which is enveloped in winter's snow, early in January the plant and animal world is awakened as if by the wave of a magic wand. The buds begin to sprout, and many animals begin to reproduce. Recently I read in [Anatole] France an observation that the most outstanding scientific and literary productions of famous men have occurred in the months of January and February. Thus, even in human existence, the winter solstice is supposed to be a critical moment and to set in motion a new flow of all the life forces. You too, Sonitschka, are such an early little flower that sprouted right in the middle of snow and ice, and therefore, all its life long shivers a little, does not feel at home in life, and needs the tender care of the greenhouse.

I was enormously pleased with the Rodin which you sent me for Christmas. I would have thanked you right away, had Mathilde not told me that you were in Frankfurt. What especially pleases me is Rodin's sense of nature, his veneration for every little blade of grass in the field. He must have been a splendid guy: open, natural, abounding in inner warmth and intelligence; he decidedly reminds me of Jaurès.

Do you like my Broodcorens? Or did you know him already? This novel moved me deeply; particularly the descriptions of landscapes are of a high poetic quality. Apparently Broodcorens, exactly like De Coster, thinks that "over the land of Flanders" the sun rises and sets much more beautifully than over the rest of the world. I feel that all the Flemish are plainly in love with their little country; they do not describe it as a beautiful bit of land, but rather as a radiant young bride. And even in the book's dark, tragic ending, I find an affinity of colors and grandiose pictures with those in Till Eulenspiegel; e.g., in the demolition of the house of ill repute. Don't you also feel that these books in their hues distinctly recall Rembrandt? The darkness of the whole picture, mixed with a sparkling old-gold tone; the most amazing realism of all the details, and still the whole is carried away into a region of fabulous fantasy.

In the *Berliner Tageblatt,* I read that a great new Titian is in the Friedrich Museum. Have you already seen it? I confess that strictly speaking Titian is not a friend of mine. For me, he is too slick and cold, too much the virtuoso—forgive me if this is perhaps a *lèse majesté,* but I cannot help following my immediate feelings. Just the same, I would be happy if I were now able to go to the Friedrich Museum to visit the new guest. Have you also seen the Kaufmann Estate about which they have made such a fuss?

My reading now includes various older studies on Shakespeare from the sixties and seventies, when in Germany people still vigorously debated the Shakespeare problem. Couldn't you get me from either the Royal Library or the Reichstag Library: Klein's *History of the Italian Drama,* Schack's *History of Dramatic Literature in Spain,* Gervinius and Ulrici on Shakespeare? How do you yourself feel about Shakespeare? Write soon! I embrace you and squeeze your hand warmly. Be calm and cheerful in spite of it all. Dearest Sonitschka, goodbye.

When will you come?! Sonjuscha, do me a favor: send Mathilde Jacob some hyacinths from me. I'll pay you back when you get here.

Your Rosa.

To Marta Rosenbaum

Breslau, February, 1918

Dearest Martchen!

I have received your greetings, but I hope—if Herr K permits—next time to get a personal kiss from you. You are much too melancholy in your letters! In spite of everything one should not be without hope. Laugh at the whole mess: Why, it's big enough for history itself to get going and sweep it up. And that it will do, don't you worry! History alone always knows how to give counsel for its own cares, and it has blasted into the air many dung heaps which stood in its way. It will succeed this time too. The more hopeless things appear the more thorough will be the cleanup—so, despite everything, keep your head high and your spirit strong.

Martchen, I have a request: you must do as much as possible for Sonja [Liebknecht]. She needs warmth, kindness, companionship and care. Transfer a part of your love for me to poor Sonja. Above all, see to it that, if possible, her birthday is celebrated. She is as sensitive as a child. Have her over often, and go for walks with her (which will do you good, too). But, still you must hold me dear! I embrace you many times, and best regards to you and yours.

Your
R.

To Franz Mehring

March 8, 1918

. . . I just can't tell you how your last letter, and particularly the news of your terrible accident, upset me. Usually I have been able to bear this slavery of mine—which is now going into its fourth year— with the patience of a lamb. In this instance, however, under the painful shock of such news, a feverish impatience and a burning longing seized me to leave at once, hurry to Berlin and see for myself, with my own eyes, how you are feeling, to clasp your hand, to chat with you a little while. That I am not able to do so, and that I must remain here in this dreary cell like a dog on a chain, with the perpetual view of the men's prison on one side and the madhouse on the other, truly shakes me up. . . . In spite of it all, however, I have the firm conviction that, by next year, we will finally be able to gather around you for your birthday. It's inconceivable that the war can go on beyond next year, and then—I count on the historical dialectic ultimately to find its way out of all the chaos, and open a great path. I don't doubt for a moment that you, along with the rest of us, will yet be able to breathe purer air than what we are breathing now. . . .

To Sonja Liebknecht

Breslau, 3/24/18

My dearest Sonitschka,

How long it has been since I wrote to you, and how often have I thought of you! With this "temper of the time," even I temporarily lose my desire to write. . . . If we could only be together now and, strolling through the fields, talk about this and that—that would be such a blessing. But right now there is no such chance. My petition has been denied, with a thorough description of my baseness and

Franz Mehring. (Courtesy Dietz Verlag)

unredeemability; so has a request for at least a brief leave. I will have to wait, then, until we have conquered the whole world. . . .

How beautiful are the pictures you sent me! No need to comment on Rembrandt. In the Titian I was overwhelmed by the horse even more than by the rider. So much royal power and nobility—I had not thought it possible to express that in a horse. By far the most beautiful thing, however, was the lady's portrait by Bartolommeo da Venezia (whom, by the way, I had not known at all). What a fervor in the colors, what finesse in the design, what mysterious charm in the expression! . . .

Of course you must keep Hans' book. I grieve that not all of his books have fallen to *us*. I would have given them to you rather than to any one else. . . .

Be cheerful; enjoy the spring. For the next one no doubt we shall be together. I embrace you, dearest. Happy Easter. Many greetings to the children, too!

Your Rosa.

To Sonja Liebknecht

Breslau 4/19/18

Your postcard yesterday cheered me heartily, even though it sounded so sad. How I would like to be with you now to get you to laugh once again, like that time after Karl's arrest when we both—do you remember—attracted some attention in the Cafe Fürstenhof with our wanton salvos of laughter. How wonderful that was at the time— in spite of everything! Our daily spring in the early morning to get an automobile on Potsdamer Platz, then the drive to the prison through the flowering Tiergarten into the quiet Lehrterstrasse with the high elms. Then, on the way back, the indispensable stop at the Fürstenhof, then your indispensable visit with me in Südende, where everything stood in the splendor of May; the comfortable hours in my kitchen, where you and Mimi would wait at the little table with the white tablecloth for the results of my culinary art (do you remember the fine *haricots verts à la Parisienne*? . . .)

With all that I have the vivid remembrance of an unchangingly radiant, hot weather and, in fact, only in such weather do we have the truly happy feeling of spring. Then, evenings, my indispensable visit to you in your lovely little room—I like you so much as a housewife, it suits you so charmingly when you, such a tiny teenage figure, stand by the table pouring tea. And finally, at midnight, when we walked each other home through the fragrant dark streets. Do you remember the fabulous moonlit night in Südende, when I walked you home and the gables of the houses, with their jagged black contours, on a background of the sweet blue of the sky, appeared to us like old knights' castles? Sonjuscha, that's the way I would always like to be with you; to amuse you, to chat with you, or be silent, so that you do not sink into your dark, despairing brooding.

You ask in your card: "Why is it all the way it is?" What a child you are! Life has been "the way it is" since time immemorial. Everything is a part of life: sorrow and separation and longing. One always has to take it along with everything, and one must view *everything* as beautiful and good. At least, I do it that way—not through any calculated wisdom, but rather simply so, from my nature. I instinctively feel that this is the only right way to take life and that's why I feel truly happy in every situation. I wouldn't have missed any part of my life, and I wouldn't have had it any other way than it was and is. If I could only bring you to this conception of life! . . .

I haven't thanked you yet for the picture of Karl. How it pleased me! It was really the nicest birthday present that you could have given me. It is standing in a good frame on the table in front of me, and it follows me everywhere with its gaze. (You know, there are pictures which seem to gaze at you wherever you put them.) The picture is a striking likeness. How happy Karl must be now about the news from Russia! But you also, personally, have reason to be happy! Now, nothing will stand in the way of your mother coming to see you. Have you thought of that yet? For your sake, I urgently hope for sunshine and warmth.

Here everything is still budding; yesterday we had snow flurries. I wonder how my "southern landscape" in Südende looks. Last year we both stood in front of the trellis, and admired the richness of the blossoms.

You shouldn't take so much trouble with letters. I want to write you often, but it is more than enough for me if you send a brief greeting on a postcard! Get out of doors often and work on your botany. Do you have my little flower atlas along? Be calm and cheerful, dearest, everything will turn out all right! You'll see!

I affectionately embrace you many times.

As always, your
Rosa

To Emanuel and Mathilde Wurm

4/22/18

Dearest Tilde,

Just as I was going to write you, your little basket arrived. Many thanks for your last package and letter. The bread was splendid and the books too. You don't even know what type of jewel you sent me: Goethe's *Wilhelm Meister's Theatrical Mission* is, after all, the original draft of the *Apprenticeship* which has been sought for a long time by Goethe philologists. It was considered lost until, completely by chance, it was discovered in Zurich seven years ago in a handwritten copy done by Barbara Schulthess, an old friend of Goethe's from the Lavater circle.[1] At the time, the discovery caused a great sensation; after all, it is the work which Goethe wrote before the *Italian Journey*, whereas the *Apprenticeship* came into existence after the trip, and after 20 years of revision. Well, you can imagine that this greatly interests me.

You wonder what conclusions you can draw from the fact that one is absolutely unable to buy *Wilhelm Meister*? Very simple: It just isn't read by the public, and that's why it isn't published separately any longer; only bibliophiles and Goethe specialists can still cope with it. His portly privy-councilor's attitude[2] really gets on my nerves, too.

The book on botany, from your husband, pleased me very much. It is of course a popular work in which, naturally, very little was new to me. But the presentation and the general slant are so admirable that I read it with great pleasure; I would very much like to see more books of this sort. I have still not completely gotten over my influenza, but I ignore it as best I can; I am all the more pleased that you are once again in full activity.

Your Rosa

Notes

[1] Johann Lavater (1741-1801): A friend of Goethe's from the Frankfurt days. Lavater, who was a priest, thought that the soul of an individual could be gleaned from his physiognomy.

[2] Goethe was a privy councilor at the court of Weimar. He first went to Weimar in 1776, which was the year he began working on *Wilhelm Meister*.

To Sonja Liebknecht

Breslau 5/2/1918

. . . I read *Candide*[1] and the Countess Ulfeldt's book,[2] and I enjoyed both of them. *Candide* is in such an exquisite edition that I couldn't bring myself to cut the leaves of the book. I read it with the leaves uncut; it was quite easy since it is bound in half sheets. Before the war, I would have thought this wicked compilation of all human misery a caricature. Now it strikes me as altogether realistic. . . . At the end, I finally found out where the saying originated which I have used myself on occasion: "Mais il faut cultiver notre jardin."[3] The book by the Countess Ulfeldt is an interesting cultural document, a complement to Grimmelshausen.[4] . . . What are you doing? Aren't you enjoying the glorious spring?

As always, your
Rosa

Notes

[1]François-Marie Arouet (Voltaire) (1694-1778): A man of letters *par excellence,* Voltaire is best known for his satirical work *Candide,* written in 1759.

[2]Countess Christina Ulfeldt (1621-1698): Rosa is no doubt referring to the Countess Ulfeldt's *Memoirs,* written during her imprisonment.

[3]The reference is to the closing line of *Candide.* After a long series of adventures, Candide says: "We must cultivate our garden."

[4]Hans Jakob Christoffel von Grimmelshausen (1625-1676): Author of the classic novel of the Thirty Years' War, *Simplicissimus.*

To Luise Kautsky

Breslau 7/25/18
[Without censor's check mark]

Dearest Lulu!

Today I got up at half past four. For a long time, I watched the little white and grey morning clouds high in the blue sky and the silent prison courtyard still asleep; then I carefully examined my flower pots, provided them with fresh water, arranged the vases and glasses, which are always filled with cuttings and wild flowers and, now, at 6 a.m. I am sitting at the desk in order to write a letter to you.

Ah, my nerves, my nerves. I can't sleep at all. Even the dentist whom I recently went to see—and although I always behave like a lamb—suddenly made the remark: "Well, your nerves are probably shot aren't they?" But, forget it.

Only admit it, incorrigible one: you have been entertaining a thousand doubts and some ideas about me because I haven't written you for so long? . . . I must look you right in the eye, as the brave knight in the fairy tale did to the monsters; no sooner do I turn away than I am done for.

Naturally, in the meantime, I have thought of you countless times; I mischievously laughed at the mistrust which has probably been newly awakened in you—but I could not write. Partly because I had already heavily overdrawn my letter-account through the bombardment of galleys and the diligent exchanges with Kestenberg,[1] partly—"besides."

At present, Kestenberg is in Switzerland; the printers, too, are taking a strategic break in their proofreading offensive—I don't know why—and I am thinking of the eleventh of August which is approaching. . . . This time I want to determine in advance where my thoughts are to find you on your birthday. Are you in Berlin, were you in Vienna, are you going somewhere for recuperation, how are you feeling? I would like to hear from you about this and many other things.

Clara [Zetkin] has been silent for quite some time. She hasn't even thanked me for the birthday letter, which is something unheard of for her. I cannot suppress a feeling of growing dread. Could you imagine what it would mean if something were to happen to one, let alone both, of her boys? Both are now at the front, and bad days are there at present. . . .

I have courage in regard to everything which concerns me. Having to bear the sorrow of others, to say nothing of Clara's, should "God forbid" something happen—for that I lack courage and strength. But all these are only my thoughts, ghosts. . . .

This psychology develops of itself, automatically, when you are in prison for a long time: every once in a while, you suffer from compulsive imaginings. You awaken suddenly, within the gravelike silence of the barred house, with the ironclad conviction that a calamity has befallen this one or that whom you hold dearest. Mostly it soon turns out to be just your imagination, a whim—sometimes not. . . .

It even occurred to me today, while I was arranging the flowers with the greatest care and occasionally consulting the botanical atlas to determine some minor point—it suddenly occured to me that I am deliberately misleading myself, lulling myself into the thought that I am still leading a normal life, while actually all around me there is an atmosphere of a world going under. Possibly the 200 "expiatory executions" in Moscow, which I read about yesterday in the papers, are what specifically affected me. . . . But, away with these thoughts, dearest! I won't have you despondent! Take heart, we will continue to meet with whatever life has in store for us. Take my word for it, together we will fight it out all right and we'll never forget to appreciate thankfully the tiniest bits of beauty and goodness that are left over.

I am enclosing a little flower from a large bouquet to which I recently treated myself on my way to the dentist. Do you know it? It has such pretty popular names: "Bride in tresses," "Maiden in Green," "Gretchen in the Bush." It must be an ancient decoration of the peasant garden for, in this area, it serves as a means of keeping the cattle from being "hexed."

What are your boys doing? I was so pleased with the jasmine blossom in your last letter and I have preserved it nicely. My mind turns to this as I think of the oldest "boy," grandpa Igel. What is he doing? From Sonja [Liebknecht] I received a wonderful volume of Flemish novellas, published by the Insel Publishing House. There are things in it which remind one of Teniers,[2] but also of "Hell-Breughel."[3] Do you know it?

Write briefly, but soon! Briefly, because, you see, I am not the only one to read the letters. . . . Oh yes, I came up with something nice for Zenzi, but it will have to wait a bit. Farewell dearest, be good and cheerful.

I embrace you many times,

Your

R.

Notes

[1]Rosa Luxemburg's publisher.

[2]The reference is probably to the religious painter David Teniers the Elder (1582-1649).

[3]The reference is probably to Peter Breughel (1525/30-1569) who painted harrowing descriptions of religious themes.

To Sonja Liebknecht

Breslau 10/18/1918

Dearest Sonitschka,

I wrote you day before yesterday. Until today, I have not received a reply to my telegram to the Chancellor;[1] it might take another few days. Anyway, one thing's for certain by now; my mood is such that to receive visits from my friends under police surveillance has become impossible for me. I have endured everything quite patiently through the years and, in other circumstances, I would have remained just as patient for years longer. But, after the general change in conditions occurred, my psychological state also collapsed. The conversations under surveillance, the impossibility of discussing what really interests me, by now has become so annoying that I would rather forego all visits until we can see each other as free human beings.

After all, it can't last much longer. Since Dittmann and Kurt Eisner have been released, they can't hold me in prison any longer and Karl will soon be free as well. So, let's rather wait to meet in Berlin.

Until then, a thousand greetings.

As always, your
Rosa

Notes

[1]Prince Max von Baden was the chancellor, and a liberal. Three weeks later, he would hand the office over to Friedrich Ebert, the right-wing social democrat. Rosa Luxemburg was only released from prison on November 9th, the day of the revolution. The amnesty of October 12th did not apply to her— ironically enough because she had not been sentenced, but rather was being held in "protective custody."

To Adolf Geck[1]

Berlin, Hotel Moltke
(my present address)
11/18/18

My dear, beloved, heartfelt friends

I just received the terrible black envelope. My hand and my heart shook even as I saw the writing and the postmark. Still, I hoped that the most terrible would not be true. I can't grasp it, and tears hinder me as I write. What you are going through—I know it, I feel it, we all know how to fathom this terrible blow.

I expected so very much from him for the Party, for humanity. One would like to gnash one's teeth. I would like to help you, yet there is no help, no comfort. You dears, don't let yourselves be overcome with grief; do not let the sun, which always shines in your house, vanish behind this atrocity. We all are subordinate to blind fate, my one comfort is the grim thought that soon I may also be dispatched into the beyond—perhaps through a bullet of the counter-revolution, which lurks on all sides. But, as long as I live, I remain bound to you in the warmest, truest, most heartfelt love and I want to share every sorrow, every pain, with you.

A thousand greetings,
Your
Rosa L.

My deepest condolences and best regards.

Your K. Liebknecht

Notes

[1]Adolf Geck (1854-1942): A social democratic functionary, he later became influential in the USPD. He also served as a Reichstag deputy for the SPD from 1898 to 1912 and for the USPD from 1920 to 1924. Geck's son was killed two weeks before the armistice marking the end of World War I.

To Franz Mehring

Hotel Moltke
November 18, 1918

My dear friend,

I can't tell you how it hurts me that I am still unable to rush to you and clasp your hand. But, from the moment I got off the train in Berlin, I have not even had the time to set foot in my own apartment in Südende, and I am staying in a hotel. From that you can imagine how this turmoil is devouring me. First there was publishing the newspaper at long last. Now, I am dying to hear your opinion, to have your advice at hand. We were all overjoyed when a friend informed us that before long we would be able to adorn the *Fahne*[1] with your name and contribution. I am awaiting that with the greatest impatience. Shortly, over the next few days, I hope finally to be able to come to you. It makes me happy to hear that you are feeling well and that you are so cheerful and ready for work. In all haste, for the present only this brief, most affectionate greeting until we meet again shortly.

Your Rosa Luxemburg

Notes

[1]*Die Rote Fahne (The Red Flag)* became the daily paper of the German Communist Party.

To Adolf Warski

[November-December 1918]

. . . Our [Polish] Party is highly enthusiastic about Bolshevism. At the same time, however, it has come out in opposition to both the peace achieved through the Treaty of Brest-Litovsk[1] and the Bolsheviks' acceptance of the slogan of "national self-determination." This shows that enthusiasm is combined with the critical spirit—what more could we wish? I, too, shared all your reservations and misgivings, but I have surrendered them in the most important issues, though in other respects I have not gone as far as you.

To be sure, terrorism indicates fundamental weakness, but the terror is directed against internal enemies whose hopes rest upon the continuation of capitalism outside Russia, and who receive support and encouragement for their views from abroad. If the European revolution takes place, the Russian counterrevolutionaries will not only lose this support, but—more importantly—their courage as well. In short, the terror in Russia is above all an expression of the weakness of the European proletariat. True enough, the new agrarian relations which have been created present the sorest and most dangerous issue for the Russian Revolution.[2] But, in this respect, as well, the truth is that even the greatest revolution can only create what it is historically possible to create. Thus, this sore spot, too, can only be healed by the European revolution. And this is coming! . . .

Notes

[1]The Treaty of Brest-Litovsk was the controversial peace treaty which the Bolsheviks made with the Germans to end Russia's participation in World War I. Trotsky, who took the position "no peace—no war," resigned as foreign secretary. Bukharin, certain Bolsheviks, and the Social Revolutionaries thought it dishonorable to conclude peace with the Kaiser. Lenin

persuaded the majority that Russia was unable to continue the war.

²These three points are made forcefully in Rosa Luxemburg's prophetic manuscript which Paul Levi later published under the title *The Russian Revolution.*

To Marta Rosenbaum

Berlin, January 4, 1919

Dear, dear Martchen!

At last, with a thousand greetings, I am sending you the first issue of *Rote Fahne.* The struggle over it has held me breathless throughout the past days from morning until night. I feel a desperate need to see you, to embrace you, to talk with you. Kurt [Rosenfeld] told me that you felt I had offended you. For my part, I felt as though a brick had fallen on my head. Through our long friendship, have I not earned enough trust that misunderstandings between us should be impossible? It was painful! Well, we must take it in stride and discuss it. Not a shadow must come between me and my dear Martchen with the heart of gold. I tried to reach you by telephone yesterday, but I couldn't. Later I didn't have a free second. I'll see if I can make it today.

In the meantime, I embrace you in the love and trust of old. A thousand greetings to you and your spouse.

Your
Rosa L.